Basic Elements

Basic Elements of Narrative

David Herman

A John Wiley & Sons, Ltd., Publication

This edition first published 2009
© 2009 David Herman

Blackwell Publishing was acquired by John Wiley & Sons in February 2007. Blackwell's publishing program has been merged with Wiley's global Scientific, Technical, and Medical business to form Wiley-Blackwell.

Registered Office
John Wiley & Sons Ltd, The Atrium, Southern Gate, Chichester, West Sussex, PO19 8SQ, United Kingdom

Editorial Offices
350 Main Street, Malden, MA 02148-5020, USA
9600 Garsington Road, Oxford, OX4 2DQ, UK
The Atrium, Southern Gate, Chichester, West Sussex, PO19 8SQ, UK

For details of our global editorial offices, for customer services, and for information about how to apply for permission to reuse the copyright material in this book please see our website at www.wiley.com/wiley-blackwell.

The right of David Herman to be identified as the author of this work has been asserted in accordance with the Copyright, Designs and Patents Act 1988.

Library of Congress Cataloging-in-Publication Data

Herman, David, 1962–
  Basic elements of narrative / by David Herman.
    p. cm.
  Includes bibliographical references and index.
  ISBN 978-1-4051-4153-6 (hardcover : alk. paper)—ISBN 978-1-4051-4154-3
(pbk. : alk. paper) 1. Narration (Rhetoric) I. Title.
  PN212.H46 2009
  808—dc22

                                                              2008023250

A catalogue record for this book is available from the British Library.

Set in 10/13pt Palatino by Graphicraft Limited, Hong Kong
Printed in Singapore by Ho Printing Pte Ltd

1   2009

For Susan, whose story is interwoven with mine

Contents

Preface

The Scope and Aims of This Book

This book outlines a way of thinking about what narrative is and how to identify its basic elements across the many communicative media in which stories are produced and interpreted, exchanged and transformed. Relevant storytelling media range from print texts, television, and spoken discourse in face-to-face interaction to comics and graphic novels, cinema, and computer-mediated environments such as e-mail, blogs, hypertext narratives, and interactive fiction. (I focus special attention here on face-to-face storytelling, print texts, graphic narratives that involve word–image combinations, and, to a lesser extent, film.) The book does not purport to offer an exhaustive survey of competing approaches to the problems of narrative study into which it delves from a specific, focused perspective. Yet that perspective, which I hope will prove relevant for creators of stories as well as narrative analysts, is itself a distillation of ideas developed by scholars working in quite disparate traditions within the field – and also in other, more or less closely neighboring fields. Thus, even as it makes its own case for how to characterize core features of narrative and cross-compare the way those features manifest themselves in various storytelling media, the book does provide a synoptic introduction to key ideas about narrative. In this sense, the book is designed both to whet the reader's appetite for more details about the traditions of narrative scholarship in which my own study is grounded, and to provide a basis for assessing those traditions from the vantage-point developed here.

Chapter 1 gives a thumbnail sketch of the overall approach. In this opening chapter I suggest that narrative can be viewed under several profiles – as a cognitive structure or way of making sense of experience, as a type of text, and as a resource for communicative interaction – and I then use this multidimensionality of narrative as a basis for analyzing it into its fundamental elements. I specify four such elements, arguing that they will be realized in any particular narrative in a gradient, "more-or-less" fashion; hence these elements in effect constitute conditions for *narrativity*, or what makes a story (interpretable as) a story. After this initial synopsis of my overall argument, chapter 2 interrupts the exposition of the model to review some recent developments in the field of narrative inquiry, providing background and context for my approach. The remaining chapters of the book pick back up with the explication of the model outlined in chapter 1, zooming in on each of the four basic elements in turn. Chapter 3 focuses on the element of *situatedness*, or how stories are grounded in (= both shape and are shaped by) particular discourse contexts or occasions of telling, providing an overview of some the frameworks that have been developed for studying this aspect of narrative. Chapter 4, which is concerned with the second basic element, *event sequencing*, steps back from my primary case studies to examine the conceptual underpinnings of the claim that modes of representation can be more or less prototypically narrative, invoking the ideas of text types and text-type categories for this purpose. The chapter uses these ideas to highlight, first, the specific kind of causal-chronological structure that serves to distinguish stories from descriptions, and second, the concern with particularized events (rather than general patterns and trends) that sets stories apart from certain kinds of explanations.

Chapters 5 and 6 bring my main case studies back into the foreground to explore, respectively, the third and fourth elements: on the one hand, *worldmaking/world disruption*; on the other hand, how stories represent – and perhaps make it possible to experience – *what it's like* to undergo events within a storyworld-in-flux. In chapter 5, I draw on Nelson Goodman's suggestive idea of "ways of worldmaking" (Goodman 1978) to examine what is distinctive about the process by which people use spoken and written discourse, images, gestures, and other symbolic resources as blueprints for creating and updating storyworlds, or global mental models of the situations and events being recounted in a narrative. In chapter 6, I probe the story–mind interface from two different perspectives, discussing how the representation of experiencing minds constitutes a critical property of narrative but also how narrative might afford crucial scaffolding for conscious experience itself. Finally, the glossary at the end of the volume assembles some keywords for narrative study, as well as a list of foundational studies where more information about these keywords can be found.

As this summary suggests, there are multiple routes through the book, which has been designed to accommodate the background and interests of different kinds of readers. Rather than following the chapters in sequence, readers who are unfamiliar with the range of recent scholarship on narrative may wish to begin with chapter 2 to get their bearings within the field, next move back to the synopsis of the model in chapter 1, and then pick up with its further development in chapters 3 and following. Readers with more expertise in narrative theory, meanwhile, may wish to concentrate instead on my characterization of the basic elements of narrative. Alternatively, advanced readers may wish to focus their attention on specific chapters dealing with particular narrative elements.

Readers should also note that the Appendix contains narrative materials to which I frequently revert in my discussion. I provide context for and synopses of all these stories, and readers may wish to familiarize themselves with the illustrative narratives before moving on to the chapters in which they feature as my primary case studies (chapters 3, 5, and 6). Included in the Appendix are: (1) a reproduction of Ernest Hemingway's 1927 story "Hills Like White Elephants"; (2) the full transcript of a story originally told in face-to-face interaction and excerpted at various points in my discussion, namely, Monica's telling of the narrative to which I have assigned the title *UFO or the Devil* (based on a phrase used by Monica as she launches her story); and (3) some pages (= sequences of panels) from Daniel Clowes's 1997 graphic novel, *Ghost World*, along with (4) screenshots from Terry Zwigoff's 2001 film adaptation of Clowes's novel. Although I also discuss a range of other illustrative texts, I use these narratives as examples throughout my analysis in part to maintain a constant focus across chapters, facilitating exploration of the constraints and affordances of various storytelling media, and in part to make the book appropriate as a standalone teaching text, complete with its own small corpus of stories. However, the model presented here is of course meant to be extensible, and those using the book in classroom settings may wish to test its possibilities and limitations by examining other narrative case studies.

Storytelling Media and Modes of Narration

At several points in my discussion (e.g., the previous paragraph) I use the term *storytelling media* to refer, in general terms, to the various semiotic environments in which narrative practices can be conducted (see also Ryan 2004). But not all storytelling media are created equal. Some afford multiple communicative channels that can be exploited by a given narrative to evoke a storyworld, whereas others afford only a single channel when it comes to designing blueprints for storyworlds. Thus, as a print narrative with only a verbal information track, Hemingway's "Hills" can be characterized as monomodal. By contrast, the graphic-novel version of *Ghost World*, though also a print text, engages in multimodal narration, since the novel exploits both a verbal and a visual information track to engage in narrative ways of worldmaking. Zwigoff's film adaptation of *Ghost World* is likewise multimodal, though what were originally word–image combinations are now remediated by way of two different semiotic channels, namely, the filmed image-track and the audiorecorded sound-track.

Meanwhile, in its original context of telling *UFO or the Devil* also involved multimodal narration, since Monica recounted her and Renee's experiences with the big ball using not only the expressive resources of spoken discourse but also (one can infer) the further information track provided by gestures. Thus, in line 5 of the transcribed version of the story, the analyst can hypothesize that pointing gestures accompanied Monica's use of the demonstrative pronoun in _this_ ↑_way_ as well as her subsequent reference to a vector of motion within her and her interlocutors' current field of vision: *comin up through here* (see the Appendix for the full transcript). But my hedges in this context ("one can infer," "the analyst can hypothesize that") are themselves pertinent to the topic under discussion, since they underscore that Monica's original narrative performance is unavailable for analysis in its own right. Instead there is an audiorecording that itself translates the narrative into a different medium – as an act of storytelling that exploits only the channel of spoken discourse. And then my transcript re-translates this remediation into the medium of print! In other words, audiorecording a face-to-face storytelling situation recasts a complex, multi-channel communicative process as monomodal narration, and the act of transcription in turn creates a differently monomodal artifact. The converse situation holds when a print narrative is adapted as a movie; in that case, single-channel, monomodal narration is translated into multimodal storytelling.[1]

These considerations suggest the relevance of the distinction that theorists such as Kress and van Leeuwen (2001) and Jewitt (2006) draw between modes and media. In their work, modes are semiotic channels (better, environments) that can be viewed as a resources for the *design* of a representation formulated within a particular type of discourse, which is in turn embedded in a specific kind of communicative interaction. By contrast, *media* can be viewed as means for the dissemination or production of what has been designed in a given mode; thus media "are the material resources used in the production of semiotic products and events, including both the tools and the materials used" (Kress and van Leeuwen 2001: 22). This distinction between modes and media captures the intuition that, as is the case with *UFO or the Devil*, a text or discourse can be designed in one kind of environment (e.g., face-to-face communication) but distributed or produced in another (e.g., as an audiorecording or a printed transcript). In short, not only do different storytelling media afford different modes of narration (cf. Herman 2004) but what is more, a variety of media can come into play during the process of transmitting, transcribing, and archiving stories, with consequences that need to be explored more fully by narrative analysts.

Acknowledgments

I taught *Ghost World* in two recent classes at Ohio State University, and I wish to acknowledge, first, some of the students whose insightful comments helped me better understand the range of Clowes's references and the importance of his achievement, as well as the complex relationship between the graphic-novel and film versions of his narrative. My special thanks go to Josh Steskal, Carrie Waibel, John Nees, Pat Carr, and Aaron Seddon. Further, I wish to acknowledge here just a few of the many other people who have helped me sharpen the arguments presented in this study, rethink the broader context of my approach, or simply maintain the conviction that I should keep working on the book until I could finish it: Porter Abbott, Jan Alber, Anita Albertsen, Jens Brockmeier, Apostolos Doxiadis, Monika Fludernik, Jared Gardner, Richard Gerrig, Per Krogh Hansen, Dan Hutto, Matti Hyvärinen, Brian Joseph, Anne Langendorfer, Barry Mazur, Paul McCormick, Brian McHale, Chris Meister, Sean O'Sullivan, Ruth Page, Bo Pettersson, Jim Phelan, Arkady Plotnitsky, Peter Rabinowitz, Andrew Salway, Debby Schiffrin, Ulrich Schnauss, Roy Sommer, Meir Sternberg, and Michael Toolan. I am also extremely grateful for the comments and criticisms offered by the anonymous reviewer, whose detailed report saved me from a number of errors and infelicities, helped me clarify several of my key claims, and more generally improved the overall quality of this book. At the press, I am grateful to Emma Bennett, Hannah Morrell, Louise Butler, and Janet Moth for their patience, professionalism, and dedication to making this the best book possible. I also thank Ohio State University's College of Humanities for the publication subvention that helped defray the cost of reprinting some of the material included in the Appendix.

I had support from other sources as well: the Lake View Trail at Prairie Oaks Park; the incredible shapeshifts of cloud and sun in the skies over Madison County, Ohio; and the sustaining power of narrative itself, the multitude of stories from which our lives are woven. But I am most grateful for the loving support of Susan Moss, whose Four Seasons lettuce, Chioggia beets, Sungold tomatoes, and Atomic Red carrots are basic elements of our own evolving story.

In some of the chapters of this book I have drawn on material published in other contexts, and though all this material has since been substantially revised, I am grateful for permission to use it here:

"Histories of Narrative Theory (I): A Genealogy of Early Developments." In J. Phelan and P. Rabinowitz (eds.), *The Blackwell Companion to Narrative Theory* (pp. 19–35). Oxford: Blackwell, 2005. Reprinted by permission.

The Cambridge Companion to Narrative, edited by David Herman. Excerpts totaling approx. 12–13 pages, taken from pp. 3–21, "Introduction," by David Herman. Copyright 2007 Cambridge University Press. Reprinted by permission.

"Storytelling and the Sciences of Mind: Cognitive Narratology, Discursive Psychology, and Narratives in Face-to-Face Interaction." Copyright 2007 The Ohio State University. Originally appeared in *Narrative* 15(3) (2007), pp. 306–34. Reprinted by permission.

"Narrative Theory and the Intentional Stance." *Partial Answers* 6(2) (2008), pp. 233–60. Copyright 2008 The Johns Hopkins University Press. Reprinted by permission.

"Description, Narrative, and Explanation: Text-Type Categories and the Cognitive Foundations of Discourse Competence." *Poetics Today* 29(3). Copyright 2008 the Porter Institute for Poetics and Semiotics, Tel Aviv University. Publisher Duke University Press. Reprinted by permission.

"Narrative Theory after the Second Cognitive Revolution." In Lisa Zunshine (ed.), *Introduction to Cognitive Cultural Studies*. Copyright 2009 The Johns Hopkins University Press. Reprinted by permission.

Ernest Hemingway's "Hills Like White Elephants" is reprinted in its entirety, in the Appendix, by permission of Charles Scribner's Sons.

Pages 21, 26, 35, and 38 of Daniel Clowes, *Ghost World* (Seattle: Fantagraphic Books, 1997) (sequences A–D in the Appendix) are reprinted by permission of Fantagraphic Books.

Screenshots 1–7 from Terry Zwigoff's film adaptation of *Ghost World* © 2001 MGM.

The Elements

A prototypical narrative can be characterized as:

(i)   A representation that is situated in – must be interpreted in light of – a specific discourse context or occasion for telling.

(ii) The representation, furthermore, cues interpreters to draw inferences about a structured time-course of particularized events.

(iii) In turn, these events are such that they introduce some sort of disruption or disequilibrium into a storyworld involving human or human-like agents, whether that world is presented as actual or fictional, realistic or fantastic, remembered or dreamed, etc.

(iv) The representation also conveys the *experience* of living through this storyworld-in-flux, highlighting the pressure of events on real or imagined consciousnesses affected by the occurrences at issue. Thus – with one important proviso – it can be argued that narrative is centrally concerned with *qualia*, a term used by philosophers of mind to refer to the sense of "what it is like" for someone or something to have a particular experience. The proviso is that recent research on narrative bears importantly on debates concerning the nature of consciousness itself.

For convenience of exposition, I abbreviate these elements as (i) **situatedness**, (ii) **event sequencing**, (iii) **worldmaking/world disruption**, and (iv) **what it's like**.

Getting Started

A Thumbnail Sketch of the Approach

Toward a Working Definition of Narrative

The overall aim of this book is to sketch an account of some of the distinctive properties of narrative. At a minimum, stories concern temporal sequences – situations and events unfolding in time. But not all representations of sequences of events are designed to serve a storytelling purpose, as we know from recipes, scientific explanations of plant physiology, and other genres of discourse. What else is required for a representation of events unfolding in time to be used or interpreted as a narrative? This book develops strategies for addressing that question, and the present chapter provides a thumbnail sketch of my approach. The next chapter then situates the approach in the context of the growing body of research on stories and storytelling, while the remaining chapters provide a more detailed description of the model presented in synoptic form here.

One of the main goals of this book is to develop an account of what stories are and how they work by analyzing narrative into its basic elements, thereby differentiating between storytelling and other modes of representation. Here at the outset, it may be helpful to provide an orienting statement of features that I take to be characteristic of narrative.[1] A relatively coarse-grained version of the working definition of narrative on which I will rely in this study, and that I spell out in more detail as I proceed, runs as follows: rather than focusing on general, abstract situations or trends, stories are accounts of what happened to particular people[2] – and of what it was like for them to experience what happened – in particular circumstances and with specific consequences. Narrative, in other words, is a basic human strategy for coming to terms with time, process, and change – a strategy that contrasts with, but is in no way inferior to, "scientific" modes of explanation that characterize phenomena as instances of general covering laws. Science explains the atmospheric processes that (all other things being equal) account for when precipitation will take the form of snow rather than rain; but it takes a story to convey what it was like to walk along a park trail in fresh-fallen snow as afternoon turned to evening in the late autumn of 2007.

Yet just as it is possible to construct a narrative about the development of science, to tell a story about who made what discoveries and under what circumstances, it is possible to use the tools of science – definition, analysis, classification, comparison, etc. – to work toward a principled account of what makes a text, discourse, film, or other artifact a narrative. Such an account should help clarify what distinguishes a narrative from an exchange of greetings, a recipe for salad dressing, or a railway timetable. This book aims to provide just this sort of account, drawing integratively on a number of traditions for narrative study to characterize the factors bearing on whether a representation of a sequence of events functions as a story. Another overarching goal of the book is to enable (and encourage) readers to build on the ideas presented here, so that others can participate in the process of narrative inquiry and help create more dialogue among the many fields concerned with stories, ranging from the humanities and social sciences (literary studies, creative writing, (socio)linguistics, history, philosophy, social and cognitive psychology, ethnography, communication studies, autobiography and life-story research, etc.) to clinical medicine, journalism, narrative therapy, and the arts.[3]

The next two sections of this chapter seek to move closer to a working definition of narrative. I begin by noting that narrative can be viewed under several profiles simultaneously – as a form of mental representation, a type of textual or semiotic artifact, and a resource for communicative interaction – and then identify four basic elements of narrative (some of them with sub-elements), which might also be viewed as conditions for narrativity, or what makes a narrative a narrative. Subsequent chapters zoom in on these elements or conditions in turn, offering a more in-depth treatment of the core features synopsized below.

Here at the outset, it is important to address a broader – indeed, foundational – issue pertaining to my attempt to identify basic elements of narrative. This issue can be approach by way of the distinction between what might be termed "etic" and "emic" approaches to narrative study – a distinction also applied to narrative research by Georgakopoulou (2007: 39ff.) in an important recent book that bears significantly on my own analysis, and that I return to at the end of this section. The etic/ emic distinction, coined by Pike (1982), is based on the contrast between phonetic and phonemic differences. Phonetic differences include, for example, all the various shades of difference among tokens of the consonant [p] that may be produced by speakers of English when they pronounce the first sound in the word *put*, such as aspirated $[p^h]$ versus unaspirated tokens. Whereas in Hindi such differences do affect the meaning of utterances containing the [p] sound (i.e., the differences are phonemic), in English these differences do not (i.e., the differences are merely phonetic). By contrast, shifting from an unvoiced to a voiced bilabial stop, that is, from [p] to [b], does change the meaning of an utterance in English, as anyone hearing or reading *put* versus *but* would recognize. To extrapolate from this distinction: whereas etic approaches create descriptive categories that are used by analysts to sift through patterns in linguistic data, whether or not those categories correspond to differences perceived as meaningful by users of the language being analyzed, emic approaches seek to capture differences that language users themselves orient to as meaningful. Accordingly, a question for any account of the basic elements of narrative is whether those elements are in fact oriented to as basic by participants engaged in storytelling practices (= emic), or whether the elements are instead part of a system for analysis imposed on the data from without (= etic).

For example, Eggins and Slade (1997) draw on Labov's (1972) approach to narrative analysis and Plum's (1988) work on storytelling genres in face-to-face discourse to differentiate between full-fledged narratives and anecdotes (defined as reports of remarkable events plus the reactions they caused), exempla (defined as reports of incidents coupled with the interpretation of those events), and recounts (defined as the giving of a more or less bare record of events).[4] But the question

remains whether these are emic categories to which participants themselves orient, using them to make sense of different kinds of communicative activity, or whether such differences go unnoticed in the business
of talk and are instead viewed by storytellers and their interlocutors
as instances of the broader category "narrative." To what extent do participants themselves discriminate between anecdotes and recounts, for
example, in their own practice, and how would we go about finding
that out? Similar questions can be posed about the model presented in
this book – for example, whether participants in face-to-face discourse,
readers of written texts, or viewers of films would discriminate among
the categories of description, narrative, and argument in the manner
suggested by my account later in this chapter and also in chapter 4.
Further, for what populations do the critical properties of narrative
outlined in this study indeed constitute basic elements of narrative,
such that texts, discourses, or mental representations lacking one or
more of those properties would be categorized by members of those
populations as something other than a story? And how robust are these
effects: within a given population, how important is a given element
identified in my approach as basic?

To be addressed adequately, these questions must be explored via
empirical methods of investigation, whether in controlled laboratory
settings, through statistical analysis of responses to questionnaires, or
in more naturalistic environments through techniques of participant
observation, followed by interpretation of the data elicited in that
fashion. I do not undertake these methods of inquiry here; instead,
I argue for a particular approach to identifying the basic elements of
narrative in the hope that it might provide a basis or at least a context
for further studies of this kind. The book draws on my own native
intuitions about stories and storytelling, coupled with traditions of
narrative scholarship, to construct a model that I argue provides emic
categories for narrative study, and not just etic ones. The possibilities
and limitations of the model will not be fully evident, however, until
others test it against their own intuitions about what constitutes a
story – as well as the intuitions of broader populations whose narrative practices might be studied through the empirical approaches just
mentioned.

This last point affords a segue back to a recent study that I mentioned
above and that I wish to return to for a moment in concluding this

section. The study in question is Georgakopoulou's (2007) ethno-graphically oriented analysis of stories told in face-to-face interaction, and more specifically in non-interview settings where peers or family members tell (and retell) stories about events from their immediate as well as longer-term past, co-narrate shared stories, engage in projections of future events, and also produce truncated yet heavily evaluated reports that Georgakopoulou terms *breaking news* (Georgakopoulou 2007: 40–56; cf. Norrick 2000, 2007). Building on Ochs and Capps' (2001) pathbreaking account (discussed below and also in my next chapter), and in particular their working assumption that "mundane conversational narratives of personal experience constitute the prototype of narrative activity rather than the flawed byproduct of more artful and planned narrat-ive discourse" (2001: 3), Georgakopoulou argues that the development of models appropriate for research on everyday storytelling has been hindered by the kinds of narratives assumed to be canonical or pro-totypical. In the domains of sociolinguistics, life-story research, and other fields concerned with narratives produced in face-to-face interaction, Georgakopoulou suggests, the canonical or prototypical narrative is the kind of story on which Labov's (1972) influential account was based: "namely, the research or interview narrative that is invariably about non-shared, personal[-]experience past events, and that occurs in response to the researcher's 'elicitation' questions or prompts" (Georgakopoulou 2007: 31).[5] By contrast, adapting a term first suggested by Bamberg (2004b), Georgakopoulou proposes to shift the focus of research on every-day storytelling to "small stories" whose structure and functions do not map directly onto the narratives featured in the Labovian model:

> small stories ... can be brought together on the basis of their main characteristic, namely that they are presented as part of a trajectory of interactions rather than as a free standing, finished and self-contained unit. More specifically, a) the events they report have some kind of immediacy, i.e. they are very recent past or near future events, or are still unfolding as the story is being constructed; b) they establish and refer to links between the participants' previous and future interactions ... including their shared stories. In this way, the stories are not only heavily embedded in their immediate discourse surroundings but also in a larger history of interactions in which they are intertextually linked and available for recontextualization in various local settings. (Georgakopoulou 2007: 40)

[handwritten margin note: Small Story]

By focusing on such noncanonical stories, and by drawing on ideas from linguistic ethnography, Conversation Analysis, and other approaches to talk-as-interaction, Georgakopoulou aims to "document local theories of what constitutes a narrative and what the role of narrative is in specific communities" (2007: 21).

Despite some terminological and methodological differences, Georgakopoulou's analysis and my own are arguably quite consonant in their underlying assumptions. Though readers are advised to come back to the following remarks after they have had a chance to read the rest of this chapter (and perhaps the subsequent chapters as well), it may be worth underscoring at this point the links between Georgakopoulou's and my approaches. For one thing, as chapter 3 explores in more detail, in the model developed here one of the basic elements of narrative is the embeddedness of stories in a specific discourse context or occasion for telling. To paraphrase Heraclitus: the same story cannot be told twice, because the context in which the first telling takes place is irrevocably altered by that initial narrational act – this being a way of capturing what Georgakopoulou terms the "social consequentiality" (2007: 148) of situated storytelling acts. Shifting to a different issue, it is true that my account is based on the premise that there are modes of representation that are prototypically narrative, and also that there are identifiable critical properties associated with those modes of representation. Yet chapter 4 begins by characterizing such properties as more or less evident in a given story and anchors them in the patterns of use by virtue of which certain texts or discourses come to count as narratives. In other words, what constitutes a prototypical story is defined in a gradient, more-or-less way, and emerges from the strategies on which people rely in their everyday narrative practices.[6] And as I also discuss in chapter 4, what is considered to be prototypical can vary across different contexts; think of the prototypical cold day in Tampa, Florida, versus Helsinki, Finland. Hence Georgakopoulou's "small stories" might be redescribed as modes of storytelling in which, because of a shift of communicative circumstances, the normal and expected range of narrative practices differs from the practices used for relatively monologic narration in an interview setting, for example. Yet both sets of practices fall within the scope of narrative viewed as a kind or category of texts, and are oriented to as such by participants.

Profiles of Narrative

Part of the challenge of analyzing stories into their basic elements is that narrative can be viewed under several profiles: as a cognitive structure or way of making sense of experience; as a type of text, produced and interpreted as such by those who generate or navigate stories in any number of semiotic media (written or spoken language, comics and graphic novels, film, television, computer-mediated communication such as instant messaging, etc.); and as a resource for communicative interaction, which both shapes and is shaped by storytelling practices.

Among the most resonant and often cited words about stories and storytelling are the following, from Roland Barthes's 1966 essay, "Introduction to the Structural Analysis of Narratives":

> The narratives of the world are numberless. Narrative is first and foremost a prodigious variety of genres, themselves distributed amongst different substances. . . . Able to be carried by articulated language, spoken or written, fixed or moving images, gestures, and the ordered mixture of all these substances; narrative is present in myth, legend, fable, tale, novella, epic, history, tragedy, drama, comedy, mime, painting . . . stained glass windows, cinema, comics, news item, conversation. Moreover under this almost infinite diversity of forms, narrative is present in every age, in every place, in every society. . . . All classes, all human groups, have their narratives. . . . Caring nothing for the division between good and bad literature, narrative is international, transhistorical, transcultural: it is simply there, like life itself. (Barthes [1966] 1977: 79)

Emphasizing in this passage the ubiquity of narrative, Barthes goes on in the rest of his essay to identify key aspects of narrative – defining traits that might be argued to be basic elements of narrative irrespective of the medium or context in which it appears.

For example, Barthes suggests at one point that we human beings have a narrative language within us that consists in part of "sequence titles" (*Fraud, Betrayal, Struggle, Seduction*, etc.) that we use to make sense of stories. According to Barthes, such titles, or labels for kinds of events, allow us to segment or "chunk" the flow of narrative information and make sense of things characters are doing (1966: 101–2). Elsewhere he suggests that "the mainspring of narrative is precisely the confusion of consecution and consequence, what comes *after* being read in narrative as what is *caused by*," such that "narrative [can be thought of as] a systematic application of the logical fallacy denounced by Scholasticism in the formula *post hoc, ergo propter hoc*" (1966: 94). In other words, if a sequence of panels in a graphic novel first shows two characters walking along a sidewalk and then shows them seated in a restaurant, readers will assume, all other things being equal, that the characters' being in the restaurant is a result of their having walked to it. This default assumption can be forestalled or dislodged only if the text provides other, supplemental information. For example, the text might rely on a different style of typography or different colors for the borders of particular panels (or different clothing and hair styles for the characters) to suggest that the restaurant scene is remembered from an earlier time rather than one the characters encounter after their stroll.

Barthes's larger point here is that narrative is not (or rather, not only) something *in* the text. To the contrary, stories are cognitive as well as textual in nature, structures of mind as well as constellations of verbal, cinematic, pictorial, or other signs produced and interpreted within particular communicative settings. In other words, narratives (the *Iliad*, an episode of the *Star Trek* television series, the film or graphic novel versions of *Ghost World*, anecdotes exchanged among friends during a party, the courtroom testimony of a witness to a crime) result from complex transactions that involve producers of texts or other semiotic artifacts, the texts or artifacts themselves, and interpreters of these narrative productions working to make sense of them in accordance with cultural, institutional, genre-based, and text-specific protocols. Indeed, as these examples suggest, different communicative situations can involve very different ground rules for storytelling. If I watch a *Star Trek* episode with the same mindset as a prosecuting attorney cross-examining a witness, or vice versa, I am apt to misconstrue the narrative at issue – with potentially disastrous consequences. By the same token, although a witness giving testimony and a screenwriter producing a screenplay for an episode in a TV series are both subject to constraints on the sorts of narratives they can generate, the constraints are radically different. Narratives that would be censured in court as too extravagant (violating for example the stricture against hearsay) might well get a screenwriter fired for being too formulaic and boring.

[handwritten margin note: narrative based on logical fallacy]

In short, an essential part of our mental lives, narratively organized systems of signs are also socially constituted and propagated, being embedded in social groups and constructed in social encounters which are themselves represented after the fact by way of narratives. Hence it behooves scholars of narrative to explore how people weave tapestries of story by relying on abilities they possess as simultaneously language-using, thinking, and social beings. Or, to put the same point another way, a truly cross-disciplinary approach to stories (only barely hinted at in the present volume) may help reveal the extent to which human intelligence itself is rooted in narrative ways of knowing, interacting, and communicating.[7]

Narrative: Basic Elements

In the approach developed in this book, stories can be analyzed into four basic elements, some with sub-elements of their own. I characterize narrative as (i) a mode of representation that is situated in – must be interpreted in light of – a specific discourse context or occasion for telling. This mode of representation (ii) focuses on a structured time-course of particularized events. In addition, the events represented are (iii) such that they introduce some sort of disruption or disequilibrium into a storyworld, whether that world is presented as actual or fictional, realistic or fantastic, remembered or dreamed, etc. The representation also (iv) conveys what it is like to live through this storyworld-in-flux, highlighting the pressure of events on real or imagined consciousnesses undergoing the disruptive experience at issue. As noted previously, for convenience of exposition these elements can be abbreviated as (i) **situatedness**, (ii) **event sequencing**, (iii) **worldmaking/world disruption**, and (iv) **what it's like**.

Consider the following two texts, both of them concerned with human emotions. The first is an excerpt from an encyclopedia article on the topic (Oatley 1999: 273); the second is a transcription of part of a tape-recorded interview with Monica, a 41-year-old African American female from Texana, North Carolina, who in the transcribed excerpt refers to the fear that she and her childhood friend experienced as a result of being pursued menacingly by a large, glowing, orange ball that Monica characterizes earlier in the interview as "[a] UFO or the devil."[8] (See the Appendix for a full transcript of the story and also for a description of the transcription conventions I've used to annotate the text here and elsewhere in the book.)

Text 1

An emotion is a psychological state or process that functions in the management of goals. It is typically elicited by evaluating an event as relevant to a goal; it is positive when the goal is advanced, negative when the goal is impeded. The core of an emotion is readiness to act in a certain way . . . it is an urgency, or prioritization, of some goals and plans rather than others; also they prioritize certain kinds of social interaction, prompting, for instance, cooperation, or conflict.

Text 2

(26)   But <u>then</u> ... {.2} for some reason I feel some heat > or somethin other <

(27)   and I < <u>look</u> <u>back</u> >

(28)   me and Renee did at the same time

(29)   it's right <u>behind</u> us. ... {1.0}

(30)   We like-... {.2} /we were scared and-/..

(31)   "<u>AAAHHH</u>" you know=

[....]

(33)   > =at the same time. <

(34)   So we take off <u>runnin</u> as <u>fast</u> as we can,

(35)   and we still lookin <u>back</u>

(36)   and every time we look back it's with us. ... {.5}

(37)   It's just a-<u>bouncin</u> behind /us/

(38)   it's <u>no:t</u>.. > touchin the <u>ground</u>, <

(39)   it's bouncin in the <u>air</u>. ... {.5}

(40)   °Just like this ... {.2} behind us°

(41)   as we <u>run</u>. ... {1.0}

(42)   We run <u>all</u> the way to her grandmother's

(43)   and we <u>open</u> the door

(44)   and we just fall out in the floor,

(45)   and we're cryin and we scre:amin

(46)   and < we just can't <u>breathe</u>.> ... {.3}

(47)   We that <u>scared</u>..

Text 1 exemplifies what Jerome Bruner (1986) calls "paradigmatic" or logico-deductive reasoning.[9] The author uses definitions to establish categories in terms of which (a) emotions can be distinguished from other kinds of phenomena (goals, events, evaluations, etc.), and (b) different kinds of emotions can be distinguished from one another. The author also identifies a core feature (readiness to act) that can be assumed to cut across all types of emotion, and to be constitutive of emotion in a way that other features, more peripheral, do not. In turn, the text links this core feature to a process of prioritization that grounds emotion in contexts of social interaction.

By contrast, text 2 exemplifies what Bruner characterizes as "narrative" reasoning. In this text, too, emotion figures importantly. But rather than defining and sub-categorizing emotions, and explicitly associating them with aspects of social interaction, Monica draws tacitly on emotion terms and categories to highlight the salience of the narrated events for both Renee and herself at the time of their occurrence – and their continuing emotional impact in the present, for that matter. Monica uses terms like *scared* (lines 30 and 47), reports behaviors conventionally associated with extreme fear (screaming, running, feeling unable to breathe), and makes skillful use of the evaluative device that Labov calls "expressive phonology" (1972: 379), which can include changes in pitch, loudness, rate of speech, and rhythm, as well as the emphatic lengthening of vowels or whole words. Thus in lines 31 and 46, Monica uses heightened volume, on the one hand, and a slower rate of speech combined with an increase in pitch, on the other hand, to perform in the here and now the emotional impact of past experiences. In other words, more than just reflecting or encapsulating pre-existing emotions, the text *constructs* Monica (and Renee) as an accountably frightened experiencer of the events reported. Monica's story provides an account of what happened by creating a nexus or link between the experiencing self and the world experienced; it builds causal-chronological connections among what Monica saw that night, her and Renee's emotional responses to the apparition, and the verbal and nonverbal actions associated with those responses. Text 1 abstracts from any particular emotional experience to outline general properties of emotions, and to suggest a taxonomy or classification based on those properties. By contrast, text 2 uses specific emotional attributions to underscore the impact of this unexpected or noncanonical (and thus reportably noteworthy) sequence of events, which happened on this one occasion, in this specific locale, and in this particular way, on the consciousness of the younger experiencing-I

– to whose thoughts and feelings the story recounted by the older narrating-I provides access.[10]

Hence, besides using principles of reasoning to develop definitions, classifications, and generalizations of the sort presented in text 1, people use other principles, grounded in the production and interpretation of stories, to make sense of the impact of experienced events on themselves and others, as in text 2. But what are these other principles? Or, to put the question differently, assuming that "we organize our experience and memory of human happenings mainly in the form of narrative – stories, excuses, myths, reasons for doing and not doing, and so on" (Bruner 1991: 4), what are the design principles of narrative itself? What explains people's ability to distinguish storytelling from other kinds of communicative practices, and narratives from other kinds of semiotic artifacts?

To capture what distinguishes text 2 from text 1, it is important to keep in mind the ideas about categorization developed by cognitive scientists such as George Lakoff (1987) and Eleanor Rosch ([1978] 2004) – ideas that Marie-Laure Ryan (2005a, 2007), among other story analysts (cf. Herman forthcoming b; Jannidis 2003), has used in her own proposals concerning how to define narrative. I return to these ideas in more detail in chapter 4, and readers may wish to read that chapter immediately after the following paragraphs to get a fuller sense of the conceptual underpinnings of the model presented in an abbreviated fashion here. In any case, the work on categorization processes suggests that at least some of the categories in terms of which we make sense of the world are gradient in nature; that is, they operate in a "more-or-less" rather than an "either-or" fashion. In such cases, central or prototypical instances of a given category will be good (= easily recognized and named) examples of it, whereas more peripheral instances will display less goodness-of-fit. Thus, a category like "bird" can be characterized as subject to what Lakoff calls *centrality gradience*: although robins are more prototypical members or central instances of the category than emus are (since robins can fly, for example), emus still belong in the category, albeit farther away from what might be called the center of the category space. Meanwhile, when one category shades into another, *membership gradience* can be said to obtain. Think of the categories "tall person" and "person of average height": where exactly do you draw the line? Narrative can be described as a kind of text (a text-type category) to which both centrality gradience and membership gradience apply.

A given story or story-like representation can be a more or less central instance of the category; further, some narratives will have properties that place them in closer proximity to neighboring text-type categories (descriptions, lists, arguments, etc.) than is the case with other narratives.[11]

Thus, whereas prototypical instances of the category "narrative" share relatively few features with those of "description," more peripheral cases are less clearly separable from that text-type, allowing for hybrid forms that Harold F. Mosher (1991) called "descriptivized narrations" and "narrativized descriptions."[12] Consider the nursery rhyme "This Little Piggy Went to Market":

> Text 3
> This little piggy went to market.
> This little piggy stayed home.
> This little piggy had roast beef.
> This little piggy had none.
> This little piggy cried "Wee! Wee! Wee!" all the way home.

Recited while one pulls each toe of the child's foot, this nursery rhyme constitutes a playful way to focus attention on and "describe" all five toes by means of a quasi-narrative that groups them together into a constellation of characters, who move along non-intersecting trajectories in a somewhat nebulous space-time environment. The quasi-story vehiculates the description – i.e., the enumeration – of the toes. Conversely, a modified version of an example discussed by Culler (1975: 167) in a different context suggests how descriptivized narration operates. If in paraphrasing Eudora Welty's short story "A Worn Path" (Welty [1941] 2006) I were to slow down the pace of narration drastically, and make Welty sound something like Robbe-Grillet, I might arrive at the following descriptivized narration of one brief phase of Phoenix Jackson's walk through the woods in quest of medicine for her ailing grandson:

> She raised her left foot two inches off the ground while swinging it forward and, displacing her center of gravity so that the foot hit the ground, heel first, strode off on the ball of the right foot . . .

This hyperdetailed paraphrase effectively moves the text in the direction of description and away from prototypical instances of narration – since the plot of Welty's story threatens to be submerged beneath the mass of descriptive detail associated with this ultra-slow-motion method of recounting. Thus the two examples discussed in this paragraph suggest the relevance of centrality gradience for members of text-type categories: narrativized descriptions and descriptivized narrations are neither prototypically descriptive nor prototypically narrative.

But what accounts for where along the continuum stretching between narrative and description (among other text-type categories) a given artifact falls? What are the design principles that, when fully actualized, result in prototypical narrative representations? As already indicated in the headnote to this section, I suggest that stories can be analyzed into four basic elements: situatedness, event sequencing, worldmaking/world disruption, and what it's like. On this account, a prototypical narrative can be construed as

(i)   A representation that is situated in – must be interpreted in light of – a specific discourse context or occasion for telling.

(ii) The representation, furthermore, cues interpreters to draw inferences about a structured time-course of particularized events.

(iii) In turn, these events are such that they introduce some sort of disruption or disequilibrium into a storyworld[13] involving human or human-like agents, whether that world is presented as actual or fictional, realistic or fantastic, remembered or dreamed, etc.

(iv) The representation also conveys the *experience* of living through this storyworld-in-flux, highlighting the pressure of events on real or imagined consciousnesses affected by the occurrences at issue. Thus – with one important proviso – it can be argued that narrative is centrally concerned with *qualia*, a term used by philosophers of mind to refer to the sense of "what it is like" for someone or something to have a particular experience. The proviso is that recent research on narrative bears importantly on debates concerning the nature of consciousness itself.[14]

The subsections that follow discuss each of these elements in turn. But some preliminary comments may provide useful context.

The first element listed gives due recognition to what Meir Sternberg has called the Proteus Principle: "in different contexts . . . the same [linguistic or textual] form may fulfill different [communicative or representational] functions *and* different forms the same function" (1982: 148). Given the proper communicative context, a simple utterance like *He walked* might serve narrative functions – cuing interlocutors to construct a fuller representational scaffolding around that simple clause that might include a character who because of disease or injury was expected never to walk again, or who, rather than driving a long distance in a car, had to walk that far because of car trouble. Accordingly, the elements of event sequencing, worldmaking/world disruption, and what it's like should be viewed, not as failsafe guarantees of the presence of narrative, but rather as critical properties of texts that circulate in communicative contexts in the manner that is characteristic of – or prototypical for – narratives. To put this another way, my aim is to diagnose critical properties of texts that can be interpreted as fulfilling a narrative function across a range of contexts; to stipulate that the properties thus identified constitute basic elements of narrative; and to specify the gradient or more-or-less manner in which those properties may be realized in a given case, resulting in more or less prototypical instances of the category *narrative*. Further, as I discuss in chapter 4, judgments about what counts as "prototypical" are themselves subject to change across different contexts.

As just indicated, some of the critical properties I have characterized as basic elements of narrative are gradient (i.e., they operate by degrees) rather than binarized: how detailed or particularized is the portrayal of the storyworld? how momentous is the disruption represented, and how extensive are its ramifications? how much impact do the events have on the experiencing consciousnesses affected by them? In turn, the gradient nature of these elements or properties helps account for variations in the degree of goodness-of-fit between the text-type category "narrative" and representations or artifacts that may be more or less prototypically story-like. The gradience also explains the existence of the hybrid forms identified by Mosher (e.g., descriptivized narration), as well as why, past a critical threshold, a given representation will lack the kinds of structure necessary for it to be interpreted in narrative terms. Thus, to anticipate my discussion below of the fourth element, what it's like, if the factor of an experiencing consciousness impinged upon by the narrated events becomes sufficiently attenuated, then past a certain point a given representation of a temporal sequence will fall outside the category of narrative and enter the domain of chronicle, synopsis, or some other genre of discourse (i.e., text type) – depending on how the representation aligns itself with other features characteristic of the texts and practices that circulate within communicative contexts under these names (see chapter 4).

In this respect, an analogue to narrative would be something like taking an examination in an academic setting. As with stories, some of the conditions for such "gatekeeping encounters" are binarized, but others are gradient. If the student does not show up for the exam, or if a fire guts the room where it was supposed to occur and there are no other rooms available, then basic conditions for the exam have not been met – just as there can be no story without a representation of one or more events involving one or more human or human-like agents. But other conditions for a successful exam, such as comprehensive mastery of the material on which the exam focuses, or the ability to deploy the conventions of scholarly argument in a relevant, field-specific way, are more-or-less rather than either-or affairs, and can lead to differences of opinion among students and their examiners. Like-wise, interlocutors in face-to-face interaction, readers of novels, and moviegoers can have differing intuitions about the degree of narrativity of certain representations – their capacity for interpretation in narra-tive terms – and such discrepancies can be attributed to the gradient nature of some of the basic elements of narrative itself.

This approach to the conditions for or basic elements of narrative can be compared with the "dimensional" approach developed by Ochs and Capps (2001), also discussed in my next chapter. As Ochs and Capps put it,

> We believe that narrative as genre and activity can be fruitfully examined in terms of a set of dimensions that a narrative displays to different degrees and in different ways. Rather than identifying a set of distinctive features that always characterize narrative, we stipulate dimensions [namely, tellership, tellability, embeddedness, linearity, and moral stance – see chapter 2 below] that will always be relevant to a narrative, even if not elaborately manifest.... The dimensions pertain both to narrating as activity and to narrative as text. Each narrative dimension establishes a range of possibilities, which are realized in par-ticular narrative performances. (2001: 19)

Although I likewise stipulate that some of the basic elements of nar-rative can be conceived as continua or dimensions, I also assume that storytelling as a communicative and representational practice does have distinctive features that set it apart from other such practices, includ-ing the representation of particular kinds of temporal sequences and the use of cues that evoke narrative worlds, or storyworlds, marked by the occurrence of disruption-causing or noncanonical events (see chapters 4 and 5). In other words, the claim that features or properties of narrative obtain in a gradient, more-or-less fashion is consistent with claim that those features are critically important for the identification of certain forms of practice as narrative in nature, as opposed to syllogistic, definitional, descriptive, and so on.[15]

Now, on to a somewhat fuller sketch of the four basic elements themselves; this sketch will be complemented by the exposition provided in chapter 4, and indeed by the rest of this book as a whole.

(i) Situatedness

In emphasizing that narrative representations are situated in specific discourse contexts, or embedded in occasions for telling, I hark back to my earlier claim that stories are the result of complex transactions involving producers of texts, discourses, or other semiotic artifacts, the texts or artifacts themselves, and interpreters of these narrative productions working with cultural, institutional, genre-based, and text-specific protocols. Insofar as narratives are *representations*, they exhibit the same twofold structure that Saussure ([1916] 1954) identified in his discussion of the relationship between *signifier* and *signified*. Thus, in parallel with the relationship that obtains between the English word *cat* and the concept evoked by that word (at least among speakers of English), a narrative representation encompasses both (a) the textual or semiotic cues used in the representing medium and (b) the characters, situations, and events (what this book terms the *storyworld*) represented by those cues. But insofar as narratives are also *communicatively situated* representations, making sense of them requires attending to how they are geared to particular communicative contexts. In other words, interpreters seeking to use textual cues to reconstruct a storyworld must also draw inferences about the communicative goals that have structured the specific occasion of the telling, motivating the use of certain cues in favor of others and shaping the arrangement of the cues selected.[16] Further, even in the case of stories not told to others, narratives are shaped by the broader sociocommunicative environment in which they are produced (cf. Bakhtin [1953] 1986). Thus, if I construct in my mind a representation of my own life story but never share it with anyone else (or perhaps mumble the story unintelligibly), I have nonetheless produced that account in a context structured by conventions for narrating the story of one's life (see Linde 1993) – conventions with which I bring myself into relation even when I seek to resist or subvert them.

Chapter 3 discusses several frameworks for inquiry that can be used to explore how stories are grounded in – necessarily interpreted with reference to – communicative occasions of this sort. Preliminarily, though, one can verify how crucially a narrative's communicative situation affects its interpretation by contrasting Monica's story (text 2) with representations that are not narrative in nature and also with a story having the same basic structure but slotted into a different discourse context. For example, stress equations used to represent forces impinging on buildings and bridges, or diagrams used to represent the radius of a circle, are not communicatively situated in the same way Monica's story is. Neither, for that matter, is the account of emotions presented in text 1 above. It makes a difference, when interpreting her story, to know that Monica is not for instance reading a script written by someone else, and thus quoting another person's first-person retrospective narration, nor a fictional character whose account is being quoted by the narrator of the text in which she appears. These altered occasions of telling would alter, too, the overall sense and also the truth status of the narrative. In the former case (Monica as script reader), the story could no longer be interpreted as firsthand testimony; in the latter case (Monica as fictional character quoted by a narrator), it would no longer make sense to ask: "But did that really happen to Monica [or the person for whom 'Monica' is a pseudonym] near Texana, North Carolina, on such-and-such a date?" By contrast, the stress equations, geometric diagram, or account of emotions could be quoted by others or inserted into dialogue among fictional characters without affecting either their basic propositional content or their truth status.

(ii) *Event sequencing*

Whereas the hallmark of narrative representations is their focus on particular situations and events, scientific explanations by their nature concern themselves with ways in which, in general, the world tends to be. Further, if particularity sets narrative apart from general explanations, narrative's temporal profile helps distinguish the prototypical narrative from many examples of description. I can in principle describe the objects on my desk in any order (left to right, back to front, smallest to largest, etc.); by contrast, narrative traces paths taken by particularized individuals faced with decision points at one or more temporal junctures in a storyworld; those paths lead to consequences that take shape against a larger backdrop in which other possible paths might have been pursued, but were not.[17]

I discuss the issues of temporality and particularity in more detail in chapter 4, but for the time being contrast text 2 with text 3 in this connection: transpose any elements of the sequence that Monica recounts and you would have a different story, whereas in text 3 the order in which the little piggies' actions are recounted is a function of the need to rhyme end-words and establish logical contrasts, not of any corresponding sequence of actions in a little-piggy storyworld. Meanwhile, insofar as text 1 outlines features of emotion in general, it does not focus on any individualized actors, nor any specific sequence of events. As discussed in chapter 5, representations of particularized sequences of events – representations that likewise have a kind of temporal structure specific to narrative – are best viewed as cues used by interpreters to construct mental representations of narrated worlds, that is, storyworlds. Even an apparently barebones verbal sequence such as *The cat raced down the hall in pursuit of a mouse that, however, cleverly eluded capture* prompts the construction of a multifaceted mental model or storyworld. That storyworld includes the cat as agent; the mouse as the (unattained) goal of the cat's pursuit; a path of motion that unfolds along an axis parallel with the hallway of a house or other building, an axis oriented such that the near end corresponds to the position from which the action is viewed; and a temporal profile that, defining the chase as a singular event rather than a recurrent scenario, situates the cat's pursuit of the mouse earlier in time than the moment from which the narrative report itself originates.

(iii) Worldmaking/world disruption

But prototypical instances of narrative involve more than particularized temporal sequences unfolding within more or less richly detailed storyworlds. Building on the work of Vladimir Propp ([1928] 1968), who characterized disruptive events (e.g., acts of villainy) as the motor of narrative, Todorov (1968) specified a further test for when an event-sequence will count as a story. Todorov argued that narratives characteristically follow a trajectory leading from an initial state of equilibrium, through a phase of disequilibrium, to an endpoint at which equilibrium is restored (on a different footing) because of intermediary events – though not every narrative will trace the entirety of this path (see also Bremond 1980; Kafalenos 2006). Todorov thereby sought to capture the intuition that stories prototypically involve a more or less marked disruption of what is expected or canonical. Making sense of how narratives represent disruption in storyworlds, then, depends on forming inferences about the kinds of agency characters have in those worlds, as role-bearing or position-occupying individuals sometimes acting at cross-purposes with their own interests and goals or those of other such individuals. In my previous example, compare the clash between the cat as aggressive pursuer versus the mouse as clever eluder.

At issue here is what Bruner (1991) characterized as a dialectic of "canonicity and breach": "to be worth telling, a tale must be about how an implicit canonical script has been breached, violated, or deviated from in a manner to do violence to . . . [its] 'legitimacy' " (11; see also chapter 5). But it is not just that stories can be recognized as such because of the way they *represent* situations and events that depart from the canonical order. More than this, narrative is a cognitive and communicative strategy for navigating the gap, in everyday experience, between what was expected and what actually takes place. Thus Bruner (1990) characterizes narrative as the primary resource for "folk psychology" – that is, people's everyday understanding of how thinking works, the rough-and-ready heuristics to which they resort in thinking about thinking itself. We use these heuristics to impute motives or goals to others, to evaluate the bases of our own conduct, and to make predictions about future reactions to events. In this context, narrative affords a kind of discourse scaffolding for formulating reasons about why people engage in the actions they do, or else fail to engage in actions that we expect them to pursue. As Bruner puts it, "the organizing principle of folk psychology [is] narrative in nature rather than logical or categorical. Folk psychology is about human agents doing things on the basis of their beliefs and desires, striving for goals, meeting obstacles which they best or which best them, all of this extended over time" (1990: 42–3). More fully,

> when you encounter an exception to the ordinary, and ask somebody what is happening, the person you ask will virtually always tell a story that contains *reasons* (or some other specification of an intentional

state). . . . All such stories seem to be designed to give the exceptional behavior meaning in a manner that implicates both an intentional state in the protagonist (a belief or desire) and some canonical element in the culture. . . . The function of the story is to find an intentional state that mitigates or at least makes comprehensible a deviation from a canonical cultural pattern. (Bruner 1990: 49–50)

Judged by the criterion of more or less markedly violated expectations, or Bruner's dialectic of canonicity and breach, text 3 ("This little piggy") would score lower in narrativity than text 2 (*UFO or the Devil*). True, the contrasts drawn in the first four lines of text 3 may suggest a rudimentary kind of narrativity, involving a disparity between plenty and dearth, hunger and satisfaction; but Monica's story in text 2 centers on a strongly (and strangely) disruptive event: the apparition of a supernatural big ball chasing Monica and her friend through the woods in the dark of night. For its part, because text 1 does not set up a concrete, particularized situation, there is no background against which a tellably disruptive event might be set off.

(iv) What it's like

Prototypically, narrative involves not only a temporal sequence into which events are slotted in a particular way, and not only a dynamic of canonicity and breach; more than this, stories represent – and perhaps make it possible to experience – what it is like to undergo events within a storyworld-in-flux. Narrative roots itself in the lived, felt experience of human or human-like agents interacting in an ongoing way with their cohorts and surrounding environment. To put the same point another way, the less markedly a text or a discourse encodes the pressure of events on an experiencing human or at least human-like consciousness, the less amenable that text or discourse will be to interpretation in narrative terms. Chapter 6 explores this nexus between narrative and mind; the chapter not only examines how the consciousness factor constitutes a critical property of narrative representations, but also draws on recent work in the philosophy of mind to speculate about the converse relation, that is, whether stories provide a basis for conscious experience itself.

In any case, as an analysis or explanation, rather than a story about time-, place-, and person-specific events, text 1 makes no attempt to capture what it's like to experience an emotion. And note also the contrast between texts 2 and 3 on this score. Whereas Monica uses emotion discourse to highlight what it was like to undergo the frightening events she reports, in text 3 the closest we get to qualia – states of conscious awareness grounded in the felt, subjective character of experience (Tye 2003) – is the fifth little piggy's cry of "Wee! Wee! Wee!" all the way home.

Having presented this synopsis of what I take to be basic elements of narrative – a synopsis upon which subsequent chapters attempt to elaborate – I pause in my exposition of this approach to provide in my next chapter a brief overview of recent scholarly developments in the field. This overview should throw light on the context from which my analysis emerges, as well as indicating for interested readers directions for further study.

Framing the Approach

Some Background and Context

Interdisciplinary Perspectives on Narrative and Narrative Theory

> Researchers have pointed to a "narrative turn" unfolding across multiple fields of inquiry over the past several decades. If, as Barthes suggested, stories are omnipresent and transcultural, by the same token the study of narrative in all of its many guises may be able to unite scholars from across the arts and sciences. The present volume emerges from and also seeks to contribute to this cross-disciplinary concern with stories and storytelling.

In his contribution to a volume titled *The Travelling Concept of Narrative*, Matti Hyvärinen traces the extent of the recent diffusion or spread of narrative across disciplinary boundaries, suggesting that "the concept of narrative has become such a contested concept over the last thirty years in response to what is often called the 'narrative turn' in social sciences. . . . The concept has successfully travelled to psychology, education, social sciences, political thought and policy analysis, health research, law, theology and cognitive science" (Hyvärinen 2006: 20). The "narrative turn," to use the term that Hyvärinen adopts from Martin Kreiswirth (2005), has also shaped humanistic fields in recent decades, thanks in part to the development of structuralist theories of narrative in France in the mid to late 1960s.

Thus, around the same time that William Labov and Joshua Waletzky (1967) developed their model for the analysis of personal experience narratives told in face-to-face interaction, thereby establishing a key precedent for scholars of narrative working in the fields mentioned by Hyvärinen, the literary scholar Tzvetan Todorov coined the term "la narratologie" (= "narratology") to designate what he and other structuralist theorists (e.g., Roland Barthes, Claude Bremond, Gérard Genette, and A. J. Greimas) conceived of as a science of narrative modeled after the "pilot-science" of Ferdinand de Saussure's structural linguistics.[1] As I discuss in greater detail below, the structuralists drew not only on Saussure's ideas but also on the work of Russian Formalist literary theorists, who studied prose narratives of all sorts, from Tolstoi's historically panoramic novels to tightly plotted detective novels to (Russian) fairy tales. This broad investigative focus helped initiate the narrative turn, uncoupling theories of *narrative* from theories of the *novel*, and shifting scholarly attention from a particular genre of literary writing to all discourse (or, in an even wider interpretation, all semiotic activities) that can be interpreted as narratively organized. That same shift helps explain why the present volume is titled *Basic Elements of Narrative* rather than *Basic Elements of the Novel* – even though I use narrative fiction as a key source of illustrative examples, written fictional texts being a highly developed form of storytelling across the world's literatures.

Taking their cue from the Formalists, and noting that stories can be presented in a wide variety of textual formats, media, and genres, structuralists such as Barthes ([1957] 1972, [1966] 1977) argued explicitly for an integrative approach to the analysis of narrative – an approach in which stories can be viewed as supporting many cognitive and communicative activities, from spontaneous conversations and historiographic writing to visual art, dance, and mythic and literary traditions. Only after the heyday of structuralism, however, did such an approach to narrative begin to emerge. Although more needs to be done to promote genuine dialogue and exchange among story analysts working in different fields (Hyvärinen 2006), it is undeniable that the past decade in particular has seen an exponential growth of cross-disciplinary research and teaching activity centering around narrative. International in scope, this activity has also spawned book series and journals in which scholarship on narrative figures importantly.[2] Other manifestations of the way narrative cuts across disciplinary boundaries include initiatives such as the Centre for Interdisciplinary Narratology at the University of Hamburg (<http://www.icn.uni-hamburg.de>); the Centre for Narrative Research at the University of East London (<http://www.uel.ac.uk/cnr/>); Columbia University's Program in Narrative Medicine (<http://www.narrativemedicine.org/>), which aims "to fortify medicine with ways of knowing about singular persons available through a study of humanities, especially literary studies and creative writing"; and Project Narrative at Ohio State University (<http://projectnarrative.osu.edu>), which brings together folklorists, scholars of language and literature, theorists of storytelling in film, digital media, and comics and graphic novels, and researchers in other fields concerned with narrative. During the same period, a number of conferences and symposia have been convened to explore the potential of narrative to bridge disciplines, in ways that may in turn throw new light on narrative itself.[3] The present book, which explores basic elements of narrative and examines how those elements manifest themselves in various kinds of storytelling media and communicative situations, can be seen as an outgrowth of this same trend toward interdisciplinarity (and transmediality) in narrative research (cf. Herman 2004).

My next section briefly outlines the (ongoing) development of frameworks for analyzing stories, and concludes with an overview of approaches to studying narrative in contexts of face-to-face interaction. In general I mean to provide a sense of how different concepts and nomenclatures have grown up around different modes of narrative practice, and to underscore the advantages of greater cooperation among scholars focusing on different kinds of storytelling situations. Granted, it may not be possible (or desirable) to transfer all the tools developed by students of cinematic narratives, say, to research on narratives told in contexts of face-to-face interaction or vice versa; attempting a wholesale transfer of this sort might focus attention on what the two storytelling media have in common, at the expense of finer-grained analyses of their specific constraints and affordances. Arguably, however, a more open dialogue among practitioners in the many fields concerned with stories and storytelling can help throw into relief the relative distinctiveness of narrative practices across various contexts, and clarify the extent to which concepts and methods used to investigate one kind of narrative practice can be brought to bear on another.

Major Trends in Recent Scholarship on Narrative

One way to map out recent developments in the study of narrative is to point to a shift from "classical" to "postclassical" approaches. Rooted in Russian Formalist literary theory, classical approaches were extended by structuralist narratologists starting in the mid-1960s, and refined and systematized up through the early 1980s by scholars such as Mieke Bal, Seymour Chatman, Wallace Martin, Gerald Prince, Shlomith Rimmon-Kenan, and others. Further, some of the scholars working in the Anglo-American tradition of scholarship on fictional narrative were influenced by and in turn influenced this Formalist-structuralist tradition.[4] Postclassical approaches, meanwhile, build on the classical tradition but supplement it with concepts and methods that were unavailable to story analysts such as Barthes, Genette, Greimas, and Todorov during the heyday of structuralism. These ideas stem from fields ranging from gender theory and philosophical ethics, to post-Saussurean linguistics, philosophy of language, and cognitive science, to comparative media studies and critical theory. In short, postclassical narratology, which should not be conflated with post-structuralist theories of narrative, contains classical narratology as one of its "moments" but also includes more recent perspectives on the forms and functions of narrative.[5]

During the same period research on narratives told in face-to-face communication has undergone an analogous shift in scope and sophistication, in recent years cross-pollinating with work by scholars interested in bridging the divide between the study of written, literary narratives and analysis of everyday storytelling.

From Russian Formalism to structuralist narratology

The Russian Formalists authored a number of pathbreaking studies that have served as foundations for later research on narrative. For example, in distinguishing between "bound" (or plot-relevant) and "free" (or non-plot-relevant) motifs, Boris Tomashevskii ([1925] 1965) provided the basis for Barthes's distinction between "nuclei" and "catalyzers" in his "Introduction" ([1966] 1977: 93–4). Renamed *kernels* and *satellites* by Seymour Chatman (1978: 53–6), these terms refer to core and peripheral elements of story-content, respectively. Delete or add to the kernel events of a story and you no longer have the same story; delete or add to the satellites and you have the same story told in a different way. Related to Tomashevskii's work on free versus bound motifs, Viktor Shklovskii's ([1929 [1990]) early work on plot as a structuring device established one of the grounding assumptions of structuralist narratology: namely, the *fabula/sjuzhet* or story/discourse distinction, that is, the distinction between the what and the how, or what is being told versus the manner in which it is told.

Another important Formalist precedent for modern narrative theory was furnished by Propp's *Morphology of the Folktale*, whose first English translation appeared in 1958. Propp distinguished between variable and invariant components of the corpus of Russian folktales that he studied; more specifically, he drew a contrast between changing dramatis personae and the unvarying plot functions performed by them (act of villainy, punishment of the villain, etc.). In all, Propp abstracted 31 functions, or character actions defined in terms of their significance for the plot, from his corpus of tales; he also specified rules for their distribution in a given tale. Harking back to Aristotle's subordination of character to plot, Propp's approach constituted the basis for structuralist theories of characters as "actants," or general roles fulfilled by specific characters. Thus, extrapolating from what Propp had termed "spheres of action," Greimas sought to create a typology of actantial roles to which the (indefinitely many) particularized actors in narratives could be reduced. Greimas initially identified a total of six actants to which he thought all particularized narrative actors could be reduced: Subject, Object, Sender, Receiver, Helper, and Opponent. Commenting on this model, Greimas remarked "[i]ts simplicity lies in the fact that it is entirely centred on the object of desire aimed at by the subject and situated, as object of communication, between the sender and the receiver – the desire of the subject being, in its part, modulated in projections from the helper and opponent" ([1966] 1983: 207).

I have already begun to discuss how the structuralist narratologists built on Russian Formalist ideas to help consolidate what I am referring to as the classical tradition of research on narrative. Founding narratology as a subdomain of structuralist inquiry, researchers like Barthes and Greimas followed Saussure's distinction between *la langue* (= language viewed as system) and *la parole* (= individual utterances produced and interpreted on that basis); they construed particular stories as individual narrative messages supported by a shared semiotic system. And just as Saussurean linguistics privileged *la langue* over *la parole*, focusing on the structural constituents and combinatory principles of the semiotic framework of language, the narratologists privileged the study of narrative in general over the interpretation of individual narratives. Already in his 1957 book *Mythologies*, Barthes had analyzed diverse forms of cultural expression (advertisements, photographs, museum exhibits, wrestling matches) as rule-governed signifying practices or "languages" in their own right (Barthes [1957] 1972; cf. Culler 1975). Barthes extended this general approach in his 1966 "Introduction"; instead of offering interpretations of individual narrative texts, Barthes sought to capture elements of the supra- or transtextual code in terms of which people are able to identify narratively organized discourse and interpret it as such.

Indeed, the use of (Saussurean) linguistics as a pilot-science shaped the object, methods, and overall aims of structuralist narratology as an investigative framework. Narratology's basic premise is that a common, more or less implicit model of narrative explains people's ability to understand communicative performances and types of artifacts as stories. In turn, just as (some) linguists have set themselves the goal of identifying the ingredients of linguistic competence, the goal of narratology is to develop an explicit characterization of the model underlying people's intuitive knowledge about stories, in effect providing an account of what constitutes humans' narrative competence. To be sure, the example of linguistics provided narratology with a productive vantage-point on stories, affording terms and categories that generated significant new research questions. Barthes, for example, used the concept of "levels of description" to develop a hierarchical model of narrative as clusters of "functions" that are subsumed under the level of characters' actions, which are in turn subsumed under the level of narration (Barthes [1966] 1977: 85–8). Genette ([1972] 1980) for his part drew on the traditional grammatical concepts of tense, mood, and voice to explore types of temporal sequence, manipulations of viewpoint, and modes of narration. Yet narratology was also limited by the linguistic models it treated as exemplary. Ironically, the narratologists embraced structuralist linguistics as their pilot-science just when its deficiencies were becoming apparent in the domain of linguistic theory itself. The limitations of the Saussurean paradigm were thrown into relief, on the one hand, by emergent formal models for analyzing language structure – for example, those proposed by Chomsky under the auspices of generative grammar. On the other hand, powerful tools were being developed in the wake of Ludwig Wittgenstein, J. L. Austin, H. P. Grice, John Searle, and other post-Saussurean language theorists interested in how contexts of language use bear on the production and interpretation of socially situated utterances. In general, the attempt by later narrative scholars to incorporate ideas about language and communication that postdate structuralist research – ideas discussed in my next chapter – has been a major factor in the advent of postclassical models for research on stories and storytelling.[6]

Anglo-American contributions

I have yet to discuss how Anglo-American scholarship on narrative fiction has contributed to the classical tradition of research on stories. An important figure in this tradition is Percy Lubbock ([1921] 1957), who took his inspiration from Henry James's novelistic practice as well as his theory of fiction. Lubbock made the issue of "point of view" the cornerstone of his account – to an extent not necessarily warranted by James's own approach (see Booth [1961] 1983: 24–5; Miller 1972: 1). In doing so, Lubbock appropriated James's ideas to produce a markedly prescriptive framework. His drew an invidious distinction between showing ("dramatizing" events) and telling ("describing" or "picturing" events), suggesting that description is inferior to dramatization, picturing to scene-making, telling to showing. As Lubbock put it, "other things being equal, the more dramatic way is better than the less. It is indirect, as a method; but it places the thing itself in view, instead of recalling and reflecting and picturing it" ([1921] 1957: 149–50). But although he may have been guilty of transforming into hard and fast prescriptions ideas that James himself proposed much more tentatively in his own critical writings, Lubbock also drew attention to specific methods or procedures that are at the heart of the craft of fiction.

In response, maintaining a focus on issues of narrative technique, but seeking to restore the complexities evident in James's original statement of his theory (as well as in his novelistic practice), Wayne C. Booth ([1961] 1983) inverted the terms of Lubbock's argument, thereby laying the groundwork for a range of rhetorical approaches to narrative.[7] Instead of privileging showing over telling, Booth accorded telling pride of place – making it the general narratorial condition of which "showing" is a localized effect. Indeed, Booth's brilliant account revealed difficulties with the very premise of the telling-versus-showing debate. He characterized showing as an effect promoted by certain deliberately structured kinds of tellings, organized in such a way that a narrator's mediation (though inescapably present) remains more or less covert. Booth also suggested that an emphasis on showing over telling has costs as well as benefits, cataloguing important rhetorical effects that explicit narratorial commentary can be used to accomplish – for example, relating particulars to norms established elsewhere in the text, heightening the significance of events, or manipulating mood.

Furthermore, Booth's wide-ranging discussion of narrative types, ranging from Boccaccio's *Decameron* to ancient Greek epics to novels and short fictions by authors as diverse as Cervantes, Hemingway, and Céline, encouraged subsequent theorists in the Anglo-American tradition to explore various kinds of narratives rather than focusing solely on the novel. This uncoupling of narrative theory from novel theory – a process that had been initiated independently by the Russian Formalists some 40 years earlier – culminated in works as broad in scope as Robert Scholes and Robert Kellogg's study, *The Nature of Narrative*. Significantly, Scholes and Kellogg's book was published in 1966, the same year that saw the publication of the special issue of the journal *Communications* devoted to "Structural Analysis of Narrative" – an issue that effectively launched the project of structuralist narratology in France.

Postclassical approaches

It is beyond the scope of this chapter to review the full range of postclassical approaches to narrative inquiry that build on the foundational work just described as well as on other early scholarship on stories.[8] Rather, the book as a whole is intended to demonstrate how concepts developed during the classical, structuralist period of narratological research can be enriched with ideas from sociolinguistics, discourse analysis, social and cognitive psychology, the philosophy of mind, and other domains. Let me nonetheless provide at least a brief sketch of some broad trends in the field.

One major trend is to continue the exploration of aspects of narrative already identified by earlier theorists, such as narration and plot, time and space, character, dialogue and thought representation, and point of view or perspective (now commonly discussed by narratologists under the rubric of "focalization"), but to extend and refine concepts outlined in the pioneering work of the Russian Formalists, structuralist narratologists, and Anglo-American theorists of fiction. Hence, for example, Michael Toolan's ([1988] 2001) updating of narratological theories with ideas from linguistics and stylistics and H. Porter Abbott's (2005, 2007, [2002] 2008) re-analysis of key ideas concerning narration, or the process by which information about storyworlds is conveyed. Another trend involves expanding the corpus of stories being studied, as well as investigating the constraints and affordances of different storytelling media (cf. Herman 2004; Ryan 2004). For example, Ryan's (2001a, 2006) work on computer-mediated narratives reflects an emergent concern with how medium-specific properties of stories may require the development of investigative tools not provided by classical theories. Likewise the focus and methods of the present book can be contrasted with Bremond's 1964 assumption that the story-level of a narrative – the *what* of a story versus the *way* it is presented – can be transposed without loss or alteration into different semiotic media. A third trend is in a sense the synthesis of the first two. It involves bringing into dialogue with established traditions of narrative scholarship ideas from fields that were not incorporated into earlier work on stories, in order to identify new frontiers of research that the structuralist narratologists, for example, could not have envisioned. This, too, is a path that I follow in the present study, and it also one described by Fludernik (2005) in her recent survey of work in narrative theory from structuralism to the present. Fludernik (2005: 44–51) notes how, during a time when the narrative turn has made stories a focal concern in many disciplines, conversely narrative specialists have added to their theoretical toolkits concepts and methods from research on conversational storytelling, feminist theory and gender studies, modes of ideology critique stemming from Marxist theory as well as research on postcolonial literature, philosophical ethics, psychoanalysis, legal studies, and linguistics and cognitive science. Examples of this third strand of research in narrative theory include the multifaceted work of Uri Margolin on character (Margolin 1990a, 1990b, 2005a, 2007), the powerful new model of plot outlined by Hilary Dannenberg (2008),

Manfred Jahn's (1996, 1997, 1999, 2005, 2007) ongoing use of ideas from cognitive science to propose new ways of understanding perspective or focalization, and the feminist-narratological research pioneered by Susan S. Lanser (1992) and Robyn Warhol (1989, 2003) and recently extended by Ruth Page (2006).

I turn now to what began as a separate tradition of narrative inquiry from the ones just described but has more recently begun to interact with these postclassical approaches. At issue are frameworks developed for the study of stories told in face-to-face interaction.

The study of stories in face-to-face communication: a brief overview

One year after the publication of Barthes's "Introduction" William Labov and Joshua Waletzky published a groundbreaking article that sketched out a sociolinguistic approach to analyzing stories told in contexts of face-to-face interaction. This approach derived from and fed back into traditions of linguistic research with which the structuralist narratologists were barely familiar. Centering on narratives of personal experience, Labov and Waletzky's model spawned a program for research still being pursued by a variety of investigators (see Bamberg 1997a for an overview). Labov and Waletzky's 1967 article (along with the follow-up article on "The Transformation of Experience in Narrative Syntax" published in 1972 by Labov) established a vocabulary for labeling the components of personal-experience narratives (abstract, orientation, complicating action, evaluation, resolution, coda; see the Glossary for definitions of these terms). It also identified clause- and sentence-level structures tending to surface in each of these components, suggesting that story-recipients monitor the discourse for signs enabling them to "chunk" what is said into units-in-a-narrative-pattern. For example, clauses with past-tense verbs in the indicative mood are likely to occur in (i.e., be a reliable indicator of) the complicating action of the narrative, whereas storytellers' evaluations depart from this baseline syntax, their marked status serving to indicate the point of the narrative, the reason for its telling. More generally, Labov's model laid the groundwork for further inquiry into both the linguistic and the interactional profile of narratives told during face-to-face encounters. Conversational narratives do consist of clause-, sentence-, and discourse-level features; yet, as I discuss in my next chapter, they are also anchored in contexts where their tellers have to have a (recognizable) point or else be ignored, shouted down, or worse (cf. Goodwin 1990: 239–57).

Note that, in founding the field of narratology, structuralist theorists had focused mainly on literary narratives as opposed to instances of everyday storytelling. Barthes drew on Fleming's James Bond novels in his "Introduction"; Genette, Greimas, and Todorov used Proust, Maupassant, and Boccaccio as their tutor-texts. Ironically, however, one of the foundational documents for structuralist narratology was Vladimir Propp's investigation of folktales rooted in oral traditions. But the structuralists neglected to consider (let alone mark off) the limits of applicability of Propp's ideas, trying to extend to all narratives, including complicated literary texts, tools designed for a restricted corpus of folktales. The result was an approach that championed the study of narratives of all sorts, irrespective of origin, medium, theme, reputation, or genre, but lacked the conceptual and methodological resources to substantiate its own claims to generalizability.

But though it was firmly anchored in empirical models for studying natural-language data, the sociolinguistic approach pioneered by Labov and Waletzky *also* lacked generalizability. Originally designed for narratives elicited during interviews, the model was manifestly incapable of describing and explaining the more complex structures found in written narratives, especially literary ones. For one thing, as Genette showed so skillfully in his brilliant discussion of Proust in *Narrative Discourse* (Genette [1972] 1980), literary narratives characteristically rely on flashbacks, flashforwards, pauses, ellipses, iterations, compressions, and other time-bending strategies not captured by Labov's definition of narrative as "one method of recapitulating past experience by matching a verbal sequence of clauses to the sequence of events which (it is inferred) actually occurred" (1972: 370). Further, noting the rise of simultaneous and prospective narration in contemporary literary works, Uri Margolin (1999) has revealed retrospective narration to be just one option within a larger system of narrative possibilities. The result is that, in literary contexts, it would be difficult to maintain that clauses with past-tense indicative verbs are the unmarked unit of narration, the baseline against which marked, i.e., evaluative or point-indicating, syntax could be measured (cf. Herman 1999b). For that matter, some avant-garde literary narratives make a point of emphasizing their apparent pointlessness, throwing up obstacles in the way of readers struggling to discern a reason for the telling.

Whereas generally speaking the onus of evaluation is on storytellers in contexts of face-to-face interaction, in experimental literary fictions the burden quite often seems to shift from teller to interpreter (but see Pratt 1977: 116 and my next chapter).

At the same time, among researchers concerned with face-to-face narrative communication, there has been a shift analogous to the one I have characterized as a transition from classical to postclassical approaches. Precipitating this shift is the recognition that the Labovian model captures one important sub-type of natural-language narratives – namely, stories elicited during interviews – but does not necessarily apply equally well to other storytelling situations, such as informal conversations between peers, he-said-she-said gossip, or conversations among family members at the dinner table. As stressed by narrative researchers working in the tradition of Conversation Analysis (Schegloff 1997), and as underscored both in Georgakopoulou's (2007) work and in my next chapter, narratives do different things, and assume different forms, in different communicative environments. In the sociolinguistic interviews from which Labov obtained his narrative data, interviewers are seeking to obtain as much (vernacular) speech from informants as possible, in contrast with conversations among peers in which different participants in the conversation may all be trying to capture the floor at once in order to tell their own version of a story under dispute. Such competition for the floor will drastically alter the shape of the stories participants (try to) tell; for example, given the communicative exigencies at work, storytellers are likely to truncate or omit all but the most essential orienting information, and conversely to bolster their efforts to signal the point of their narrative, why they should be heard out rather than interrupted with a competing story. Meanwhile, the narratives told in this context are likely to bear on the social status or "face" of their tellers in ways that they might not in the context of interviews.

Precisely this sort variability in the structure of stories produced during conversational interaction caused Elinor Ochs and Lisa Capps (2001: 1–58) to propose the dimensional model of narrative mentioned in my previous chapter; according to this model, stories told in contexts of face-to-face interaction can be situated along the five dimensions of *tellership* (to what extent is the story told by a single narrator or co-narrated?); *tellability* (a given narrative may be a rhetorically effective rendition of reportable events, or it may be only a teller's halting attempt to make sense of a situation with low tellability); *embeddedness* (is the narrative told in a lengthy turn relatively detached from the surrounding conversational environment, or is it embedded in the flow of the surrounding discourse, conveyed in a turn at talk no longer than those that precede and follow it?); *linearity* (does the story depict events as part of a single, linear causal-temporal path, or does it rather suggest, in a more open and uncertain way, multiple paths?); and *moral stance* (to what extent does the teller include an explicit judgment of self and others?). More generally, in suggesting that "mundane conversational narratives of personal experience constitute the prototype of narrative activity rather than the flawed byproduct of more artful and planned narrative discourse" (2001: 3), Ochs and Capps helped set a new course for study of the structure and functions of storytelling in face-to-face interaction. Rather than making autonomous narrative "set-pieces" (like the ones favored in the Labovian tradition) paradigmatic for narrative inquiry, Ochs and Capps shifted the attention to "small stories" (Bamberg 2004b, 2007; Georgakopoulou 2007) and their status as micro-interactional resources for identity construction.[9]

Although Labov and Waletzky developed their model for the analysis of narratives told in contexts of face-to-face communication just as structuralist narratologists were proposing their key ideas, initially there was little interaction between narratology and (socio)linguistic, social-psychological, and other social-scientific traditions of research on storytelling. But now there is interest in building an integrative theory that can accommodate both the study of written, literary narratives and the analysis of everyday storytelling (see, e.g., Fludernik 1996; Herman 2004). For example, Monika Fludernik's (1996) argument that conversational storytelling constitutes the primordial narrative situation – the basis for later, written narratives, no matter how elaborate and ludic – harmonizes with Ochs and Capps' account of mundane conversational stories as the prototype of narrative activity. Other recent research that seeks to integrate narratological concepts with ideas drawn from linguistic and more broadly social-scientific traditions of narrative scholarship includes Herman (1999b, 2000, 2001a, 2003a, 2007b), Hyvärinen (2006), Kraus (2005), Mildorf (2007), Palmer (2004), Sternberg (1990, 1992), Thomas (2002), and Toolan ([1988] 2001).[10]

Along the same lines, in focusing on what I have characterized as the first basic element of **situatedness** – the grounding of stories in specific discourse contexts or occasions of telling – my next chapter suggests strategies for synthesizing work on everyday storytelling and research on written, literary narratives. The chapter draws on multiple traditions of scholarship to characterize stories as a form of communicative practice that cuts across the various media for storytelling, even as that form of practice is differently inflected by the constraints and affordances of a given semiotic environment.

Back to the Elements

Narrative Occasions

(i) **Situatedness**. *Narrative is a mode of representation that is situated in – must be interpreted in light of – a specific discourse context or occasion for telling.*

Situating Stories

> Narratives are both structured by and lend structure to the communicative contexts in which they are told. Ideas from multiple fields of study, including sociolinguistics, social psychology, and narratology, can throw light on narrative occasions taken in this double sense – as communicative environments shaping how acts of narration are to be interpreted, and, reciprocally, as contexts shaped by storytelling practices themselves.

As discussed preliminarily in chapter 1, one of the basic elements of narrative is its situation in a particular discourse context or occasion for telling. In the three-level model of narrative that Bal ([1980] 1997) inherited from Genette ([1972] 1980; cf. Rimmon-Kenan [1983] 2002), the *story* level (= the narrated content or storyworld) is a mental representation built up on the basis of cues included at the level of the *text*, and the text level can in turn be viewed as a result (or record) of the communicative processes that occur at the level of *narration*.[1] Acts of narration are grounded in occasions for telling in two senses. On the one hand, interpreters using textual cues to reconstruct a storyworld (see chapter 5) must also draw inferences about the communicative goals that have structured the specific occasion of the telling, motivating the use of certain cues in favor of others and shaping the arrangement of the cues selected. For example, what communicative design informs Hemingway's use of the (unnamed) male character in "Hills Like White Elephants" as the predominant "reflector" in this story told in the third person – that is, as the center of consciousness through whose perceptions and attitudes the narrator's account is refracted? How do interpreters of the story factor in this narrative design or strategy when trying to make sense of the text, and what interpretive adjustments would they need to make if Jig were the predominant reflector, or if the story were recast as a first-person account told by Jig, by the male character, or for that matter by the waitress that serves them at the train station? (I return to these questions below.)

On the other hand, processes of narration not only emerge from but also lend structure to particular discourse contexts, molding them into (constituting them as) occasions for telling in a second sense. For instance, Monica begins her story with what Labov (1972) would call an abstract, that is, a pre-announcement of the gist of the narrative, used to clear the floor for the relatively long turn at talk required to tell a story:

(1)   So that's why I say..UFO or the devil got after our <u>black</u> <u>asses</u>,
(2)   for showing out.

By announcing that she has something noteworthy to tell, Monica cues her interlocutors (in this case, the two sociolinguistic fieldworkers present when Monica recounts *UFO or the Devil*) to collaborate in the production of the story by withholding turns at talk that they might otherwise be inclined to take, particularly in the context of an interview where question-and-answer pairs are a typical and therefore expected discourse structure. Note, too, that given the overall structure of their interaction, Monica's interlocutors would likely feel cheated if she devoted a lengthy turn to a report of unremarkable events (that is, events that are low in tellability in this communicative context). Indeed, if Monica's interlocutors were her peers rather than interviewers constrained by a somewhat more formal speech situation, they might interrupt a story with no readily apparent point before she

ever finished it. Readers of Hemingway's story, like Monica's interlocutors, in effect cede the floor to the narrator, co-creating the narrative
by adopting the role of story-recipients. They also use an assumption
of tellability to orient themselves to the story: interpreters of literary
narratives like Hemingway's expect the payoff from reading the text
to be commensurate with the amount of "floor space" or interpretive
engagement the text itself requires – although some (postmodern)
works actively manipulate readerly expectations of this sort, frustrat-
ing attempts to attribute significance to events sometimes narrated in
painstaking detail (cf. the tradition of the *nouveau roman*, as practiced
by writers such as Alain Robbe-Grillet [1957, 1959] 1965).[2]

In the sections that follow, making frequent reference to "Hills Like
White Elephants," *UFO or the Devil*, *Ghost World* (in both its graphic-
novel and film versions), and other texts as test cases, I discuss several
frameworks for inquiry that can be used to explore narrative occasions
defined in both of the two senses just mentioned – as communicative
environments shaping how acts of narration are to be interpreted
and, reciprocally, as contexts shaped by storytelling practices themselves. My next section reviews sociolinguistic approaches to narrative occasions, drawing on Erving Goffman's (1981) rethinking of the
speaker–hearer pair in terms of what he called production formats and
participation frameworks. This section also discusses how research
on turn-taking processes, some of which I have already alluded to, is
relevant for the study of narrative occasions. Then I move to the theory
of positioning (Harré and van Langenhove 1999) developed by social
psychologists to suggest how narratives are both a cause and a result
of discourse practices, in which participants use utterances to position
themselves and others in overarching "storylines" more or less subject
to dispute. Finally, I discuss how narratologists have developed yet
another approach to narrative occasions; refined by rhetorical theorists
of narrative, this approach, sometimes referred to as "the narrative
communication model" (Chatman 1978; Herman and Vervaeck 2005a;
Martin 1986; Rimmon-Kenan [1983] 2002; Shaw 2005), distinguishes
among actual authors, implied authors and narrators on the production side of the storytelling process, and, on the interpretation side, the
corresponding roles of actual readers, (types of) implied readers, and
narratees (the audience implicitly or explicitly addressed by the narrator
in the text).

Sociolinguistic Approaches

Goffman (1981) suggested that by decomposing the "global folk categories" of speaker and hearer into more finely grained "participant statuses," analysts can better understand what talk is and the various ways in which people participate in it. Though focusing on discourse in general, Goffman's approach also throws light on the situated nature of storytelling in particular, revealing how narratives are embedded in (that is, both structure and are structured by) complex, multidimensional communicative processes. Conversation Analysis, a complementary model for sociolinguistic inquiry with a special focus on the dynamics of turn-taking in communicative interaction, provides further insight into how stories fit within a broader ecology of discourse, with different kinds of stories having different niches within that ecology.

Production formats, participation frameworks,
and narrative occasions

Goffman's rethinking of the speaker–hearer pair in terms of production formats and participation frameworks (Goffman 1981: 124–49) can be traced back to his earlier work (Goffman 1974) on how people make sense of the world by creating *frames* that channel and delimit the sorts of inferences that need to be made about particular activities and zones of experience. Consider, for example, the different protocols on which people rely to interpret stories told in a classroom, in an experimental literary fiction, or during an argument among family members. We bring different strategies to bear on these storytelling situations because we frame them as different kinds of activities (cf. Levinson [1979] 1992; Wittgenstein [1953] 1958). Likewise, Goffman suggests that participants in talk contextualize what is going on by framing communicative transactions in ways that allow them to assign various kinds of statuses or roles to themselves and others. They then modify both the frames and the role-assignments that those frames entail (or *footings*, as Goffman calls them) if the nature of a transaction changes in mid-course. Reciprocally, shifting to a different frame or altering one's footing can change the nature of a given transaction, as when a business person stops making small talk with a potential client and begins presenting the sales pitch he or she was instructed to deliver.[3]

Thus, in place of older, dyadic models of communication, based on the "global folk categories" of *speaker* and *hearer*, Goffman decomposes these supposedly primitive terms "into smaller, analytically coherent elements" (1981: 129). For Goffman, the terms speaker and hearer are insufficiently nuanced to capture the many (and fluctuating) statuses that one can have as a participant in talk. Relevant statuses include, on the one hand, those associated with the various production formats an utterance can have – formats that include speaking as an *author*, *animator*, *principal*, or *figure*. On the other hand, the folk category of hearer needs to be broken down into a range of other possible participant statuses, including those of *addressee*, unaddressed but ratified participant (= *bystander*), or unaddressed and unratified participant (= *eavesdropper*).

On the production side of things, I may animate utterances authored by someone else, as when a political candidate gives a speech written by a speechwriter; or I may speak for the sake of someone I am defending from an accusation, who then becomes the principal of the utterance. Further, the topic of my talk may be something that I myself said in another place and time, such that the earlier self whose words I animate is a figure, the author of words that my present, speaking self animates (example: someone's production of an utterance such as *Back then I used to tell people that I was from Canada*). Meanwhile, on the reception side of things, if I am involved in a conversation with multiple parties, I may have to shift frequently (and rapidly) from having the status of an addressee to having the status of a bystander, and if the interaction splits into two subgroups I may also find myself eavesdropping on a conversation that two or more of the interlocutors intended me *not* to hear. All these statuses affect the way discourse is designed and interpreted, as participants in talk constantly change their footing, defined as "the alignment [they] take up to [themselves] and the others present as expressed in the way [they] manage the production or reception of an utterance" (Goffman 1981: 128).

But how do Goffman's ideas bear on narrative communication in particular?[4] How can they illuminate the role of context in shaping narrative occasions, as well as the role of narrative in shaping communicative contexts? Both production formats and participation frameworks can be thought of as strategies for formulating responses to questions – questions that we pose as we seek to orient ourselves within the communicative situations we must navigate: am I the intended recipient of this person's story, or am I an unratified and unaddressed recipient, an eavesdropper catching a gossipy tale to which I was not meant to be privy? Does the narrative text I am reading represent the words of someone speaking in his or her own behalf, as in the case of an autobiography, or the words of someone speaking for the sake of another, as in the case of a *Bildungsroman*, testimonial, or story told in the context of a eulogy? Further, is the narrative at issue being conveyed by a character within the overarching narrative, a framed tale or story-within-a-story, or is the teller both author and animator of the account? What sort of encounter is going on here anyway? In other words, is my interlocutor's story being put to the service of a dispute or a complaint, or are there other communicative purposes at stake, such as memorializing a dead loved one or entertaining an audience of educated readers of fiction? Interpreting stories requires formulating tentative answers to questions like these, that is, attending to how a given story is grounded in a particular kind of narrative occasion.

Consider how Goffman's ideas about production formats and participation frameworks might be brought to bear on the example narratives included in the Appendix. In "Hills Like White Elephants," readers have the status of addressees for whom the text authored by Hemingway was intended. But though in one sense the narrator of the story can be viewed as the animator of the account of which Hemingway is author, in another sense Hemingway himself can be described as having the dual status of animator as well as author. His text emerges from prior conventions for storytelling that provide both an orienting context and a basis for narrative innovation, such as the "tip of the iceberg" technique which became one of the hallmarks of Hemingway's method of composing short stories.[5] At another level, Goffman's ideas can be brought to bear on the conversational interaction, or "scene of talk" (Herman 2006b), represented within Hemingway's text. Throughout the scene, we readers are unaddressed but ratified participants in the communicative encounter taking place in this fictional world. (If the waitress in the story were to overhear what Jig and the male character say to one another, she could be characterized as an eavesdropper.) Interpreters' ability to understand Hemingway's text as a narrative hinges on their capacity to reconstruct the scene portrayed in the story as a coherent whole – a whole whose coherence derives in part from their own specified mode of participation in it.

Within the scene itself, the way the characters frame their own interaction affords them various sorts of footings over the course of their encounter. Hence the text models the process by which people take up and test out the footings that they adopt as participants in talk. For example, the male character appears to be solicitous toward Jig, that is, to treat her as the principal in whose behalf he formulates his remarks about the simplicity of the abortion procedure, etc. However, the male character's encouraging words and displays of concern for Jig can be read as part of a self-interested attempt to disencumber himself of inconvenient domestic obligations. More generally, insofar as it is a story *about* the structure and dynamics of participation in discourse, Hemingway's representation of this scene of talk is metacommunicative, using the resources of written, literary narrative to throw light on processes of face-to-face interaction and the complex, often covert, motives shaping who says what to whom – and how (cf. Herman 2006b).

Further, the production formats and participation frameworks associated with *UFO or the Devil* and *Ghost World* can be cross-compared with those structuring interpretation of "Hills"; indeed, differences among the formats and frameworks involved help account for the intuition that these are different *kinds* of stories. For one thing, as Dorrit Cohn (1999) has argued, one of the key structural contrasts between factual (e.g., historical or autobiographical) and fictional discourse is that in factual accounts the roles of author and narrator (or animator) converge, erasing the distinction between the author and a separate, autonomous narrator that is by contrast one of the signposts of fiction (cf. Lejeune 1989; Ryan 2001b). Definitionally, in fictional accounts, including fictional first-person testimonials such as Ian McEwan's *The Cement Garden* (1978) or W. G. Sebald's *Austerlitz* (2001), the roles of author and animator/narrator diverge. Whereas readers are warranted in conflating, say, the narrator of *Survival in Auschwitz* (Levi 1961) with Primo Levi, the biographical individual who authored the text, and can legitimately assume that events recounted by the narrator are ones that Levi himself experienced in the Nazi death camp, adopting the same interpretive strategy for McEwan's and Sebald's texts would generate erroneous inferences concerning the life-histories of those two authors.[6] Although it is conveyed through the medium of spoken discourse rather than written text, the production format of *UFO or the Devil* is in this respect more similar to that of Levi's account than McEwan's or Sebald's. In other words, we are warranted in assuming that Monica herself underwent the life-changing experience recounted in the story.

Cutting across the different kinds of stories just mentioned, factual as well as fictional, is their use of retrospective first-person (or homo-diegetic) narration, in contrast with Hemingway's use of third-person or heterodiegetic narration in "Hills." As a result, in *UFO or the Devil*, as in the first-person accounts by McEwan, Sebald, and Levi, there are opportunities for the younger experiencing-I to appear as what Goffman would call a figure and what Emmott (1997) would term an *enactor*, that is, another, earlier version of the speaking agent produc-ing a narrative or of a character included in it. In Monica's narrative, the figure is a younger version of the self whose words the older narrating-I animates in the here and now of the storytelling situation (cf. lines 18, 25, 31, and 49). Hemingway uses a third-person narrator who is removed from the events of the storyworld – in Genette's ([1972] 1980) terms, a extradiegetic-heterodiegetic narrator. This narrating agent does not at any point appear in the represented scene and thus cannot take up any sort of footing toward an earlier self constructed as figure or enactor. By contrast, Monica's self-representation creates possibilities for alignment (and disalignment) between narrator and enactor that do not arise in Hemingway's text. Indeed, as I discuss in more detail in my account of positioning theory in the next main section of this chapter, Monica uses a variety of expressive resources to signal her alignment with her earlier self and against the traditional or received wisdom animated by the grandmother.

Turning from production formats to participation frameworks, note the commonalities and contrasts between Hemingway's scene of talk and the analogous though briefer scene represented in lines 48–55 of Monica's story – that is, the scene in which (as Monica recounts it) Monica and Renee engage in a dispute with Renee's grandmother concerning the exact nature of their experiences. Though the process of "ratification" is different in each case, both readers of Hemingway's story and also readers of the transcript (or listeners to the tape-recorded version) of *UFO and the Devil* are ratified albeit unaddressed participants. Readers of "Hills" are ratified participants because of the conventions surround-ing fictional texts, which specify that reading an account of a conver-sation among fictional characters does not constitute eavesdropping. For her part, Monica consented to have her discourse recorded as part of a larger sociolinguistic research project designed to gather information about the linguistic and cultural traditions of multiple communities across the state of North Carolina.[7] Monica's informed consent is what makes analysts of this recorded interaction ratified participants in the communicative situation. Indeed, academic research institutions now have strict protocols for research on human subjects – protocols designed, in effect, to prevent "eavesdropping" from becoming an institutionalized data-gathering technique.

Finally, in the case of graphic novels such as *Ghost World*, the multimedia profile of these narratives sometimes entails quite complex production formats, constellations of authorial agents of a sort more characteristic of movies than print texts. Thus, whereas Daniel Clowes created both the text and the drawings in *Ghost World*, in *Watchmen* (Moore, Gibbons, and Higgins 1987), a graphic novel which won the 1988 Hugo Award for Achievement in Science Fiction (in the "Other Forms" category), Alan Moore wrote the text, Dave Gibbons served as illustrator and letterer, and John Higgins was the colorist. All three expressive components of the work – textual content, drawings/lettering, color – bear crucially on the process by which interpreters reconstruct the storyworld associated with this graphic novel, just as film narratives result from the combined efforts of cinematographers, screenplay writers, producers of soundtracks, and other agents of cinematic narration. At the same time, insofar as *Watchmen* draws reflexively on the types of action-sequences, drawing and lettering styles, and bold color choices used in the superhero comics that it recycles and recontextualizes, this authorial collective, as it might be called, also animates prior narrative conventions, graphic styles, and thematic motifs. Given its focus on two teenage girls trying to navigate the transition from high school to post-high-school life, *Ghost World* stands out contrastively against the backdrop afforded by this same tradition of superhero comics. Far from possessing superhuman powers, Enid Coleslaw[8] and Rebecca Doppelmeyer struggle with familial and romantic relationships, resist the stereotypes their peers try to impose on them, and are brought face to face, on more than one occasion, with the fragility and tenuousness of their own friendship.

Both *Ghost World* and *Watchmen* were authored in a context defined in part by prior formal and thematic conventions, resulting in a production format in which the authorial agents orient themselves (as animators) to techniques and themes that pre-exist their narrative designs. Yet it should also be pointed out that the convergence of author and animator/narrator roles that functions as a signpost of factual narrative can also occur in comics and graphic novels. In other words, there is nothing intrinsically fictional about the medium of comics, or any other narrative medium for that matter. Rather than being an attribute of narrative media, the status of a given narrative representation as factual or fictional derives from the semantic profile of its storyworld (is the world evoked by a narrative an autonomous or stand-alone domain, or can accounts of situations and events within it be compared with other, competing accounts?) and also from its pragmatic situation (if my interlocutor cues me to interpret his or her propositions about an imaginary domain as claims about how the world really is, then he or she is lying rather than engaging in the production of fictional discourse). Thus Joe Sacco's graphic journalism, as practiced in works such as *Palestine* and *Gorazde* (Sacco 1994, 2000), exemplifies nonfictional graphic narrative, just as print texts can be the bearers of both factual reports and literary fictions.

For another perspective on how practices of storytelling are grounded in (that is, both shape and are shaped by) particular communicative occasions, I turn now from Goffman's ideas to a different tradition of sociolinguistic research sometimes referred to as Conversation Analysis. A special focus of this tradition are the speech-exchange systems, or processes of turn-taking, that function differently in (and serve to identify) different kinds of sociocommunicative practices – for example, interviews versus ritualized exchanges of insults versus storytelling.

Conversation Analysis: narrative and the economy of turn-taking

Conversation Analysis is an approach to the study of communicative interaction with roots in the traditions of sociological analysis that emerged from phenomenology (cf. Schutz 1962). Those traditions, pioneered by Harold Garfinkel (1967) under the rubric of ethnomethodology, study how participants display their understandings of an ongoing interaction precisely by making particular kinds of contributions to the course of the interaction itself, and thereby jointly construct it as the *kind* of interaction that they understand it to be.[9] For example, I signal my understanding of an interaction as a conversation versus a formal lecture or a eulogy by performing particular kinds of verbal and nonverbal behaviors in the context of the interchange, which, thanks to my and the other participants' coordinated performances, *becomes* (= counts for us as) a conversation.

One of the main ways in which participants display their understanding of a type of interaction, and thereby co-construct that interaction *as* one that falls within a particular category or kind, is through the methods they use to take turns at talk. In their classic account of "A Simplest Systematics for the Organization of Turn-Taking for Conversation," Sacks, Schegloff, and Jefferson argued that "[f]or socially organized activities, the presence of 'turns' suggests an economy, with turns being for something valued – and with means for allocating them, which affect their relative distribution, as in economies" (1974: 696). As this foundational study revealed, in the case of conversational interaction, as opposed to other types of activity involving speech such as formal debates, professional storytelling performances, or classroom lectures, there is a preference for small turns. Speakers want to produce their utterances in such a way that the risk of being interrupted by others prematurely is minimized, whereas other parties to the conversation are looking for the first available opportunity (what Sacks, Schegloff, and Jefferson [1974] termed "transition relevance places") to make their contributions to the discourse. Hence, pressure for smallest possible turn size comes from two directions simultaneously: from the direction of the current speaker, who wishes to complete his or her turn, and from the direction of (potential) next speakers, who monitor the ongoing discourse for cues that it is now possible for them to take a turn at talk – in other words, to self-select as next speaker. In consequence, as Schegloff (1981) stresses in a later study that builds on the "Simplest Systematics," extended discourse in a conversational setting is not tantamount to activity on the part of the speaker and passivity on the part of an interlocutor (or group of interlocutors). Rather, given that participants in conversation must jointly overcome the bias toward smallest possible turn size to produce multi-unit turns at talk, extended discourse productions (including narratives) should be viewed as an interactional achievement.

The process of telling stories thus helps constitute communicative occasions of a particular sort, organizing the turn-taking behavior of the parties engaged in the production and interpretation of narratives – whether in the context of face-to-face interaction or that of viewing a film or reading a literary fiction or a graphic novel. In some storytelling contexts, at least, a hallmark of narrative is an overall preference for the current speaker's turn at talk to continue, and a dispreference for potential next speakers to truncate that turn by self-selecting. That said, as a number of story analysts have shown, in other storytelling contexts collaborative telling or co-narration is an accepted, even expected, practice (see, e.g., Georgakopoulou 2007: 50–6; Norrick 1992, 2000, 2007; Ochs and Capps 2001; Ochs et al. 1992). Thus, members of a family or other social unit often gain a sense of cohesion or shared group membership through processes of co-telling or co-rehearsing already well-known narratives, which are co-narrated precisely for this purpose of signaling or confirming membership in the group. In any case, both in relatively more monologic and relatively more dialogic (or shared) modes of storytelling, narratives require a dovetailing of sequencing strategies by interpreters as well as producers of the discourse. All parties must actively enable the production of the narrative through a coordinated sequence of behaviors performed and behaviors withheld. Interpreters of spoken narratives make storytelling possible by refraining from taking turns at crucial moments, co-producing the story either by letting a single teller relay the narrative or by intervening at strategic points to collaborate in the process of narration. For their part, readers likewise make narrative possible by an analogous recentering of their attention, at strategic points in time, on a discourse not their own. As Mary Louise Pratt puts it, in literary narrative as well as some forms of "natural" narrative (those in which no co-narration is involved), the role structure of participants in the speech situation remains similarly marked vis-à-vis "the unmarked situation among peers, in which all participants have [in principle] equal access to the floor" (1977: 113).[10]

Readers of "Hills Like White Elephants" and *Ghost World*, like Monica's interlocutor(s), assume the role of an audience ceding its floor rights to discourse producers who must as a result live up to "increased expectations of delight" (Pratt 1977: 116).[11] In other words, a common feature cutting across these storytelling situations, and helping constitute them as narrative occasions in the first place, is their reliance on turn-taking procedures distinct from those used in other, non-narrative systems for speech exchange. In stories told in face-to-face interaction, narrators can use abstracts like that contained in the first two lines of Monica's account to pre-announce their intention to tell a story. Likewise, producers of written narratives can issue requests for "floor space" by using a variety of paratextual as well as textual means. Paratextual cues include the publication of a text in a volume containing other texts labeled as narratives, such as *The Complete Short Stories of Ernest Hemingway*, or in a graphic novel that includes an array of images among which readers are prompted by the context to assume sequential, narrative-based connections. Textual cues include formulaic openings such as "Once upon a time," as well as openings that include noun phrases with definite articles (and demonstrative pronouns) right from the start, as in the first two sentences of Hemingway's story: "*The hills* across the valley of the Ebro were long and white. On *this side* there was no shade and no trees and *the station* was between two lines of rails in the sun" (Hemingway [1927] 1987: 211, emphases added).[12] As I discuss more fully in chapter 5, these sorts of patterns economically evoke the storyworld (or "text world" in Werth's [1999] terms) to which readers of a fictional text must imaginatively relocate if they are to interpret referring expressions (*the hills, the station*, etc.) and deictic terms (*this side*) properly – mapping them onto the world evoked by the text rather than the world(s) that the text producer or the text interpreter occupies when producing or decoding these textual signals.[13]

Further, some written narratives originating from cultures in transition from oral to literate practices demonstrate particularly clearly how producers and interpreters of literary narrative are caught up in a socio-interactional situation that remains anchored at essential points to the communicative dynamics of face-to-face storytelling (Herman 2001b, 2004). For example, the first word of the Old English epic *Beowulf* is *Hwæt* – literally, "Listen" – suggesting a hybridized narrative situation. Here written language is used to issue a request for the floor but in a manner that harks back to traditions of spoken storytelling, in which a narrator might indeed have to ask his or her interlocutors to "listen up."[14] What is more, *Beowulf* itself foregrounds ways in which storytelling shapes contexts of social interaction. When Unferth and Beowulf publicly recount dueling narratives about Beowulf's swimming contest with Breca (*Beowulf* 1993: 33–4), with Unferth casting doubt on Beowulf's abilities by way of a verbal challenge known as a *flyting* (Clark 1990: 60; Clover 1980), the poem highlights how telling a story involves not a monologic speech act but a coordination of verbal as well as non-verbal activities on the part of multiple participants.[15] Thanks to the surrounding social context in which their exchange unfolds, Unferth's narrative functions to impugn Beowulf's valor, whereas Beowulf's counternarrative reasserts his bravery and obliges him to live up to the heroic self-image presented in his version of the story. In the world portrayed in the poem, then, these stories take on particular forms and functions because of the situation in which they are told and the identities of their tellers. Reciprocally, the alternation between story and counter-story affords protocols used by the participants to make sense of the situation at hand. Stories and storytelling not only emerge from communicative interactions structured as narrative occasions, but can at another level *represent* the process by which social interchanges assume a narrative profile – and with what consequences and effects.

Likewise, the sample narratives included in the Appendix represent (at a second-order or metacommunicative level) the way storytelling is embedded in communicative contexts. The narratives show how extended turns at talk required to tell a story must be slotted into those contexts in ways jointly negotiated by participants, with the stories themselves shaping such negotiations as they unfold. Hemingway's story, for instance, suggests that the possibilities for narration are constrained by the exigencies of the characters' current circumstances, whose profile might very well be altered by acts of narration Jig and the male character could conceivably produce but do not. Thus in the lines marked with arrows in the excerpt below, Jig twice uses questions to invite the male character to produce an account that puts their current situation in a larger temporal context. When he proposes only a very minimal account in response, Jig herself produces an ironically truncated narrative about the happiness of other women who have opted to terminate pregnancies under similar circumstances.

> "I'll go with you and I'll stay with you all the time. They just let the air in and then it's all perfectly natural."
> → "Then what will we do afterwards?"
> "We'll be fine afterwards. Just like we were before."
> → "What makes you think so?"
> "That's the only thing that bothers us. It's the only thing that's made us unhappy."
> The girl looked at the bead curtain, put her hand out and took hold of two of the strings of beads.
> "And you think then we'll be all right and be happy."

"I know we will. You don't have to be afraid. I've known lots of people that have done it."

→   "So have I," said the girl. "And afterwards they were all so happy."

"Well," the man said, "if you don't want to you don't have to. I wouldn't have you do it if you didn't want to. But I know it's perfectly simple." (Hemingway [1927] 1987: 212–13)

In one sense, the brevity of these turns indexes the male character's and Jig's understandings of the kind of interaction they are having – understandings which are not necessarily congruent. Faced with a momentous decision that is also likely to be a turning-point in their relationship, the male character's contributions to the discourse reveal that he orients himself toward their encounter in the way that participants orient themselves to an ongoing dispute, in which turns are moves in a language-game that involves the staking out and defending of positions. By contrast, Jig's questions might be construed as probes by means of which she tests the male character's willingness or ability to shift to a different discourse footing – from that of a participant in a dispute or argument to that of a more cooperative interlocutor who engages in the joint construction of a narrative by means of which both parties might jointly think their way through to a different mutual understanding of their overall situation. From this perspective Jig's own terse contribution, marked with the third arrow, represents her abandonment of any attempt to co-produce with her interlocutor a story about what her and the male character's future might look like, and a reversion to more dispute-like turn-taking behaviors – that is, to a construal of the interaction as one falling into the category of an argument or dispute. This is not to say that in other contexts, narratives themselves cannot be used as moves in an argument, as when one attempts to undercut an interlocutor's current position by telling a story about his or her past conduct (Goodwin 1990). But in the scene of talk represented by Hemingway, the characters' dispute curtails possibilities for narration, discourse possibilities that, if actualized during the encounter, might have enabled them to reconstrue the encounter itself – indeed, to dissolve the basis for the dispute of which the encounter functions as both a symptom and a contributing cause.

Meanwhile, *Ghost World* remediates the dynamics of turn-taking through the placement and configuration of speech balloons, text-filled spaces within panels that allow utterances (and sequences of utterances) to be attributed to characters whose appearance, demeanor, and non-verbal actions are simultaneously represented through modes of visual narration, in particular, drawing and coloration (Carrier 2000; Eisner 1996; Ewert 2004, 2005; McCloud 1993). For example, in the first two panels of sequence A included in the Appendix, semiotic cues prompt readers to assume that the characters produce a particular sequence of utterances – a sequence that forms part of the narrative being conveyed by *Ghost World* but that does not itself represent an act of narration, as it would if one of Clowes's characters were herself telling a story. In the first panel, the musical notes, the proximity of the represented words to stereo equipment, the Ramones album propped up next to the stereo (the words in the first two interconnected speech balloons are in fact lyrics to the Ramones' song "Carbona Not Glue"), and the positioning of the three "tails" of the balloons (two tails are pointed toward the stereo speakers and the third toward Enid) all indicate that Enid is singing along with the lyrics of the song. By contrast, the separate speech balloon for the woman represented on the TV screen indicates that she is producing (at some indefinite point during the sequence of words contained in the song lyrics) a non-synchronized speech act. Further, the smaller lettering used to convey the woman's words suggests that the utterance represented as emanating from the TV is not a primary focus of Enid's attention.[16]

Then in the second panel of sequence A, the left-to-right reading conventions associated with English-language texts cue the inference that Rebecca produces what Conversation Analysts would characterize as a "first pair-part" of a structure called an adjacency pair, here a question-answer pair, only to have Enid answer with a question of her own. (Note, too, how the use of boldface text allows Clowes to represent emphasized words – that is, prosodic details of the sort that I have tried to capture through other means in my transcription of *UFO or the Devil* in the Appendix.) In this instance, the unexpected arrival of Rebecca on the scene, and the unexpected appearance of Enid's hair (revealed to be green in a subsequent panel in this chapter), proves inauspicious for an extended discourse production, whether narrative or otherwise. Instead, the occasion prompts an exchange of questions designed to put the encounter back on a stable footing after the introduction of startling information (Enid's green hair, Rebecca's presence) that requires both participants to rebuild a workable framework for interaction.

By contrast, in sequences C and D (panels that are part of the same chapter of the novel but separated by intervening material not reproduced in the Appendix), Clowes *does* represent communicative situations favorable to (and structured by) storytelling on the part of the characters. Representing events that transpire on different narrative levels, these panels show Rebecca and Enid on the telephone (note the jagged tails of the speech balloons that indicate contributions by the party on the other end of the phone in a given panel); Enid requesting a story from Rebecca; and Enid producing her own story when Rebecca demurs – a story in which Enid appears as a figure (in Emmott's [1997] terms, an enactor) sitting in a restaurant booth *telling a story* to Enid's and Rebecca's mutual acquaintance, Naomi. Whereas the panels in sequence A represent a type of communicative interaction in which the participants must focus on establishing a basis for further talk, sequences C and D portray scenes in which that basis has already been accomplished. At the first or primary level (termed the "diegetic" level by narratologists), the scene is a drawn-out, late-night phone call between close friends (one of the panels in sequence D shows a blank TV screen and a clock that reads 1:41, the lack of a picture on the TV suggesting that the time is 1:41 in the morning rather than the afternoon). At the second, embedded (= hypodiegetic) level, the scene is a storytelling situation about which Enid in turn tells Rebecca story, a conversation among peers in the context of a shared meal. Both encounters afford opportunities for more extended discourse productions of the sort Enid initiates at both narrative levels, with both Rebecca and Naomi (at their respective levels) enabling these productions by refraining from taking turns when, in principle, it might have been possible for them to do so.

Reciprocally, readers' assumption that storytelling scenarios are in play at multiple levels shapes how they interpret Clowes's representation of the characters' talk in this part of the novel. Thus in sequence C the bounded rectangular text-box containing the words "No, I mean my story . . . I can't keep yours straight . . ." can be interpreted as a response to a question from Rebecca ("You told her about me and Martin?") at the primary or diegetic level, not a turn taken during Enid's exchange with Naomi in the earlier time-frame. This way of representing the characters' speech is followed by panels containing unbounded lines of text above depicted scenes; in this way, Clowes suggests that Enid is narrating to Naomi events from a still earlier time-frame preceding their conversational interaction in the restaurant booth. Hence, just as the characters use storytelling practices to frame their encounters with one another as particular kinds of interaction, regulating their communicative conduct accordingly, readers of Clowes's text draw on their understanding of the protocols for narration to form inferences about the relationship between elements within panels and about the sequential links across different panels.

More generally, in face-to-face interaction as well as other communicative contexts, stories at once emerge from and organize particular modes of practice, enabling participants to collaborate on the accomplishment of extensive, multi-unit discourse productions. Allowing interlocutors to overcome conversation's interactionally motivated bias toward the smallest possible turn size, stories told face to face promote the creation of carefully structured, pre-planned discourse segments – stretches of talk such as *UFO or the Devil*, whose production and interpretation require participants to reflect on and evaluate previous, ongoing, or possible experiences. In this way, storytelling contributes primordially to the sense-making activities jointly accomplished by social interactants, affording one of the basic means by which people make sense of themselves, one another, and the world (Herman 2003a). Written and multimodal narratives like Hemingway's and Clowes', respectively, build on this same legacy of sense-making, and do so by exploiting medium-specific properties of printed texts (including graphic-novel texts). Because of their deliberate or "worked over" nature in contrast with the relative spontaneity of spoken discourse (Chafe 1994), as well as the longer span of time allowed for interpretation of printed narratives than for stories told face to face, texts like those of Hemingway and Clowes can use scenes of *represented* storytelling to comment reflexively on the processes of saying and interpreting at work in narrative occasions, among other environments for communication.

My next section draws on ideas from social psychology – specifically, the theory of positioning – to outline another approach to the situated nature of narrative representations. This work, too, suggests that narratives emerge from sociointeractional contexts on which their telling in turn has a shaping effect; but it deploys a different descriptive vocabulary than that used by Goffman or the Conversation Analysts.

Positioning Theory

In the terms afforded by positioning theory (Harré and van Langenhove 1999; cf. Bamberg 1997b, 2004a, 2005), a method of analysis proposed by researchers working in the subfield of social psychology known as discursive psychology (cf. Edwards 1997, 2006; Edwards and Potter 1992; Harré 2001; Harré and Gillett 1994; Harré and Stearns 1995), speech acts are used to assign positions to social actors. Positions, in this model, are places along scales or continua that correspond to polarities of character such as "strong versus weak," "flashy versus understated," etc. Over time, self- and other-positioning speech productions help build overarching storylines in terms of which we make sense of our own and others' doings. Reciprocally, those overarching narratives provide the means for linking particular position-assignments with particular utterances, as when a snide or affirming remark about someone does its work thanks to the way it shores up (or undercuts) a larger story about that person. Positioning theory thus provides another way of characterizing as a basic element of narrative its grounding in contexts for communication. The telling of narratives functions to position both teller and recipient, and in some cases to contest positions associated with competing storylines, while conversely individual speech acts contribute to the formation of more or less convergent or conflicting storylines about self and other. In addition, the process of narration positions characters in storyworlds.[17]

Positioning in UFO or the Devil

This section draws on research in discursive psychology to characterize narrative occasions in terms of positions – with stories both allowing people to assign positions to themselves and one another and also emerging from that same process of position assignment.[18] In Harré and van Langenhove's account (1999: 1–31), one can position oneself or be positioned in discourse as powerful or powerless, admirable or blameworthy, etc. In turn, a position can be specified by characterizing how a speaker's contributions are taken as bearing on these and other "polarities of character" in the context of an overarching storyline – a narrative of self and other(s) being jointly elaborated (or disputed) by participants, via self-positioning and other-positioning speech acts. Hence positions are selections made by participants in discourse, who use position-assigning speech acts to build "storylines" in terms of which the assignments make sense. Reciprocally, the storylines provide context in terms of which speech acts can be construed as having a position-assigning force. It should also be pointed out, though, that self- and other-positioning acts are not always intentionally or volitionally performed. An utterance I produce may allow others to position me in ways I neither planned for nor desire – as when Renee's grandmother uses the girls' report about their experiences to position them as unreliable narrators (see lines 48–55 and below). Conversely, I may position another person in unintended ways when I produce utterances that connect up with (reinforce, undercut) storylines of which I am unaware, as when I compliment someone on his or her punctuality in the presence of others who have constructed a larger narrative about that person's obsessive concern with being on time.

In *UFO or the Devil*, Monica engages in self-positioning via speech acts concerning racial as well as generational polarities. As suggested above, the abstract of Monica's story (lines 1–2) functions to situate Monica and Renee within a complex network of ethnic identities. By referring to herself and her friend in terms of "our black asses," Monica on the one hand can be heard as claiming for herself an identity that is based on skin color and that, in this respect, stands in polar opposition to the identity "white" – even though the composite ethnic heritage of black Appalachians as a group undercuts dichotomous (self-)identifications of this sort (see the background on Texana provided in the Appendix). At the same time, as Mallinson (2006) has shown, Monica is one of the residents of Texana who associates herself with urban black culture and language practices. From this perspective, Monica's abstract can be interpreted as a means by which she aligns herself with a distinct subgroup of the broader African American population – one that is not immediately present in Texana itself, but that nonetheless constitutes a point of reference for Monica's strategies for self-presentation. In either interpretation, Monica's abstract can be construed as a positioning strategy: on the one hand, by positioning

Monica and Renee as part of a proximate minority community vis-à-vis
the dominant local culture of a county that is more than 98 percent white;
on the other hand, by positioning both girls as members of another,
larger, and spatially nonproximate minority community vis-à-vis a
supraregional culture that is also predominantly white. In either case,
the abstract marks the story about to be told as a counternarrative
opposed to the narratives circulating within and defining the majority
white culture. Yet the minority status that Monica attributes to herself
here is, in effect, a double-edged sword: even as it prepares the way
for a recounting of experiences to which members of the dominant communities may not have access, because of their association with master
narratives or the normative order of discourse, Monica's counternarrative also positions her as a kind of self whose experiences may
not carry weight or authority when juxtaposed against such master
narratives and the assumptions and expectations that they entail.[19]

This dialectical logic of positioning, whereby authoritative experiential (or "firsthand") knowledge opposes itself to the discourses that
undermine the self's claims to such authority and such knowledge,
also structures the polarity that Monica sets up between herself and
Renee's grandmother toward the end of *UFO or the Devil* (lines 48–55).
The grandmother is represented as dismissing Monica's and Renee's
experiences by constructing a storyline in which those experiences are
in reality the deluded imaginings of overexcited, possibly hysterical,
young girls. Specifically, the grandmother attempts to other-position
Monica and Renee as unreliable narrators by proposing instead of their
supernatural account a naturalistic explanation of the apparition as a
formation of "minerals," distorted somehow by the girls' own overheated
condition (lines 50–4). In turn, however, Monica uses the expressive
resources of talk, including prosody,[20] to discredit the grandmother's
purported explanation, that is, the storyline according to which Monica's
mind has merely fabricated the big ball. For one thing, Monica uses a
slower rate of speech and heightened pitch and volume for purposes
of emphasis in lines 46 and 47, where she underscores the effect on her
and Renee of the encounter with the big ball. Further, Monica manipulates both pitch and rhythm to construct dismissive, sing-song-like
reproductions of the grandmother's discourse in lines 51 and 53–4; here
the downward shifts in pitch are rhythmically timed to co-occur with
words that index the grandmother's purported explanation(s) of events,
suggesting the extent to which Monica disfavors and seeks to distance

herself from any such account. At the same time, Monica uses nonce words (*bah bah* ↓ *bah* ↓ *bah*) in line 53 to suggest how, in general, the grandmother's account is discourse devoid of relevant semantic content. She also produces, in line 55, an explicit evaluation (*Bullshit*) of her interlocutor's counternarrative about what must have happened. Monica uses a word-internal downward shift in pitch in *Bullshit*, together with sentence-final intonation at the end of this line of the transcript. Whereas utterances ending with rising pitch (e.g., questions) can be used to implicate various kinds of uncertainty (Ward and Hirschberg 1985), Monica's utterance in line 53 suggests both prosodically and lexically that she is committed to the truthfulness of her own account in contrast with the grandmother's.

Thus, exploiting a variety of expressive resources available to participants in face-to-face interaction, Monica other-positions the grandmother's discourse as a monolithic voice of authority that in fact has no authority when it comes to this domain of experience. The storytelling process entails a complex embedding or lamination of self- and other-positioning acts, of a kind that narratively structured discourse environments are uniquely able to create and sustain. At a global level Monica uses her narrative as a means for self-positioning even though – or rather, precisely because – at a local level it recounts another person's attempt to other-position Monica and Renee. Monica embeds a report of Renee's grandmother's other-positioning speech act within her own account, critically evaluates it, and thereby puts it in the service of a story about the power of firsthand experience to trump received accounts of the way the world is.

Monica's mode of narration also positions her interlocutors vis-à-vis the (inter)action unfolding within the storyworld (cf. Bamberg 2004a, 2005). The narrative relies heavily on what narratologists would term internal focalization: once the story is launched, events are refracted through the vantage-point of an individuated participant in the storyworld, namely, the younger experiencing-I who undergoes the encounter. That said, Monica uses discourse resources available in the here and now (including tense shifts, deictic references, and prosody) to animate earlier events, whose life-transforming impact thus emerges through the interplay between different time-frames. The same dual positioning is marked lexically in line 55. At this juncture, Monica's evaluation of the action is ambiguously external and internal, in Labov's (1972) sense of those terms: *Bullshit* marks the fusion of the evaluative stance of the younger experiencing-I with that of the older narrating-I. Then, in lines 56 and following, the focalization shifts unambiguously back to the vantage-point of the older narrating-I: Monica speaks summatively about how her behavior changed after the encounter with the big ball.

Overall, though, using the current discourse to stage the main action of the narrative from the perspective of the experiencing-I, Monica aligns her interlocutors (and analysts) with her younger self's vantage-point. Relevant here is Dorrit Cohn's (1978) account of the discourse strategy that she characterized as consonant self-narration, where the older narrating-I does not enjoy any cognitive privilege with respect to his or her earlier experiencing self. As the foregoing remarks suggest, however, the term "cognitive privilege" might need to be reformulated as "direction of flow": is the discourse organized such that the narrating-I animates the experiencing-I's perspective on the storyworld, or is it organized such that past events become the means for staging current conceptions of self and world? In the case of *UFO or the Devil*, by positioning her interlocutors *with* her younger self Monica in effect positions them *against* other discourses that might claim authoritative status – discourses such as those represented by the grandmother. The repositories of received wisdom, these discourses purport to invalidate the experiences whose formative role Monica's narrative, by contrast, enacts.

Positioning in "Hills" and Ghost World

Likewise, drawing on the expressive resources of a different medium for storytelling, Hemingway's mode of narration in "Hills" is communicatively situated in ways that positioning theory can help account for. To reiterate, positioning is a relevant parameter for analysis on several levels: the level of the characters; the level of the reader's engagement with the text, given the specific narrative techniques deployed; and the level of narrative's bearing on more or less dominant storylines, or master narratives, about the way the world is. At the first level, "Hills" portrays the unnamed male character and Jig as engaged in both self- and other-positioning acts. At the second level, Hemingway's mode of narration – in particular, his use of what F. K. Stanzel ([1979] 1984) would characterize as the figural narrative situation (= third-person or heterodiegetic narration in which events are refracted through the vantage-point of a particular consciousness or "reflector") – positions interpreters of the overarching narrative concerning the characters' encounter. And at the third level, the story engages with master narratives associated with gender roles in particular.

Although there are shifts of perspective over the course of the story, the male character functions as the main internal focalizer or reflector figure, whose vantage-point provides a window on the action being recounted. Thus, almost all of the nonverbal actions recounted in the story are performed by Jig, confirming that the dominant reflector or perceiver (the one witnessing Jig's actions) is the male character. The use of the male character as the focalizer tends to align the reader with his vantage-point: we literally see things through his eyes. Yet, for reasons already mentioned, the text ultimately invalidates both the storyline he proposes and his attempt at other-positioning Jig in terms of that storyline. What the male character presents as empathy and concern for Jig can be read otherwise, as a self-interested attempt to sidestep what he views as onerous domestic obligations. The tension between (1) the male character's status as the main source of perceptual information about the storyworld and (2) his self-centered approach to his and Jig's situation creates a kind of dissonance in the positioning logic of the narrative. Hence, whatever Hemingway's conscious stance toward dominant conceptions of gender in the epoch during which he wrote, his text positions readers simultaneously with and against the male character, thereby disrupting sexist master narratives in which men are the repositories of authoritative knowledge and sound judgments while women lack these attributes and are therefore unreliable.[21] More generally, to reconstruct the storyworld in "Hills" readers must draw inferences about the larger communicative situation in which Hemingway's textual cues are embedded and which the story in turn represents, through its portrayal of the interaction (or "scene of talk") involving Jig and the male character. The larger communicative situation at issue is thus complex and multi-layered; in it, readers are positioned vis-à-vis the male character's attempts to position both Jig and himself.

In the case of *Ghost World*, the graphic-novel medium affords still other expressive resources by means of which interpreters of the text can be positioned – and through which, in the storyworld evoked by the narrative, characters' own attempts at self- and other-positioning can be represented. Likewise, aspects of the text serve to position Clowes's account vis-à-vis dominant storylines or master narratives circulating in the culture at large. Consider the positioning logic at work in sequence B, for example. The verbal-visual organization of the sequence aligns readers with Rebecca and Enid, while distancing them from the back-grounded male characters about whom the two friends converse (or argue). Clowes deploys here the multimodal equivalent of a print text's use of third-person or heterodiegetic narration that moves along a spectrum from relatively more external to relatively more internal views – that is, from external focalization, where the vantage-point on events is not associated with a character in the storyworld, to internal focalization, where the vantage-point is in fact a character's.[22] For instance, in the third panel of sequence B, readers can use the communicative context established by the visual design of first two panels as a basis for drawing an inference concerning the status of the image represented in this panel. Specifically, they can infer that this image of the former bass player is mediated through the perceptions of one of the two main characters – most probably Rebecca, given her physical location and the orientation of her torso and gaze in the preceding panel. That inference is reinforced by the absence of a speech balloon in the third panel, even though the bass player is shown talking on the phone. Readers can assume that, because of the male character's location at the far side of the restaurant, Rebecca cannot hear what he is saying on the phone. By contrast, in the case of the (self-incriminating) utterance that is represented by means of a speech balloon in the second panel, readers can assume that this remark ("You guys up for some reggae tonight") was made within Rebecca's and Enid's perceptual range and is therefore included in the report of their perceptions at this point in the unfolding action.[23] Both the design of individual panels and sequential links among panels thus align readers with particular vantage-points on the storyworld, and prevent or at least inhibit other identifications and alignments.

The net result of this logic of identification, enacted through the progression of the text's word–image combinations, is that readers are prompted to construct a storyline concerning Rebecca's and Enid's difficulties with identifying potential romantic and life partners – and, by extension, a larger storyline about the similar difficulties that any intelligent, independent-minded young woman is likely to experience in this connection. The verbal and visual details found in individual panels and panel sequences cue readers to attach local textual details to this (emergent) storyline, while that storyline in turn provides context for interpreting the actions, postures, and speech productions of characters represented within a given panel or across panels. Further, as the screenshots also included in the Appendix suggest, Terry Zwigoff's film version of *Ghost World* picks up with and indeed amplifies this same global storyline. Screenshot 1 reproduces Rebecca's and Enid's perspective on the reggae-lover's self-incriminating remark. Meanwhile, portraying scenes not included in the graphic-novel version of *Ghost World*, screenshots 4, 5, and 6 bolster the storyline concerning the dearth of potential romantic or life partners – given the unpromising conduct and demeanor of the patrons registered by the camera (which corresponds here to Enid's gaze).

At the same time, sequence B exploits the modulation between relatively more internal and relatively more external perspectives to present alternating views of Enid's and Rebecca's table as the primary vantage-point on the situations, events, and characters inhabiting the storyworld. Panels 4 and following prompt readers to pull back from the internalized view of the ex-bass player in panel 3 and adopt shifting perspectives during Rebecca and Enid's dispute concerning what Rebecca characterizes as Enid's impossibly high standards for men. (Apparently, only a "famous cartoonist" named "David" Clowes would be up to snuff!) In a manner reminiscent of the shot/reverse-shot technique in cinematic narratives, the text first provides, in panel 4, an over-the-shoulder view of Rebecca from Enid's perspective, followed in panel 5 by an over-the-shoulder view of Enid from Rebecca's perspective. Then in panel 6 the perspective shifts again, to a more externalized view that captures Enid's angry expression as she defends her preference for the cartoonist over the "guitar plunkin' moron" (= ex-bass player) whom Rebecca had alluded to favorably. By showing both Enid's angry reaction and the now discredited male characters in the restaurant, and by attributing to Rebecca the utterance "Still, I just hate anybody who likes cartoons," panel 6 aligns readers with Enid's position, fracturing the global storyline concerning the lack of viable male partners into competing storylines about life choices for young women in Enid and Rebecca's position. Making sense of both individual panels and panel sequences thus requires situating them in a broader logic of positioning and counter-positioning, thanks to which Clowes's panels serve particular communicative functions and which in turn takes shape because of how the panels themselves are sequenced.

In short, the idea of positioning, although originally developed by discursive psychologists for the purposes of analyzing everyday, face-to-face communicative interactions, can also throw light on the communicative strategies by which readers are positioned vis-à-vis literary narratives like Hemingway's and multimodal texts such as Clowes's. This work suggests that framing inferences about the stance one is being prompted to adopt toward particular positions represented in a narrative is a fundamental part of the process of reconstructing that narrative's storyworld, no matter what the medium in which it is presented. Reciprocally, concepts and methods originating in narratology, such as internal focalization, consonant self-narration, and the contrast between authorial and figural narrative situations, can lead to finer-grained analyses of positioning logic, as can research on modes of narration made possible by the medium-specific properties of comics and graphic novels, for example (cf. Baetens 2002; Carrier 2000; Eisner 1996; Ewert 2004, 2005; Groensteen 2007; McCloud 1993).

I turn now to a third broad approach to the study of narrative occasions – one "homegrown" within the field of narrative theory itself. In parallel with Goffman's work on production formats and participation frameworks but using a different analytic scheme, this third, indigenous, approach aims to identify the parties to narrative transactions and how different relations among them affect the process of telling and interpreting stories, which can in turn affect how these parties orient to one another.

The Narrative Communication Model

In this final section of the chapter, I discuss how narratologists have created their own indigenous vocabulary for describing and analyzing narrative occasions. This approach, sometimes referred to as "the narrative communication model" (Booth [1961] 1983; Chatman 1978; Genette [1972] 1980, [1983] 1988, [1991] 1993; Herman and Vervaeck 2005a; Leech and Short [1981] 2007: 206–30); Iser 1974; Phelan 2005a; Prince 1982; Rimmon-Kenan [1983] 2002; Shaw 2005), focuses on the constitutive factors of narrative communication and explores how those factors come into play differently in different kinds of storytelling situations. In the version developed by rhetorical theorists of narrative, the approach distinguishes among actual authors, implied authors, and narrators on the

production side of the storytelling process, and, on the interpretation side, the corresponding roles of actual readers, (types
of) implied readers, and narratees (the audience implicitly or
explicitly addressed by the narrator in the text). According to this
model, telling and interpreting narratives must be situated
within a multi-layered process of narrative communication, in
which an implied author, for example, might communicate
something to an implied reader by having a narrator tell a particular kind of story in a particular way to a specific narratee.
Reconstructing a storyworld thus requires framing inferences
about the dynamically unfolding relations among the parties to
a given narrative transaction – relations that are both an emergent result of textual designs and a basis for understanding how
those designs form part of larger narrative occasions.[24]

The narrative communication model has roots in both structuralist
narratology (Chatman 1978; Genette [1972] 1980; Prince 1973) and the
rhetorical approach to narrative pioneered around the same time by
Wayne C. Booth ([1961] 1983). As discussed in chapter 2, the narratologists, influenced by Saussure's emphasis on the linguistic system versus
particular speech acts made possible and intelligible by that system
(Saussure [1916] 1959), focused not on particular authors and readers
but on the system of structural options available to producers as well
as interpreters of narrative texts. This general approach led narratologists to create a taxonomy of narrators and narratees, agents of narrative production and reception about which inferences can be formed
based on features immanent to the text. For his part, Booth took issue
with then prevalent Formalist (New Critical) approaches to literary analysis and conceived of fictional works not as autonomous artifacts that
had to be bracketed from their contexts of production and interpretation to be understood but rather as elements of a purposeful communicative process in which authors and readers participate, but in ways
that are mediated by the rhetorical designs that structure the text.

Narratological foundations

In the narratological framework, narration can be conceived as a
communicative process in which information about the story level is

conveyed by a particular kind of narrator to a particular kind of narratee. Gerald Prince defines the narratee as "[t]he one who is narrated to, as inscribed in the text" ([1987] 2003: 57), and contrasts this participant role with both the real reader and the implied reader (see below). Hence, in contrast to the biographical critics who pre-dated them or the reader-response theorists who came later, the narratologists focused not on authors and readers and their role in narrative transactions but on narrators and narratees viewed as communicative positions correlated systematically with identifiable textual markers. In other words, whereas authors and readers are dimensions of "narrative *parole*," particular instances of narrative discourse, the narratologists' main concern was narrative *langue*, or the underlying semiotic system that makes narrative production and understanding possible in a given case. Hence, adapting folk models of the communicative process, based on the three components or participants of sender, message, and receiver –

sender → message → receiver[25]

– the narratologists developed an analogous model of the participants involved in the process of narrative communication:

narrator → narrative message → narratee

As noted by Rimmon-Kenan ([1983] 2002: 95–106) in her exposition of Genette's ([1972] 1980) foundational work, narratologists have classified narrators as well as narratees according to *narrative level*, *extent of participation* in the storyworld, and *degree of perceptibility*; further, under the influence of rhetorical approaches to narrative that can be traced back to Booth's work and that I discuss more fully in my next subsection, *degree of (un)reliability* has come to constitute an additional parameter for comparing and contrasting narrators in particular.[26]

With respect to narrative level, narrators are extradiegetic if they do not inhabit the storyworld evoked by their discourse (as in Hemingway's text); intradiegetic if they are characters within the storyworld and tell a story within the story (as in lines 48–55 of *UFO or the Devil*, when Monica narrates the narrative that she and Renee told to the grandmother); or hypodiegetic if, within an embedded narrative, a character narrator tells yet another story (as in sequences C and D from *Ghost World*, where within Clowes's narrative Enid tells Rebecca a story about how she told her loss-of-virginity story to Naomi on a previous occasion). Whereas Hemingway's story does not feature an explicitly characterized narratee, that is, a textually evoked recipient of the narrator's discourse, successful interpretation of Monica's narrative and of *Ghost World* requires sorting out who is the narratee at a given point. Thus, I will misconstrue *UFO or the Devil* if I fail to realize that two sets of narratees are in play in lines 48–55: on the one hand, the two fieldworkers to whom Monica is conveying her account (and to whom she addresses the three instances of the locution *you know*[27] found in these lines); on the other hand, the grandmother, to whom in the earlier time-frame being recounted here she and Renee tell their story about the encounter with the big ball. Not only do interpreters need to keep distinct these different narratees; what is more, they can infer that Monica is communicating something to the fieldworkers (the extradiegetic narratees) by constructing the grandmother as an unsympathetic audience (intradiegetic narratee). Likewise, in *Ghost World*, readers must sort out who is being addressed at what moments in Enid's account, and frame inferences about (1) what Enid seeks to communicate to Rebecca by telling her the story of her narration of her loss-of-virginity story to Naomi, and (2) what Clowes seeks to communicate to the reader by having Enid attempt to communicate this to Rebecca.

Shifting from the question of narrative levels to that of extent of participation in the story, analysts have drawn on the narrative communication model to distinguish among autodiegetic, homodiegetic, and heterodiegetic narrators. Autodiegetic narration constitutes a special case of first-person or homodiegetic narration in which the narrator does not only participate in the action being recounted but is also the main character in the storyworld evoked by the text. To put the same point another way, a homodiegetic narrator is one who has participated (more or less centrally) in the circumstances and events about which he or she tells a story, with completely central participation yielding the autodiegetic mode.[28] In heterodiegetic narration, by contrast, the narrator has not participated in the circumstances and events about which he or she tells a story. Furthermore, narrators can be extradiegetic-homodiegetic, like the older Pip who narrates his earlier life experiences in Charles Dickens's *Great Expectations*; extradiegetic-heterodiegetic, like Henry Fielding's narrator in *Tom Jones*, who comments evaluatively on but does not participate in events in the storyworld; intradiegetic-homodiegetic, as when Marlow, in his role as a character narrator in Conrad's *Heart of Darkness*, tells about his experiences in the Congo; or intradiegetic-heterodiegetic, as when in Chaucer's *Canterbury Tales* the Miller tells a bawdy tale (specifically, a fabliau) centering on events in which he himself did not take part.[29]

In these terms, Hemingway's narrator is extradiegetic-heterodiegetic, whereas *UFO or the Devil* involves both extradiegetic-autodiegetic narration (when Monica tells the interviewers the story of her earlier encounter with the big ball) and intradiegetic-autodiegetic narration (when she tells the story of how she told a previous version of that same story to Renee's grandmother, just after the events in question transpired). *Ghost World*, meanwhile, features extradiegetic-heterodiegetic narration (because the narrating agent who produces the primary diegetic level does not inhabit the storyworld evoked by the graphic novel, and does not figure as a participant in the narrated action[30]) along with instances of intradiegetic-autodiegetic and hypodiegetic-autodiegetic narration (as in sequences C and D). Also, in the film version of *Ghost World*, Enid is herself a fledgling comic artist, and her sketchbook images of Seymour (a character not included in the original graphic-novel version) constitute further instances of intradiegetic narration, further stories-within-the-story, some of them heterodiegetic in focus.

The broader point to emphasize here is that, as was the case with textual cues prompting interpreters to draw inferences about who is communicating with whom at what point and on what narrative level, recipients of narrative discourses and texts make sense of storyworlds in part by figuring out a narrator's degree of participation in or involvement with narrated events – how a narrator fits into the overall participant structure of the communicative transaction in which they engage while interpreting a story. Indeed, as Lubomír Doležel (1998) has argued, modes of narratorial participation bear crucially on the process by which circumstances and events in storyworlds are "authenticated" (or not) as fictional facts – as things that must be assumed to be true about the storyworld if one is to build up a coherent interpretation of it. As Doležel puts it, "entities [and events] introduced in the discourse of the anonymous third-person narrator are *eo ipso* authenticated as fictional facts, while those introduced in the discourses of the fictional persons are not" (1998: 149, quoted in Margolin 2005b: 33; cf. Doležel 1980). In other words, fictional facts reported by third-person narrators have an authority, or mark a degree of certainty, lacking in first-person reports given by characters or character narrators occupying specific positions in a storyworld.[31]

In sequences C and D from *Ghost World*, for example, the content of the phone conversation between Enid and Rebecca is authenticated in a way that Enid's own report of the story she tells to Naomi is not. The phone conversation framing this story-within-the-story can be taken as fictional fact, whereas Enid's assertion that she did not tell Naomi about Rebecca's own loss-of-virginity story remains a (disputable) assertion made by Enid in her role as an intradiegetic (or character) narrator. Indeed, this assertion seems to be undercut by the panel that precedes the one in which Enid makes this claim in sequence D; here Naomi is shown reacting ("Oh God . . .") to Enid's remark that Rebecca's "first time was with this completely fruity guy she met on a *computer bulletin board!*" – as if, in a jump back up to the primary diegetic level on which Rebecca and Enid are having their phone conversation, Enid is recalling what Naomi looked like at precisely the moment when she (Enid) *did* tell her the story at issue. In the dialectical interplay at work in narrative occasions, then, the truth status of a given narrative act (or narrator's report) can be determined only in light of the larger context of telling of which it forms a part, and, vice versa, localized acts of storytelling shape interpreters' understanding of the overall narrative sequence to which they contribute.

Rhetorically oriented theorists have also explored the structure and dynamics of what Doležel called narrative authentication, or the process by which narrative texts prompt interpreters to sort propositions about the storyworld into factual and nonfactual assertions – and conversely to build up a global understanding of the storyworld precisely through that sorting process. As I discuss in my next subsection, though, rhetorical narrative theorists have approached this issue from a different direction, attempting to link the semantics of narrators' statements about fictional worlds with the pragmatics of audience participation. To construct this link, they have proposed new inflections of the narrative communication model, and thus new ways of grounding narrative itself in communicative processes.

Rhetorical inflections

When it was integrated with the ideas of Wayne Booth and Wolfgang Iser that came into prominence around the same time that structuralist theories of narrative were being developed and disseminated, the basic model of narrative communication acquired additional nuances, as suggested by the form it took in Seymour Chatman's study, *Story and Discourse* (1978: 151, reproduced in Rimmon-Kenan [1983] 2002: 86; a slightly simplified version of the diagram is presented here):

Real author ⋯> Implied author → Narrator → Narratee → Implied reader ⋯> Real reader

In this version of the model, the dotted arrows indicate how individual authors and readers are not in themselves targets of this approach to narrative analysis; rather, they are relevant only insofar as they adopt communicative roles (compare Goffman's "participant statuses") in order to take part in narrative transactions. On the production side of things, authors of fictional narratives create a persona that Booth called the *implied author* and that can be defined as "the governing consciousness of the work as a whole, the source of the norms embodied in the work" (Rimmon-Kenan [1983] 2002: 87–8). In other words, the implied author can be defined as a "streamlined version of the real author, an actual or purported subset of the real author's capacities, traits, attitudes, beliefs, values, and other properties that play an active role in the construction of the particular text" (Phelan 2005a: 45); this streamlined version of the implied author can be assumed to be "responsible for the choices that create the narrative text as 'these words in this order' and that imbue the text with his or her values" (Phelan 2005a: 216).[32]

Shaped in part by the New Critics' strictures against what they called "the intentional fallacy" (Wimsatt and Beardsley [1947] 2001), according to which the attempt to use an author's assumed intentions as a yardstick for literary interpretation results in a version of the genetic fallacy, or arguments based on origins, Booth's ([1961] 1983) approach avoids committing the analyst to claims about the intentions of the actual author. Instead, Booth suggested, authors adopt a "second self" (if an author produces multiple works, this persona becomes a "career author") for the purpose of engaging with readers in communicative acts mediated by texts featuring particular kinds of rhetorical designs. In turn, readers scan fictional texts for these designs – that is, for cues that enable them to pick up on the attitudes, norms, and values associated with the implied author, the persona adopted by the actual author for the purposes of engaging in such rhetorically situated acts of narrative communication. Interpreting a narrative entails searching the text for signals that convey information about these underlying norms and values, which in turn enable recipients to detect favored versus disfavored character traits, modes and degrees of unreliable narration, and other dimensions of the broader communicative occasion in light of which particular textual details acquire specific narrative functions.

Thus, in a text like Robert Browning's *My Last Duchess*, a dramatic monologue told by a Renaissance-era Duke who has had his wife murdered (one assumes) because of his own pathological jealousy and possessiveness, reconstructing the storyworld requires recognizing the gap between the norms and values of Browning's implied author and those displayed by the Duke in his role as narrator. Or, in the case of Hemingway's short story, which involves not unreliable narration but rather a clash of attitudinal and practical stances vis-à-vis a conflict-causing turn of events within the storyworld, invoking the concept of the implied author would allow the rhetorical theorist to reformulate in yet other terms some of the interpretations that I have used Goffman's ideas, accounts of turn-taking strategies in discourse, positioning theory, and narratological work to advance in previous sections in this chapter. For example, I have suggested that Hemingway's male character frames his utterances such that Jig appears to be the principal for whose sake the utterances are spoken, when in reality they are spoken for his own sake; that he treats his and Jig's interaction like a dispute in which each turn at talk constitutes a move within a competitive game, whereas Jig makes tentative efforts to move beyond this dispute-like discourse environment to one in which she and the male character can work together to envision a future for themselves; and that there is a tension between the male character's status as the source of most of the perceptual information in the story and the self-interested storyline that he attempts to foist upon Jig. Recasting these claims in the language used by rhetorical theorists, one could argue that Hemingway's textual designs indicate a disparity between the norms and values informing the male character's words and actions and those that contribute to the profile that interpreters assign to the implied author, viewed as the source of the work's underlying norms and values. Interpreters work to reconstruct this profile in order to make sense of the communicative strategies motivating the use of particular textual choices to represent the characters' relations to one another in the storyworld, even as the choices themselves provide grounds for this process of reconstruction.[33]

Reciprocally, the *implied reader* is Iser's (1974) term for the communicative role that must be adopted by actual readers if they are to discern the gap between an implied author and an unreliable narrator like Browning's Duke or a less than ideal partner like Jig's interlocutor in "Hills" – or, for that matter, between the governing norms and values of Zwigoff's film version of *Ghost World* and the male characters who come across as grossly inappropriate candidates for romantic relationships in screenshots 1, 4, 5, and 6 included in the Appendix.[34] In the terms afforded by the (rhetorically inflected) narrative communication model, only to the extent that readers occupy the role of implied reader will they recognize the irony in Browning's treatment of his unreliable narrator, whose words provide at best oblique cues for making sense of what has transpired in the world of the narrative, or the irony associated with Hemingway's and Zwigoff's treatment of their respective male characters. In other words, the implied reader is the intended addressee or target audience of the implied author. This reader knows that the Duke's words are not to be taken at face value, that Jig's interlocutor does not necessarily have her best interests at heart, and that Enid would be ill advised to attempt a relationship with any of the male characters glimpsed in those screenshots.

But what is more, rhetorical theorists of narrative seeking to improve upon earlier versions of the narrative communication model have retained the distinction between actual readers and narratees but divided implied readers into two kinds, the authorial audience and the narrative audience, to use terms proposed by Peter J. Rabinowitz ([1977] 1996, 1998). The authorial audience can be described as the implied author's target audience, the hypothetical reader who is able to pick up on all the norms, attitudes, and values that are inferable (in principle) from every textual design included in a narrative text. By contrast, to the extent that they take up a position within the narrative audience, readers construe as truthful a narrator's reports concerning what is going on in that world. On this model, further, to engage fully with fictional texts, actual readers have to enter both audiences simultaneously, maintaining an awareness of the characters as serving the larger design of the work even as they get caught up in the characters' situation, as if they were real-world individuals. The model is meant to explain why actual readers can be "taken in" enough to empathize with the characters and experience curiosity, suspense, and surprise (Sternberg 1990, 1992) on the characters' behalf, but not so taken in that they jump onto the stage during the performance of a play to "rescue" a character being threatened by a villain, say. As a member of the narrative audience of Clowes's *Ghost World*, I experience suspense about how Enid's and Rebecca's attempt to make the difficult transition to adult life will turn out, as well as curiosity about the situations and events that have led them to where they are for the time-span covered by the narration. But as a member of the authorial audience, I construe these characters' utterances and actions as signals designed to cue inferences about the constellation of norms and values informing the storyworld that has been constructed by Clowes. Thus, in sequence B, I recognize that Clowes has used Rebecca and Enid to stake out different positions vis-à-vis the possibility of forming romantic attachments with their male peers, and in this light I read their conversation as a dialectical interplay between the conflicting stances represented by the characters interpreted as theme-bearing textual designs.[35]

After these refinements are factored in, along with others described by Martin (1986: 154) and Herman and Vervaeck (2005a: 22), something like the following picture emerges:

Sender: author → implied author → dramatized author → (un)dramatized narrator

⇓

Narrative message

⇓

Receiver: (un)dramatized narratee → narrative audience → authorial audience → real reader

A dramatized author uses "I," unlike the implied author, which is the persona or belief-set adopted by an actual author for the purpose of creating a particular narrative text; a dramatized narrator is an intradiegetic or character narrator, like the younger Monica who, in the account given by her older, narrating self, tells Renee's grandmother the story about the big ball in lines 48–55 of *UFO or the Devil*; a dramatized narratee is a characterized recipient of a story, like Rebecca and Naomi (at different narrative levels) in sequences C and D in *Ghost World*, or like Renee's grandmother in Monica's story-within-the-story

Not all of these participants roles will come into play in every narrative transaction; indeed, as already discussed in the first section of this chapter, one of the signposts of fictional narrative is a disparity between author and narrator that does not obtain in the case of nonfictional narratives (biographies, autobiographies, histories, witness testimony in court) (Cohn 1999). But the rhetorical theorist would argue that the communicative roles that *are* pertinent in a given storytelling context will have the structure indicated here. Admittedly, some ludic, experimental narrative texts toy with this linear arrangement of communicative roles, as when Denis Diderot in *Jacques the Fatalist* uses an elaborate structure of narrative frames, coupled with techniques of frame-breaking, to create uncertainty or at least hesitation about what sort of communicative agent (dramatized author? dramatized narrator who is himself a character within a higher-level story?) is narrating the tale and in what context. But such disruptive effects become palpable against the backdrop afforded by the expectation that narrative transactions will generally have the kind of structure suggested by the diagram. For example, in a fictional narrative featuring a dramatized narrator (like Enid telling Rebecca the story of how she told her own loss-of-virginity story to Naomi), the default assumption is that this narrator is a textual design created by the actual author rather than the other way around. (The biographical individual named Daniel Clowes conjured Enid Coleslaw and Rebecca Doppelmeyer, but not vice versa.) By the same token, the way a fictional text deploys a dramatized narrator is likely to generate inferences about that narrator's relation to the implied author. For example, in the case of sequences C and D in *Ghost World*, Enid comes across as a partly unreliable narrator, given that she appears to tell (that is, to experience a memory of telling) to Naomi Rebecca's loss-of-virginity story, despite reassuring Rebecca that she did not. In Rabinowitz's terms, this discrepancy translates into a disharmony between the roles of the narrative and the authorial audiences – between the belief-set readers adopt in order to engage fully with Enid's story-within-the-story, and the belief-set they adopt in order to make sense of the functions of her embedded narrative within *Ghost World* as a whole. The rhetorical approach thus suggests that "authentication" (or not) of particular situations and events as fictional facts depends not only on whether they are presented through first-person, third-person, or figural modes of narration, but also on the audience positions those narrative modes invite readers to occupy.

More generally, the approach complements those used by sociolinguists and positioning theorists to study the dialectical interplay between specific textual features and storytelling occasions, narrative texts and the larger communicative contexts in which they are told and interpreted.

Conclusion

The sociolinguistic, discursive-psychological, and narratological approaches reviewed in this chapter stem from quite different traditions of inquiry, and practitioners have up to now worked largely independently – some concerned mainly with natural-language narratives told in contexts of face-to-face interaction, others focusing chiefly on stories conveyed through literary or cinematic art. (A fully developed narratology of graphic narratives, despite the promising beginnings made by scholars such as Baetens 2002, Ewert 2004, 2005, and Groensteen 2007, remains a goal for the future.) Taken together, however, these investigative frameworks provide complementary tools for studying the structure and dynamics of narrative transactions – while also revealing the extent to which common storytelling processes unite narratives presented in different semiotic media. More than this, despite their different disciplinary origins and distinctions among the kinds of texts on which their practitioners characteristically focus, these approaches afford convergent insights into what I have described as the first basic element of narrative, namely, its status as

(i)   a mode of representation that is situated in – must be interpreted in light of – a specific discourse context or occasion for telling.

As all of the approaches suggest, although it may be possible to identify the bare propositional content of a storyteller's utterances without factoring in the context in which his or her narrative is told, detaching the utterances from that surrounding context is like focusing on the semantic content of a compliment without stopping to consider whether it is being said earnestly or ironically (compare *What a great guy!* said of a humble philanthropist versus someone convicted of stealing medicine from the elderly). I may issue a compliment, or tell a story, either to praise or to shame; and just as storytelling shapes the discourse contexts in which it unfolds, those contexts are what give any story its point or reason for telling.[36]

Temporality, Particularity, and Narrative

An Excursion into the Theory of Text Types

*(ii) **Event sequencing**. Narrative representations cue interpreters to draw inferences about a structured time-course of particularized events.*

From Contexts of Narration to Narrative as a Type of Text

To approach the second basic element of narrative identified in my thumbnail sketch in chapter 1, the present chapter turns from discussion of my main case studies to more general considerations of the concept of "text types" on which the overall approach is based. To explore where stories fit within a larger constellation of textual kinds – to identify the patterns of event sequencing that are distinctively associated with narrative – I examine commonalities and contrasts among *describing*, *narrating*, and *explaining*, viewed both as cognitive activities and as forms of communication, that is, text types embedded within interactional, social, institutional, and other contexts for communicative practice. Further, the chapter relates issues of text types to research on categorization processes in cognitive science, exploring what might constitute the "basic" level of a taxonomy of text types (i.e., the most cognitively fundamental level), and also what might be considered prototypical features of descriptions, explanations, and stories (i.e., the features found fully realized in exemplars or standard cases of these types). My account suggests that, like examples of birds,

cups, and chairs, instances of the category *narrative* adhere to a
logic of graded centrality, with specific story artifacts (or story-like
mental representations) being more or less prototypically narrative
in nature.

Having discussed in my previous chapter the dialectical relationship
between narrative texts and their contexts of production and interpretation – the way narrative transactions, regardless of medium, are
always and irreducibly grounded in particular discourse contexts or
communicative occasions – in this chapter and the ones that follow I
shift my emphasis to the text side of this text–context dialectic, without,
however, assuming that texts can be accessed or interpreted apart from
particular contexts of interpretation.[1] Rather, my focus shifts from consideration of how communicative contexts shape and are shaped by
the narratives circulating within them to analysis of the critical properties of texts that *do* circulate in the manner characteristic of stories. To
put this point still another way, although contexts or occasions help
determine the meaning or function of storytelling acts, analysts can work
to identify structural properties of those (situated) acts themselves –
properties thanks to which they function as instances of narrative
rather than as syllogisms, recipes, warehouse inventories, sayings in
greeting cards, or mathematical theorems, as the case might be.

The elements of **event sequencing, worldmaking/world disruption,**
and **what it's like,** the focus of this and my next two chapters, are meant
to capture some of these critical properties of narrative viewed as a
type of text as well as a cognitive structure.[2] In the present chapter,
I begin the process of characterizing key traits of narrative by sketch-
ing a map of the place of stories within a broader ecology of kinds of
texts. More specifically, to explore where stories fit within a larger constellation of text types – to determine what methods for sequencing
events might be distinctively narrative in nature – I examine commonalities and contrasts among *describing, narrating,* and *explaining,* viewed
both as cognitive activities and as forms of communication, that is,
text types embedded within interactional, social, institutional, and
other contexts for communicative practice. Although my analysis con-
siders only three text types and is meant to be illustrative rather than
exhaustive, it will allow me to zoom in on distinctive features of stories.

More specifically, a text-type approach can bring into relief key issues associated with the element of event sequencing; the approach highlights the specific kind of temporal structure that functions as a critical property of narrative representations, but not descriptions, as well as the concern with particularized events (rather than general patterns and trends) that sets stories apart from certain types of explanations. Building on this discussion of narrative's distinctive temporal structure and its focus on particularity, my next two chapters turn to other key properties of the narrative text type, including the way it functions as a blueprint for worldmaking and its foregrounding of an experiencing consciousness within the storyworld thereby evoked.

As I discuss in more detail in my next section, text types such as description, narrative, and explanation stand in complex relations with one another and with other representational strategies and artifacts. In line with research in the cognitive sciences that I go on to review – research suggesting that people make sense of things in the world by grouping them into multi-level systems of categories – this network of relationships among kinds of texts can be plotted along horizontal and vertical axes. Vertically, the text types in question are members of a category subordinate to the category that contains all the phenomena classifiable as texts, but superordinate to the category containing, say, particular kinds of narratives or explanations.[3] In other words, (kinds of) text types have a place within a hierarchical taxonomic system, with the categories becoming narrower or more specific as you move downward through the hierarchy:

texts
text types (e.g., narrative)
genres (e.g., science fiction)
subgenres (e.g., cyberpunk fiction)

Horizontally, realizations of text types can be more or less clearly distinct from one another, depending on how many features a given artifact or representation shares with central, prototypical instances of the type of which it is a token. Furthermore a single text can simultaneously embody several text types through operations of conjunction, alternation, embedding, etc. Novels, for example, can contain many descriptive passages yet still be considered narratives; in this case, a text that is globally narrative embeds local instances of description, with narrative segments of the text being conjoined to or alternating with descriptive segments.[4] Conversely, describing a person's everyday behavior might entail quoting the humorous anecdotes he or she likes to tell; in this case, a text or discourse that globally realizes the category of description embeds local instances of narration. Explanations of physical or social processes may also embed detailed descriptions of their initial conditions and their effects. Yet a text, discourse, or mental representation that addresses the central concern of explanations, namely, the question of *why?*, differs in crucial respects from one that addresses the central concern of descriptions, namely, the question of *what?* (see Hempel [1948] 1998). Less intuitively clear is how telling a story about a situation or an event relates to explaining that situation or event.[5] I consider the nature of the relationship between narrative and explanation in a "coda" on narrative and science provided in the final part of this chapter.

In the sections that follow, after discussing recent work on text types, I relate that work to research on what cognitive theorists have termed *basic-level* and *prototype* effects in categorization processes; here I explore what might constitute the "basic" level of a taxonomy of text types (i.e., the most cognitively fundamental level), and also what might be considered prototypical features of descriptions, explanations, and stories (i.e., the features found fully realized in standard cases of these types). I argue that, like other members of a category, instances of the category *narrative* adhere to a logic of graded centrality, with specific story artifacts (as well as story-like mental representations) being better or worse examples of narrative. Accordingly, whereas prototypical instances of the category *narrative* (what Hogan 2003 terms *exemplars*) share relatively few features with those of *description*, more peripheral cases are less clearly separable from that text type, allowing for hybrid forms such as "descriptivized narrations" and "narrativized descriptions" (Mosher 1991). A further question is whether narrative shares a similarly porous boundary with the text-type category *explanation*, making possible "narrative explanations" (Adams 1996) that blend attributes of these two kinds of texts. In any case, the existence of hybridized or "fuzzy" forms does not mean that narrative is, at a deep level, equivalent to description or explanation. Rather, such forms again suggest the graded versus binarized, either-or nature of text-type categories, and the way non-prototypical instances of those categories can verge on neighboring textual kinds.

Building on the taxonomy outlined earlier in the chapter, especially the account of core features of explanation, the coda at the end of the chapter uses the taxonomy to investigate how narrative relates to description and explanation in contexts of scientific inquiry in particular. Here my discussion uncovers something of a paradox or at least a tension: whereas some aspects of scientific inquiry may be indissolubly bound up with narrative modes of representation, other kinds of scientific explanation appear to be not just non-narratively structured but also antithetical or at least resistant to narrativization – to being conceptualized in narrative terms.

Text Types and Categorization Processes

The first part of this section reviews work on the concept of text types. I then connect that work with research on categorization processes and the vertical as well as horizontal relations between categories within taxonomies, or systems for organizing the world into kinds and instances of those kinds. I focus on two key concepts: basic-level effects, whereby one category within a hierarchy of levels (such as texts > text types > genres > subgenres) functions in a more cognitively basic way than the categories at other levels, and prototype effects, by which instances of the same category may be more or less prototypical examples (or "exemplars") of that category. My argument is that both sorts of effects are relevant for understanding how narrative provides a specific method for sequencing events – this method being one of the distinctive properties of stories that in turn accounts for how narrative relates to other types of texts.

Categorizing texts: an overview

In Chatman's account, a *text* can be defined as "any communication that temporally controls its reception by the audience" (1990: 7), i.e., "a time-regulating structure" (1990: 8). But different kinds of texts regulate time in different ways, and one of the motivations of the theory of text types is to capture the differences at issue.

Theorists of texts types have proposed a number of taxonomic principles and nomenclatures (see, e.g., Adam 1985; Chatman 1990; Fludernik 2000; Görlach 2004; Virtanen 1992; Virtanen and Wårvik 1987; Werlich 1975, 1983). In this book I assume that *text types* are broader in scope than literary *genres* (*Bildungsroman*, the psychological novel). Instead, they can be compared with the "primary speech genres" characterized by Bakhtin ([1953] 1986: 60) as relatively stable types of utterance which develop within particular spheres of language use, and from which "[s]econdary (complex) speech genres – novels, dramas, all kinds of scientific research, major genres of commentary, and so forth – arise in more complex and comparatively highly developed and organized cultural communication (primarily written) that is artistic, scientific, sociopolitical and so on" ([1953] 1986: 62). For his part, Görlach (2004) defines *text type* as

> a specific linguistic pattern in which formal/structural characteristics [e.g. the lexical patterns found in patient histories written by physicians, or the question-answer turn-taking sequence of police interrogations] have been conventionalized in a specific culture for certain well-defined and standardized uses of language so that a speaker/hearer or writer/reader can judge:
>
> a) the correct use of linguistic features obligatory or expected in a specific text type . . .
> b) the adequate use of the formula with regard to topic, situation, addressee, medium, register, etc.;
> c) the identification of intentionally or inadvertently mixed types, or their misuse;
> d) the designation of the text type [e.g., speakers not only know what features characterize a *political speech* but also know the name].
> (2004: 105)

As Görlach notes, judgments of this sort form part of language users' overall communicative competence; hence "the lack of knowledge of textual conventions can carry the same degree of stigmatization as the incorrect use of syntax or pronunciation" (2004: 105). In an academic debate, for example, foul-mouthed exchanges of insults are neither obligatory nor expected (a), nor am I likely to address my interlocutor in such a debate using the formula *Hey, bud* or *Yo, dude* (b), unless I am inadvertently or intentionally (humorously) mixing the text types of public academic debate and streetcorner dispute (c). Further, my ability to frame this example, and to refer to academic debates versus street-corner disputes by name, stems from my knowledge of the repertoire of text types that constitutes my overall communicative competence (d), i.e., my knowledge of what to say, how, and under what circumstances (cf. Hymes 1974; Saville-Troike 2002).

Insofar as text types are heuristic constructs used to make sense of more or less heterogeneous semiotic practices, text-type categories can be related to categorization processes in general – that is, the processes whereby people use categories to make sense of the world. Originating in the work of cognitive anthropologists, anthropological linguists, and psychologists examining categorization processes both intraculturally and interculturally, the study of category systems has highlighted the extent to which humans rely on categories in everyday perception, reasoning, and communication. Inspired by the pathbreaking work of Eleanor Rosch and her colleagues (Rosch 1973, [1978] 2004; Rosch et al. 1976; cf. Lakoff 1987, [1987] 2004), theorists working in this tradition have focused on two key aspects of categorization processes; these aspects have been termed *basic-level effects* and *prototype effects*.[6] On the one hand, basic-level effects arise from the way categories are arranged hierarchically in terms of degrees of inclusiveness; in such hierarchies, one level of the system can be described as being more cognitively basic than the others, and certain "effects" flow from this hierarchical structure: e.g., in empirical tests, it is the level at which members of the category are most rapidly identified. Such basic-level effects, discussed more fully below, thus manifest themselves along the "vertical" axis of a category system and apply to the basic category *tree* versus subordinate categories *maple* or *red maple* – and also versus the superordinate category *living thing*. On the other hand, prototype effects concern not the hierarchical relations among more and less inclusive categories but rather the relations among more or less prototypical instances of the same category – and also among neighboring categories themselves. Research on this second kind of effect suggests that certain members of categories tend to be perceived as more central or prototypical than other members (cf. robins versus emus as instances of the category *bird*). Further, the research suggests that boundaries between categories are permeable, such that less standard cases of neighboring categories can be difficult to situate in one category versus the other – as is the case with certain non-prototypical instances of the category *tree* as compared with exemplars of the category *shrub*.

In my next subsection, I explore how accounts of these two kinds of effects within category systems can help illuminate relations among text types such as narrative, description, and explanation.

Are text types cognitively basic?

Cognitive-anthropological research (Atran 1990; Berlin 1992; Berlin, Breedlove, and Raven 1973; Ellen 1993) has revealed cross-cultural regularities in the structure of folk taxonomies of living organisms – regularities pointing to basic-level effects in category systems. In Atran's characterization, a culture's folk taxonomy consists of "a stable hierarchy of inclusive groups of organisms, or taxa, which are mutually exclusive at each level of the hierarchy" (1999: 317). These levels or ranks encompass FOLK KINGDOMS (e.g., *animal, plant*), LIFE FORMS (*insect, mammal, bird, tree*), FOLK GENERICS (*mosquito, dog, starling, oak*), FOLK SPECIFICS (*schnauzer, white oak*), and FOLK VARIETALS (*miniature schnauzer, swamp white oak*). Across cultures hierarchically differentiated ranks, not the taxa (groups of organisms) that they contain, are universal. Further, names for taxa of the same rank tend to have (across different languages) similar morphological/lexical properties. Whereas most folk generics are assigned names consisting of unanalyzable lexical stems (such as *oak* or *dog*, in English) subordinate taxa usually receive binomial or polynomial labels, which consist of an attributive word or phrase attached to a lexical stem: *willow oak, southern red oak* (for a more detailed account of linguistic reflexes of folk taxonomies, see Herman and Moss 2007).

The similar structure of names for folk generics across different languages (as attested in Malt 1995) provides evidence that categories at this (intermediate) level of taxonomic systems are cognitively fundamental, that is, "functionally and epistemologically primary with respect to the following factors: gestalt perception, image formation, motor movement, knowledge organization, ease of cognitive processing (learning, recognition, memory, etc.), and *ease of linguistic expression*" (Lakoff [1987] 2004: 144, my emphasis). In other words, the research on basic-level effects suggests that "categories are not merely organized in a hierarchy from the most general to the most specific, but are also organized so that categories that are cognitively basic are 'in the middle' of a general-to-specific hierarchy. Generalization proceeds 'upward' from the basic level and specialization proceeds 'downward'" (Lakoff [1987] 2004: 144). In this model, the middle level of a taxonomic hierarchy such as

superordinate level = animal
basic level = dog
subordinate level = retriever

has the following attributes – it is:

the highest level at which category members have a similarly perceived
  overall shape;
the highest level at which a single mental image can reflect the entire
  category;
the highest level at which a person uses similar motor actions for interacting with category members;
the level at which subjects are fastest at identifying category members;
the level with the most commonly used labels for category members;
the first level named and understood by children; and
the first level to enter the lexicon of a language. (Lakoff [1987] 2004: 168)

But how might this work supporting the notion of basic-level categorization bear on text-type classifications – and on narrative texts in particular? Prior to being made the object of academic study (for example,
through accounts of literary genres or analyses such as the one outlined
in the present chapter), a culture's system for classifying text types
and their superordinate and subordinate categories is likewise a folk
taxonomy. In parallel with other taxonomies, such classificatory systems
are in principle subject to basic-level effects. But consider whether a
taxonomy like the following captures categorization processes underlying the use of texts, at least in some cultures and subcultures:

superordinate level = "time-regulating" phenomena (Chatman 1990: 7)
  interpretable as texts (print texts, cinematic texts, spoken discourses,
  structured mental representations that could in principle be textualized, etc.)
basic level = text types (narrative, description, explanation, instruction,
  etc.)
subordinate level = genres (detective novel, *Bildungsroman*, legal
  explanation, forensic explanation, etc.)

Some reflexes of basic-level effects appear to be absent from this
taxonomy, including reflexes associated with category labels. Hence

among the terms that Görlach (2004: 79) lists as definitions of *story*, several are in actuality competing labels for this text type, used in more or less free variation with *story*: *narrative, account, tale*. In other words, it would be difficult to establish that any of the lexical items in the set *story, narrative, account, tale* is more "basic" than any of the other items. Yet in other respects – e.g., categorical representativeness and motor responses – basic-level effects might in fact be attributed to members of the middle or text-type-level category in this taxonomy. It could be argued that the text-type level is the highest level at which a single mental image can reflect the entire category, with the concept "narrative" reflecting key properties of all the narrative genres and subgenres that can be ranged under that category. Likewise, it could be argued that what Meir Sternberg (1990, 1992, 2001) characterizes as the narrative universals of curiosity, suspense, and surprise orient my (simulated) motor responses to agents and events when I transpose my spatial and temporal coordinates to those orienting characters within mentally projected storyworlds (no matter what the specific genre or subgenre of narrative involved) – whereas descriptions and explanations do not trigger responses of this kind.[7] Then again, when I consult my own intuitions about the highest level at which inferences about overall shape first become possible, I find that I am more likely to draw those inferences at a lower level of the taxonomy – in connection with the plot structure of detective novels, say, or the processes of identity formation in the *Bildungsroman*.[8] So which is more basic, in the sense at issue: the text-type level or the level of genres?

The mixed picture that emerges from this taxonomic thought-experiment may account for the proliferation of text-type classifications among text linguists, for example.[9] The research reveals a lack of convergence in this context – i.e., a lack of consensus about how to create a hierarchy of levels in this domain of categorization, let alone a common list of items within each such level. We may therefore speculate that ways of understanding the domain of textual phenomena are changing more rapidly than ways of understanding and categorizing the domain of biological organisms, for example. Similar intuitions seem to motivate what might be characterized as the anti-taxonomy sketched by Barthes ([1968] 1977), who uses the capitalized word *Text* as a mass noun, like *water* or *space*, and the lower-case word *text* as a count noun, like *cat* or *pencil*. In this way, Barthes suggests particular texts are merely strategic demarcations of a generalized textual field or, rather, process

– a citational process by which ever more Text is produced. The work, any particular textual instantiation, now becomes epiphenomenal or "the imaginary tail of the text" (Barthes [1968] 1977: 156–7). As Barthes puts it, "the Text does not stop at (good) Literature; it cannot be contained in a hierarchy, even in a simple division of genres. What constitutes the Text is, on the contrary (or precisely), its subversive force in respect of the old classifications" ([1968] 1977: 157).

In characterizing the Text as superordinate to specific literary genres, Barthes builds on his own earlier account of narrative as a trans- or super-generic phenomenon in "Introduction to the Structuralist Analysis of Narratives" ([1966] 1977), where narrative stands out as an object of inquiry precisely because of the way it occupies a level above particular story genres and media, whether popular or elite, traditional or avant-garde. Situating narrative at a super-generic level allowed Barthes to explore what he took to be critical properties of narrative in general as opposed to novels, autobiographies, news broadcasts, etc. But this strategy invites, in turn, questions about prototype effects arising from "horizontal" relations among narratives and other types of texts, including descriptions and explanations.

Text types, category gradience, and prototype effects

Just as basic-level effects are evident along the vertical axis of text-type taxonomies, prototype effects are evident along the horizontal axis. They concern not the hierarchical relations among more and less inclusive categories but rather the relations among more or less prototypical instances of the same category – and also among neighboring categories themselves.

As Lakoff (1987: 12–22) points out, and as sketched preliminarily in chapter 1, along the horizontal dimension of taxonomic systems, relations among categories and category members are subject to two forms of gradience, membership gradience and centrality gradience. These two forms of gradience are defined, respectively, by "the idea that at least some categories have degrees of membership and no clear boundaries" and by "the idea that members (or subcategories) which are clearly within the category boundaries may still be more or less central" (Lakoff [1987] 2004: 144). For example, members of the category *tall people* will belong to that category on a more-or-less basis (is someone who stands 5 feet 11 inches [1.8 meters] tall or not?), and there will be no clear dividing line between the categories *tall people* and *people of medium height*. Rather, a person who is 6 feet 6 inches will, by the standards of current-day North America, be "more" (or more strongly) a member of the category of *tall people* than will someone who is 5 feet 11 inches. By contrast, unlike the category *tall people* the category *bird* is a bounded one; despite having the ability to get airborne, neither a plane, nor a human cannonball at the local carnival, nor a flying squirrel is a bird. However, particular birds will still be more or less central or prototypical realizations of the category, with robins and sparrows having more of the prototypical features of *bird* than emus or penguins, neither of which can fly. *Bird*, then, is subject to centrality gradience but not membership gradience, whereas *tall people* is subject to membership gradience; this in turn entails that certain instances of the category *tall people* will be more representative or "central" than others, with centrality now being defined as full possession of the properties that members of the gradient category can have on a more-or-less basis.

Hogan (2003: 45–7, 71–6) offers an excellent synopsis of some of the issues raised by research in this area. As Hogan notes, prototypes are in essence standard cases. But the cognitive process by which those cases come to be viewed as standard is richly structured. As Hogan puts it:

> prototypes add "average" properties to defaults. . . . [This] averaging is "weighted" by saliency. The prototypical man for any given person will involve average properties, not of all men, but of men who are highly salient in that person's experience.[10] . . . Perhaps more interestingly, the weighting of averages is also bound up with *contrast effects*. In other words, the saliency of particular instances of one category is in part a function of their contrast with instances of some opposed category. . . . Thus, if a square jaw is associated with men and not women, then the prototypical man will have a squarer jaw than will the actual statistically average man. (2003: 46)

As Hogan's characterization suggests, although processes of categorization in general and assessments of relative prototypicality in particular may be grounded in basic cognitive abilities and dispositions, contexts of interpretation affect judgments about how specific instances of categories pertain to prototypes and where to draw the boundary between a non-prototypical instance of one category and an equally peripheral member of a neighboring category. Prototype effects, accordingly, may emanate from underlying cognitive capacities and tendencies, but they are also anchored to features of the situations in which those abilities and dispositions are deployed. This way of thinking about prototypes raises key questions: how are judgments of what constitutes a prototypical narrative affected by the contexts in which those judgments are formulated, and what sorts of contrast effects come into play with judgments about (or analyses of) standard cases of stories vis-à-vis descriptions, explanations, or other text-type categories?

The contextual grounding of prototype effects can be illustrated by dropping down one level in our hierarchy of textual phenomena, from text types to genres. Theorists of literary genre have long recognized the presence of prototype effects in systems for classifying genres. According to Jacques Derrida, in an argument that perhaps underestimates the role of exemplars or standard cases in generic systems, a given text submits itself only more or less to the law of any particular genre (Derrida [1980] 1991), orienting itself to multiple generic norms simultaneously. Conversely, genre distinctions make their presence felt even (or perhaps especially) in texts that actively violate dominant generic conventions (cf. Dubrow 1982: 3–4). Suppose a western were to include a scene with alien invaders or a hardboiled detective novel were to recruit extensively from the techniques used in eighteenth-century sentimental fiction. The subversive force of such generic transpositions becomes palpable only because they cut against the grain of established categorization practices, which organize people's understanding of the textual domain and establish cuts or boundaries between textual kinds. Yet as reception theorists as well as students of genre have discussed, such boundaries between genres may change over time, since particular texts can claim generic status while also pushing against the boundaries of established generic norms.[11] To paraphrase Jauss (1982): the novel was never the same after Joyce's *Ulysses*.

The appearance of generically creative or subversive works like Joyce's can reset the system of generic classifications, demonstrating how context impinges on assessments of prototypicality. In other words, what counts as a novel (for example) can be altered by texts eventually if not immediately recognized as instances of the novel form. *Ulysses* altered the conditions for novel-writing in general, as attested by such follow-up works as Woolf's *Mrs Dalloway* (1925), Döblin's *Berlin Alexanderplatz* (1929), and Faulkner's *The Sound and the Fury* (1929). This process suggests that different contrast effects came into play at different points in the history of *Ulysses'* reception. Its degree of prototypicality as a novel increased as the generic categories that formed the main comparison set were themselves reconfigured by the publication of Joyce's novel and other, affiliated, novels; those novels' focus on the flux of consciousness reduced the contrast effect between e.g. novelistic discourse and the expressive dimensions of lyric, and thus the saliency of features (action, plot) which had been factored into the determination of what made for a prototypical novel.

In short, generic categories function more like *tall people* than *bird*, with cut-off points between one genre and another being subject to variation over time. But, moving back up one level in the hierarchical systems, are instances of text-type as well as generic categories also gradient in nature? Is it the case that texts, discourses, or representations can be more or less narrative in kind, such that the frontiers of narrative are less like borders between autonomous nation-states than contested property lines between neighboring communities, which share some practices but not others? When compared with central, prototypical instances of the narrative text type, are certain non-prototypical narrative representations less readily distinguished from descriptions – in the same way that some trees are quite shrub-like? Further, to return to Hogan's (2003) synopsis of recent research on prototypes, how do the issues of contextual grounding and contrast effects play out at the level of text types? Are different kinds of features going to be identified as prototypically narrative or descriptive or explanatory depending on context? In parallel with the way the standard case of *dog* changes when one moves from the farm in Maine to an apartment in Manhattan, does the prime exemplar of the category *story* change when one moves from the family dinner table to a scriptwriting class? And will different sorts of contrast sets cause different features of narrative to be weighted with special salience? Does my own analysis weight particular aspects of narrative more heavily because I have chosen description and explanation as my contrast set, whereas different critical properties might be foregrounded if the contrast set consisted of drama and lyric?

In the following sections I signal the relevance of these questions while moving forward with my more general account of how research on categorization might be synthesized with text-type theory to explore basic elements of narrative.

Narrative as a Text-Type Category: Descriptions versus Stories versus Explanations

In this section, I explore conceptual underpinnings of the approach developed in this book, a thumbnail sketch of which was presented in chapter 1. Specifically, I outline what can be construed as features of prototypical instances or standard cases of the three text-type categories under consideration, description, narrative, and explanation – though, again, I acknowledge the relevance of context and of contrast effects when it comes to the identification of prototypes. Attempting to isolate core features of each textual kind, I also examine how forms of category gradience might apply in this domain. To reiterate, since my next two chapters investigate the elements of worldmaking/world disruption and what it's like, I focus here on the role of event sequencing in stories – and discuss the extent to which a specific method of sequencing events distinguishes the narrative text type from descriptions and explanations.

Description

Description can be conceived as a cognitive activity that may or may not be realized as a discourse or text falling within the text type *description*. If textualized, descriptions can in turn be embodied in a variety of media and shaped by diverse representational conventions, from mathematical symbolism and flow charts to inventories of personality traits and ethnographic practices.

As Chatman notes, description has long held a special fascination for narratologists, who tend to treat it as "the most interesting of the other text-types because its relation to Narrative is the most subtle and complex" (1990: 16). As I go on to discuss, the area of overlap between narrative and description can indeed be substantial, since representations and discourses falling under both rubrics have the net effect of coupling properties with situations, events, or objects (compare ascribing to someone the trait of being poor against telling the story of how he or she came to be impoverished). But Lukács ([1936] 1970), in his critique of modernist fiction, emphasized the difference. For Lukács, to describe constitutes in some contexts a refusal to narrate, when "mere" description is measured against the realist narrative practice of emplotting events within a larger chain of occurrences in a richly social context. In making this argument, Lukács builds on a (rhetorical) tradition that, as Hamon (1982) and Chatman (1990: 23) point out, long viewed description as secondary or derivative, i.e., as inferior to (or an interruption of) what is properly narrative. Again, however, contrast Sternberg's (1981) functionalist account, according to which descriptive and narrative functions can be fulfilled by one and the same textual structure – and reciprocally, many different structures can serve, say, a descriptive function – depending on the particularities of communicative contexts. From this perspective, attempts to draw an invidious distinction between narrative and description are misguided, especially since, as discussed below, context alone determines whether one and the same statement functions as a description of some aspect of a storyworld or rather as narration via a character's thought-processes.

For his part, Pflugmacher suggests that "[d]escription is a text-type which identifies the properties of places, objects, or persons" (2005: 101). Pflugmacher's definition might be expanded as follows: representations and discourses that are central instances of this text-type category entail the ascription of properties to entities within a mental model of the world (whatever the modality status of that mentally projected world – e.g., real, fictional, dreamed, etc.). Furthermore, such ascriptions can be either static or dynamic. On the one hand, stative propositions involve property ascriptions at a moment in time or, as in (1), ascriptions of enduring attributes over an undifferentiated span of time.

1   Water is H_2O.

On the other hand, active propositions, or process statements, involve property ascriptions over a differentiated time-course within the mentally projected world; cf. (2) and (3):

2   The trees lost their leaves during the transition from fall to winter.
3   Mondays, Wednesdays, and Fridays I have toast for breakfast, but on Tuesdays and Thursdays I have cereal.

(2) and (3) can be captured by Pflugmacher's definition if they are translated into their underlying logical structure, along the lines of "At time

t the trees possess property L, and at time t + 1 property ~L (where L = being fully leaved and ~L = being leafless)." Here, however, the limits of both the classical accounts of description and the classical model of categorization become evident. Precisely because descriptions can focus on temporally emergent phenomena, the boundary between description and narration should be thought of as porous and variable rather than as impermeable and fixed (cf. Genette [1966] 1982; Kittay 1981; Ronen 1997). Likewise, specific instances of description and narrative will pertain to these text-type categories in a gradient, more-or-less rather than binarized, all-or-nothing manner.

Pointing to forms of category gradience, Mosher (1991) identified mixed modes that he termed descriptivized narration and narrativized description, already discussed in chapter 1. Mosher's analysis suggests the relevance of centrality gradience for members of text-type categories: narrativized descriptions and descriptivized narrations are neither prototypically descriptive nor prototypically narrative. But what is more, it is not always clear which text type is dominant and which is subservient in a given discourse context, raising the question of whether a description is being narrativized or a narrative descriptivized. In these cases membership gradience also makes its relevance felt. If I read a clause such as *the house was dark* in a novel, only context can determine whether this is a statement by the narrator ascribing a property to the house or, rather, a report of some perceiving agent's reaction to the house at a specific point in the unfolding action (cf. Jahn 1997). In other words, is this clause a piece of descriptive text embedded within and subserving a more global narrative, or is the clause itself a narrative report of a character's perceptions – with the character's consciousness suffusing the third-person voice?

Chatman is surely right to suggest that (thanks to a kind of higher-order grammar that applies to texts versus words, phrases, and clauses) readers and speakers are able "to distinguish between Narrative and Description as text-types, on the one hand, and sentences in the surface of a text which are loosely called 'narrative' or 'descriptive', on the other" (1990: 16). Arguably, however, membership gradience affects classifications at both of these levels. As discussed in chapter 3, interpretations of surface-level structures are shaped by their situation in a larger discourse context; so are assessments of global text-type categories – for example, when one has to determine the communicative function of the first utterance spoken by one's interlocutor at the beginning of a conversational interchange. Thus, to get a better sense of the (fuzzy) boundary between description and narrative, it is necessary to work toward an account of the elements that are prototypical for narrative.

Narrative

Like description, narrative is a cognitive activity, which may or may not be realized as an artifact falling within the text type *narrative*. That text-type category in turn encompasses a variety of media and representational conventions, ranging from those used in sign language and cinematic narrative to face-to-face storytelling and avant-garde literary narratives.

Again, my analysis in this chapter focuses on just one of what I have presented as a set of basic elements or critical properties of narrative:

(ii) Narrative representations cue interpreters to draw inferences about a structured time-course of particularized events.

As discussed more fully in my next subsection, the degree to which represented events are particularized provides a parameter along which narratives can be distinguished from explanations. Whereas stories are prototypically concerned with particular situations and events, it can be argued that explanations by their nature concern themselves with ways in which, in general, the world tends to be. Particularity is, however, a scalar, more-or-less notion, with context determining whether a text or a discourse counts as more or less particularistic. I am expected to go into detail when telling ghost stories around the campfire; the threshold for sufficient particularity is high in such contexts. But the same level of particularity would be judged excessive in the give-and-take of normal conversation (see the final section of my next chapter, and also Norrick 2007: 135–6). Again the contextual grounding of judgments about prototypes or standard cases manifests itself.

If particularity sets narrative apart from explanation, the kind of time-course represented in stories serves to distinguish the prototypical narrative from instances of description. But how can the temporal profile of narrative, its distinctive method of sequencing events, best be characterized? Example (3) suggests that a fairly widely used definition of narrative as a sequential representation of a sequence of events (cf. Chatman 1990; Genette [1972] 1980; Rimmon-Kenan [1983] 2002) is too broad:

3   Mondays, Wednesdays, and Fridays I have toast for breakfast, but
    on Tuesdays and Thursdays I have cereal.

Example (3) is a sequentially ordered representation of things that happen in a sequence, but arguably it is still not a narrative – taken on
its own, at least. For one thing, the representation lacks particularity;
like a recipe or a list of measurements read off a scientific instrument,
it concerns a general pattern or protocol for activity or behavior as
opposed to a series of particularized events. Further – to anticipate my
discussion of the element of worldmaking/world disruption below and,
more fully, in my next chapter – no disruptive or noncanonical events
figure in (3), of the sort that are prototypical for narrative representations. The absence of the noncanonical explains why converting (3) to
a series of statements about particular breakfasts, as in (3′), would not
in itself produce a narrative representation:

3′   On Monday, Wednesday, and Friday I had toast for breakfast, but
    on Tuesday and Thursday I had cereal.

However, with a shift in context – and in accordance with the Proteus
Principle (Sternberg 1982; see note 1 of this chapter) – both (3) and (3′)
might start to acquire narrativity. Thus, if either representation
occurred in the context of a discourse in which a cruel foster-parent
had just said to his or her new foster-child, "In this house, we do not
eat breakfast," and the child had replied by uttering (3) or (3′), the result
would be challenge to the dominant order, a breaking out of the disruptive or the noncanonical, that would serve to shift this representation across the (fuzzy) boundary separating descriptions from stories.
Likewise, in (3″),

3″   From Monday to Thursday I had toast for breakfast. But on Friday
    I had cereal.

a modicum of world-disruptiveness accounts for the intuition that the
representation has shifted its position along the continuum or cline linking description with narrative.[12]

In any case, as discussed in chapter 2, the tradition of thinking about
narrative as a collation or coordination of two levels of temporality has
its roots in the *fabula/sjuzhet* or story/discourse distinction proposed

by Russian Formalist theorists such Viktor Shklovskii ([1929] 1990) and further developed by structuralist narratologists. At issue is the distinction between the *what* and the *how*, or what is being told versus the manner in which it is told. From this perspective, narratives feature two different layers or levels of temporal sequence that can be more or less (dis)aligned, namely, the sequence of events in the storyworld evoked by the narrative, and the sequence in which those events are ordered in the narrative representation itself. In strictly chronological narration (ABC), these sequences match up; in what Genette ([1972] 1980) termed *analepses* (= flashbacks of the form BCA or BAC) and *prolepses* (= flashforwards of the form ACB), the two sequences diverge.

Drawing on this work, Sternberg (1990, 1992, 2001) points to the peculiarly double temporality of stories as the constitutive condition for narrativity, or what makes narrative narrative, as well as the basis for the three narrative universals he names: suspense, curiosity, and surprise. As Sternberg puts it,

> narrativity lives between the processes uniquely run together by the genre [or, in the terms used here, the text type]: actional and communicative, told and telling/reading sequence. This interplay between temporalities generates the three universal narrative effects/interests/dynamics of prospection, retrospection, and recognition – suspense, curiosity, and surprise, for short. *Suspense* arises from rival scenarios for the future. . . . Its fellow universals rather involve manipulations of the past, which the tale communicates in a sequence discontinuous with the happening. Perceptibly so, for *curiosity*: knowing that we do not know, we go forward with our mind on the gapped antecedents, trying to infer (bridge, compose) them in retrospect. For *surprise*, however, the narrative first unobtrusively gaps or twists its chronology, then unexpectedly discloses to us our misreading and enforces a corrective rereading in late re-cognition. (2001: 117)

The question, however, is whether the two layers of temporality operative in stories are sufficient to account for suspense, curiosity, and surprise as distinctively narrative phenomena or effects. As already noted, example (3) likewise involves both a sequence of represented events and a sequential structure in the representation itself; however, in representations like (3), opportunities for suspense, curiosity, and surprise would seem to be minimal or nonexistent. For this very reason, perhaps, (3) is a better candidate for inclusion in the text-type category of description than that of narrative; but my larger point is that double-layered temporality cannot be used as a criterion for narrativity – nor as an explanation for the presence of Sternberg's three key narrative effects – if layered temporality can obtain in descriptions as well as stories.

In this connection, it should be noted that Sternberg (1981) has elsewhere sketched a continuous, more-or-less rather than discrete, either-or relationship between narrative and description – in a way that harmonizes with the account developed in the present book. In Sternberg's terms, because "actional mimesis presupposes a descriptive element, however implicit or even camouflaged" (1981: 72), "action and description form not givens but inferences, constructs, opposed but not divorced frames of coherence. Whether in tense or harmonious opposition, they may cohabit in the very same piece of text; and it is only according to the dominant function – or primary frame of intelligibility – that we can reasonably speak of actional or descriptive writing" (1981: 73). Hence, "[a]ctional and descriptive discourse . . . form a polar rather than ungradable contrast; and the position of a given textual piece on that continuum can be determined not in formal but in functional terms alone, involving all the contextual operations of reading" (1981: 76). But what combination of textual and contextual factors accounts for judgments about where a given text or discourse falls along this continuum stretching from descriptive to actional (= narrative) representations? Granted that, in accordance with the Proteus Principle (Sternberg 1982), neither temporal sequence nor any other formal feature serves as a guarantee for narrativity, do certain kinds of temporal structures *inhibit* the interpretation of texts as narratives?

For his part, Prince (1973, 1982) argues that event sequences are a necessary but not a sufficient condition for stories; i.e., narratively organized sequences have a higher-order structure not found in all strings of events classifiable as descriptive sequences. More precisely, narratives represent time- and place-specific transitions from some source state S to a target state S'. In Prince's (1973) account of "minimal narratives," the target state S' is the inverse of the source state S, with an event mediating between them. Thus contrast the higher-order structure evident in (5) but not (4):

4   The politician had a reputation for hypocritical self-righteousness. The politician had a reputation for integrity. The politician's illegal acts came to light.

5   The politician had a reputation for integrity. Then the politician's illegal acts came to light. As a result, the politician now had a reputation for hypocritical self-righteousness.

The structure manifest in (5) but not (4) at least affords the possibility for the sort of choice, risk, consequence, and irreversibility that Kittay (1981) and Chatman (1990) characterize as distinguishing features of narrative versus description – specifically, the risk assumed by the politician in committing illegal acts in the first place, and the irreversibility of the consequences of his choosing to commit those acts. Bremond (1980) addresses similar issues in his discussion of the logic of narrative sequences, which, he argues, pass through three phases: the opening of a possibility (the possibility of committing illegal acts); the actualization or non-actualization of that possibility (the politician's commission of the acts); and, if the possibility is actualized, the end result (the politician's losing his reputation for integrity and gaining one for hypocritical self-righteousness instead). Accordingly, narrative does not merely involve a (dual) temporal sequence – the sequentially organized representation (= *sjuzhet*) of a sequence of events (= *fabula*) – but also traces paths taken by particularized individuals faced with decision points at one or more temporal junctures in a storyworld; those paths lead to consequences that take shape against a larger backdrop of consequences in which other possible paths might have eventuated, but did not. Hence, what Sternberg characterizes as the narrative universal of suspense arises, not just because of narrative's double temporality, but also because of the structure of risk or irreversible consequence that certain kinds of temporal structures afford. Likewise, surprise is rooted not just in temporality but also in expectation, or rather in the violation of what is expected based on a standard or canonical pattern of events (cf. Bruner 1990, 1991).

To put these same points another way, prototypical instances of narrative involve more than particularized events unfolding within more or less richly detailed storyworlds. Thus, as noted in my preliminary discussion in chapter 1, Todorov (1968) argued that narratives characteristically follow a trajectory leading from an initial state of equilibrium, through a phase of disequilibrium, to an endpoint at which equilibrium is restored (on a different footing) because of intermediary events – though not every narrative will trace the entirety of this path (cf. Bremond 1980; Kafalenos 2006; Propp [1928] 1968). In this account, stories prototypically involve a more or less marked disruption of what is expected or canonical, and being able to recognize such disruptions depends on forming inferences about the kinds of agency characters have in storyworlds, as role-bearing or position-occupying individuals sometimes acting at cross-purposes with their own interests and goals or those of other such individuals. Thus, in example (5), the disruptive event is the politician's own self-destructive conduct.

By the same token, the narrative universal of surprise (Sternberg 1990, 2001) is rooted not just in temporality but also in expectation, or rather in the violation of what is expected based on a standard or canonical pattern of events – as when stories portray politicians as engaged in precisely those forms of illegality on whose detection and prosecution they had staked their earlier careers. Yet it is not only that narrative can be recognized as such because of the way it represents non-normal situations and events; more than this, narrative is a cognitive and communicative strategy for navigating the gap, in everyday experience, between what was expected and what actually takes place. Thus Bruner (1990) characterizes narrative as the primary resource for "folk psychology" – that is, people's everyday understanding of how thinking works, the rough-and-ready heuristics to which they resort in thinking about thinking itself. From this perspective, as discussed more fully in chapter 6 (cf. Herman 2008b), narrative affords a kind of discourse scaffolding for formulating reasons about why people engage in the actions they do, or else fail to engage in actions that we expect them to pursue. Accordingly a further narrative about the politician's upbringing and familial relationships, or perhaps about a problem connected with addiction or some other disability, would be the most appropriate instrument for accounting for the turn of events represented in example (5).

My next chapter revisits issues of event sequencing and narrativity by providing something of a primer on how to build – and disrupt – a storyworld. The chapter also argues that, by starting with worldmaking/ world disruption as a basic cognitive and communicative function served by storytelling, and then working backward to the formal structures that support this root function of narrative, it is easier to motivate – to provide warrant for – fine-grained analyses of both the temporal and the spatial dimensions of storyworlds. Meanwhile, I return now to the factor of particularity vis-à-vis distinctively narrative methods of sequencing events. This factor is of key importance when it comes to studying the relationship between stories and explanations.

Explanation

Explanation, like narrative and description, is a cognitive activity that may or may not be embodied in a material artifact belonging to this text-type category, which encompasses multiple representational media and proof procedures. In this subsection I review a prominent theory of explanation as well as attempts to reconcile narrative and explanation, that is, to assimilate (at least some) narratives to the text-type category *explanation*, and vice versa.

In the philosophy of science, a focal point for recent research on explanation has been the Covering Law Model (CLM) that was originally developed by Carl Hempel and Paul Oppenheim (cf. Hempel [1948] 1998), refined in later work by Hempel during the 1950s and 1960s, and then disputed or at least recontextualized by subsequent theorists (see Klemke et al. 1998 for important contributions to the debate). In essence the CLM suggests that phenomena can be explained if they are characterized as instances of more general patterns or trends capturable as laws, whether deductive (or "nomological") or inductive (or statistical) (Lambert and Britten [1970] 1998). From this perspective, the *explanandum*, or thing to be explained, is accounted for by virtue of its being subsumed under or "covered" by a law-like regularity that applies in analogous circumstances, all other things being equal. If the circumstance in question obtains, then that initial condition, coupled with its falling under the scope of the covering law, provides the *explanans*, or principle of explanation for the circumstance at issue. Hence the predictive power of covering laws, as when one predicts that if there is a pool of water and the temperature reaches 0 degrees Celsius, then all other things being equal that water will freeze.[13] The nomological and statistical types of explanation are exemplified by (6) and (7), respectively:

6   All human beings are mortal. I am a human being. Therefore [by modus ponens], I am mortal.
7   Human beings tend to live longer than cats. Baby X, born on the same day as kitten Y, is a human being. Therefore [by modus ponens], baby X will probably go on to live longer than the cat that kitten Y will become.

Classical accounts of the CLM do not address how explanation might relate to narrative, however. Can there even be such a thing as a narrative explanation – given that narrative concerns itself with the particular and the contingent, with how specific things were, are, or will be (Margolin 1999) versus how in general they have to be? Arguing that "the reason for telling a narrative is to explain what happened" (1996: 3), Adams answers this question in the affirmative; he attempts to reconcile the notion "narrative explanation" with the CLM. Adams suggests that

> Narrative is a type of explanation that has a past event (or state of affairs) as its explanandum, and a sequence of events as its explanans: narrative explains an explanandum, a single event, and tells an explanans, a sequence of events. The logic of narrative explanation lies in the assumption that a sequence of events explains a single event by leading up to it. (1996: 110)

However, in contrast with Adams's attempt to link narrative to CLM explanations, researchers such as Ankersmit (2005a, 2005b), Bruner (1986, 1991), Danto (1985), and Mink (1978) have drawn a broad contrast between these two explanatory modes, suggesting that if narratives in fact explain the world they do so in a way that differs from instances of explanations that are affiliated with the CLM.

For example, as noted in chapter 1, Bruner (1991) distinguishes abstract, logico-deductive, or paradigmatic reasoning from narrative reasoning; he argues that, just as basic and general principles of reasoning ground the domain of logical-scientific reality construction,

> the construction of the social order is [also] well buttressed by principles and procedures. It has an available cultural tool kit or tradition on which its procedures are modelled . . . we organize our experience and memory of human happenings mainly in the form of narrative – stories, excuses, myths, reasons for doing and not doing, and so on. (Bruner 1991: 4)

For Bruner, narrative explanations are a kind of original, "folk" explanatory mode from which academic and scientific explanations have evolved to create more technical, specialized types of explanatory accounts (see Herman 1998 for fuller discussion; cf. Lyotard [1979] 1984 on the complex historical interactions between narrative and scientific forms of knowledge). A key question in this context is whether, having bifurcated from a common root, the two explanatory modes have now effectively become distinct text types separated by firm boundaries, or whether their common origin has resulted in a more porous border between them, comparable to that separating description and narrative. Or, to use Bruner's terms, is it only the comparatively recent ascendancy of paradigmatic reasoning that has made CLM-type explanations the litmus test for explanation in general, and banished narrative explanations to peripheral status at best – on the grounds that they are "soft," lacking scope, rigor, and generality? In short, it may be time to conduct a genealogical investigation of the story and the syllogism as competing varieties of and models for explanation – an inquiry into their intertwined histories as means of accounting-for.

One way to explore the border between narrative and explanation is to examine the commonalities and contrasts between quantitative and qualitative explanations. Once we stop trying to answer questions about how much (the degree to which) and how often (the frequency with which) data display a given property or set of properties, and begin to address instead questions about how and why those data have the character that they do (Johnstone 2000), it can be argued that we are shifting from quantitative explanation to something different – namely, a qualitative, case-study mode of explanation. But stories, too, are told in order to address questions about how and why. Hence, mapping the boundary between narrative and explanation requires coming to terms with what may be an internal split within explanation itself, assuming that qualitative and quantitative explanations are both bonafide instances of this text type. More precisely, studying how narrative relates to explanation will entail a two-pronged investigation: an inquiry into the relation between quantitative and qualitative modes of explanation, coupled with an inquiry into the relation between stories and qualitative explanations in particular.

The concluding section of this chapter explores some further puzzles about relationship between narrative and explanation.

Coda: Text Types, Communicative Competence, and the Role of Stories in Science

In this concluding section, I relate the fuzzy, more-or-less rather than binary, either-or logic of text types to people's everyday communicative competence – that is, their ability to recognize, understand, and create not just prototypical exemplars of text-type categories but also borderline instances and hybrids or blends. Furthermore, I draw on work in the philosophy of science and the sociology of scientific knowledge to tease out further issues pertaining to the study of narrative vis-à-vis the neighboring text types of description and explanation.

My analysis assumes that at least a baseline ability to correlate individual texts with text-type categories, and to recognize degrees of membership within such categories, is a necessary ingredient of everyday discourse competence. For example, my discourse competence, my familiarity with a higher-order grammar of texts, enables me to avoid conflating descriptive and narrative sequences. I do not find myself reading the phone book as if it were a novel by Zola, or, conversely, fleeing from Martian invaders after watching *War of the Worlds*. As I have also suggested, however, the grammar of text types itself instantiates the category of "fuzzy grammars" (Aarts et al. 2004). As the complicated relationships among description, narrative, and explanation suggest, the very notion "kind of text" is a gradient, more-or-less affair, rather than being binarized, i.e., all or nothing. Thus, beyond licensing a variety of text-type combinations and embeddings, discourse competence requires that speakers and writers of a language be fluent in their use and interpretation of fuzzy forms such as descriptivized narrations and narrativized descriptions. Indeed, a fundamental mechanism of human creativity appears to be the ability to engage in the strategic deformation of prototypes – for example, through the blending of properties associated with categories usually viewed as separate or discrete (Hogan 2003: 70–86; Turner 2006). Phenomena such as metaphor and allegory, as well as roleplaying and performative re-enactment, can be explained in these terms.

The discreteness of the categories *narrative* and *description* can also be questioned from the vantage-point of research on the nature and origins of scientific knowledge. Based in part on Quine's (1951) holistic model of scientific knowledge as a web of beliefs, according to which all scientific theories are underdetermined by experience and observation statements are thus necessarily theory-laden (since experience is not *given* as theory-neutral data but rather *constructed* by virtue of its relation to some conceptual framework or another), recent inquiry into science has disputed what Barnes (1990) characterizes as the rationalist account of scientific knowledge. This account holds that "[a]ny reasonable agent could infer which beliefs deserved to count as established scientific knowledge by comparing their logical implications with the indications of observation and experiment" (Barnes 1990: 62). By contrast, holistic models of scientific knowledge lead away from this "individualistic rationalist" account toward a "collective conventionalist" account (Barnes 1990: 63; cf. Longino 1990, 2002; Nelson 1990). Insofar as narrative constitutes a primary resource for constructing and disseminating more or less collectively held conventions for interpretation, descriptions or observational reports can be viewed as necessarily embedded in stories, rather than as raw experiential inputs out of which stories and other kinds of representations are subsequently built up.[14] For example, as noted earlier in this chapter, storytelling practices interconnect with the process of ascribing motives, or reasons for acting, to self and others. There are thus grounds for arguing that, rather than assembling observations of individual behaviors into narratives of human conduct, people make sense of observed behaviors in terms of prior narrative templates – what Hutto (2008), building on Bruner's (1990) work, has characterized as folk-psychological narratives. From this perspective, the chief analytic goal is not to disentangle descriptions from narratives (an impossible task), but instead to study narratives as both causes and symptoms of the webs of belief in which any (scientific or other) description of the world must be situated.

By the same token, the boundary between the text types of narrative and explanation may differ from that separating descriptions and narratives. From a microanalytic perspective at least, narrative sequences can be conceived as building additional structure (for example, a certain kind of temporal structure) on foundations provided by the elements contained in descriptive sequences. By contrast, some modes of scientific explanation, especially those of the inductive-statistical variety, may be radically resistant to narrativization, that is, radically at odds with narrative explanation. Abbott (2003), for example, discusses narrative-resistant aspects of Darwin's theory of evolution by natural selection. Abbott suggests that it is not possible to tell a "story" about evolution at the species level, insofar as, in Darwin's account, neither natural selection nor species function as entities with agency, but are rather part of a non-goal-directed process involving random mutation and selective adaptation. In other words, even though Darwin's theory of natural selection is a way of understanding change over time and thus invites attempts at narrativization, it simultaneously defeats those attempts by assuming that evolution stems from a cascade of processes that operate in truly random fashion. In a different way, accounts of the so-called "explanatory gap" in cognitive science (Levine 1983) may also prove resistant to narrativization, defeating any attempt to map story or story-like templates onto causal processes of literally mind-boggling complexity. At issue is the gap between physical brain states and the condition of conscious awareness that may or may not be supervenient on those states. Even if cognitive neuroscience develops an inductive-statistical explanation of the link between complex neuronal activity in the brain and the equally complex phenomenality of conscious awareness, it is doubtful that an explanation taking into account the multivariate statistical relationships involved could ever lend itself to narrativization.

The previous examples raise general questions about the status that narrative, as a radically particularized, non-quantitative mode of accounting-for, might have in fields of inquiry that traditionally rely on quantitative methods, such as evolutionary biology, physics, and neuroscience. But further research in this area should also explore whether stories shape (overtly or covertly) what might on first blush appear to be non-narrative modes of explanation. In the domain of theoretical physics, for example, it may be that explanations based on the fourth basic element of narrative, what it's like, need to be construed as intrinsic to the work of science, given the key role accorded the observer in quantum theory – for example, the observer of Schrödinger's Cat, or the observer to whom Heisenberg's uncertainty principle applies. Such explanations involve the impact of events on the real or imagined consciousnesses that register them; they can thus be argued to share with stories the consciousness factor characterized as a basic element of narrative in chapter 6. Does the ineliminability of the observer's role in quantum-theoretical experiments – a structural requirement that invites comparison with the impossibility of narration without a viewpoint – give the lie to accounts of scientific knowledge claims as detached from particular perspectives and their attendant biases?

In any case, assessing how narrative bears on the production and organization of scientific descriptions and explanations will require more extensive interchange among philosophers and sociologists of science,

science practitioners, text linguists/discourse theorists, and analysts of narrative. A key question is whether scientists use narrative as a vehicle for what remains at heart a descriptive and explanatory enterprise, or whether stories in fact play a fundamental, even constitutive, role in the work of science.

The present chapter has made a foray into the theory of text types and research on the cognitive dimensions of categories to unpack what I have characterized as the second basic element of narrative, namely, event sequencing. At issue are narrative's distinctive temporal structure and its special concern with particularized situations and events, rather than general trends. I have also taken this opportunity to discuss aspects of a key concept on which my analysis relies, namely, the idea of the prototype or standard case. My next two chapters shift the focus from the conceptual underpinnings of the model back to a more direct exposition of the approach itself, focusing on what I have labeled as the third and fourth basic elements of narrative: respectively, the representation of disruption or disequilibrium in a storyworld involving human or human-like agents, and an emphasis on how real or imagined consciousnesses are affected by what goes on in such storyworlds-in-flux.[15]

The Third Element; or,
How to Build a Storyworld

(iii) **Worldmaking/world disruption.** *The events represented in narrative are such that they introduce some sort of disruption or disequilibrium into a storyworld involving human or human-like agents, whether that world is presented as actual or fictional, realistic or fantastic, remembered or dreamed, etc.*

Narratives as Blueprints for Worldmaking

Storyworlds can be defined as the worlds evoked by narratives; reciprocally, narratives can be defined as blueprints for a specific mode of world-creation. Mapping words (or other kinds of semiotic cues) onto worlds is a fundamental – perhaps *the* fundamental – requirement for narrative sense-making; yet this mapping operation may seem so natural and normal that no "theory," no specialized nomenclature or framework of concepts, is necessary to describe and explain the specific procedures involved. In the present chapter, I argue for the need to slow down and de-automatize the rapid, apparently effortless interpretive processes involved in experiencing narrative worlds. Exploring the third basic element of narrative necessitates taking the measure of these processes – that is, identifying what is distinctive about narrative ways of worldmaking as opposed to other methods for using symbol systems to make and unmake worlds.

The classical, structuralist narratologists failed to come to terms with the referential or world-creating properties of narrative, partly because of the exclusion of the referent in favor of signifier and signified in the Saussurean language theory that informed the structuralists' approach (see chapter 2). Over the past couple of decades, however, one of the most basic and abiding concerns of narrative scholars has been how readers of print narratives, interlocutors in face-to-face discourse, and viewers of films use textual cues to build up representations of the worlds evoked by stories, or *storyworlds*. Such worldmaking practices are of central importance to narrative scholars of all sorts, from feminist narratologists exploring how representations of male and female characters pertain to dominant cultural stereotypes about gender roles, to rhetorical theorists hypothesizing about the kinds of assumptions, beliefs, and attitudes that must to be adopted by readers if they are to participate in the multiple audience positions required to engage fully with fictional worlds, to analysts (and designers) of digital narratives interested in how interactive systems can remediate the experience of being immersed in the virtual worlds created through everyday narrative practices. New ways of characterizing the third basic element of narrative, its intrinsic concern with more or less richly detailed storyworlds, have arisen from this re-engagement with the referential, world-creating potential of narrative. That re-engagement has received additional impetus from foundational theoretical studies of narrative worlds – studies that I discuss later in this chapter and that draw on ideas developed by philosophers, psychologists, linguists, and others concerned with how people use various kinds of symbol systems to refer to aspects of their experience.

In parallel with the account developed in Herman (2002a: 9–22), I use the term *storyworld* to refer to the world evoked implicitly as well as explicitly by a narrative, whether that narrative takes the form of a printed text, film, graphic novel, sign language, everyday conversation, or even a tale that is projected but never actualized as a concrete artifact – for example, stories about ourselves that we contemplate telling to friends but then do not, or film scripts that a screenwriter has plans to create in the future. Storyworlds are global mental representations enabling interpreters to frame inferences about the situations, characters, and occurrences either explicitly mentioned in or implied by a narrative text or discourse. As such, storyworlds are mental models of the situations and events being recounted – of who did what to and with whom, when, where, why, and in what manner. Reciprocally, narrative artifacts (texts, films, etc.) provide blueprints for the creation and modification of such mentally configured storyworlds.[1]

Storytellers use the semiotic cues available in a given narrative medium to design these blueprints for creating and updating storyworlds.[2] In print texts, the cues include the expressive resources of (written) language, including not just words, phrases, and sentences, but also typographical formats, the disposition of space on the printed page (including spaces used for section breaks, indentations marking new paragraphs, etc.), and (potentially) diagrams, sketches, and illustrations. In graphic novels such as *Ghost World*, by contrast, the nonverbal elements play a more prominent role: the arrangement of characters in represented scenes, the shapes of speech balloons, and the representations of the scenes in panels that form part of larger sequences of images and textual elements, can convey information about the storyworld that would have to be transmitted by purely verbal means in a novel or short story without a comparable image track. Likewise, interlocutors in contexts of face-to-face storytelling, readers of short stories and novels, and members of the audience watching a film draw on such medium-specific cues to build on the basis of the discourse (or *sjuzhet*) a chronology for events (or *fabula*) (what happened when, or in what order?); a broader temporal and spatial environment for those events (when in history did these events occur, and where geographically?); an inventory of the characters involved; and a working model of what it was like for these characters to experience the more or less disruptive or noncanonical events that constitute a core feature of narrative representations, which may in turn be more or less reportable within a particular discourse context or occasion for telling.[3]

At the same time, as discussed in chapter 3, interpreters seeking to build a storyworld on the basis of a text will also take into account complexities in the design of the blueprint itself – complexities creating additional layers of mediation in the relationship between narrative and storyworld. Such mediation affects the interpretive process in, for example, cases of unreliable narration such as Browning's *My Last Duchess*, where the teller of a story cannot be taken at his or her word, compelling the audience to "read between the lines" – in other words, to scan the text for clues about how the storyworld really (or probably) is, as opposed to how the narrator says it is. Likewise, in *Ghost World*, during a sequence in which Enid fantasizes about one of her teachers,

Mr. Pierce, the use of a distinctive font or typeface within the speech balloons (not to mention the content of the sequence – e.g., Enid naked in the shower with Mr. Pierce clad in a formal suit) indicates that the represented scenes and utterances are ones that Enid has imagined, rather than events that took place within the storyworld to which the characters orient as actual or real (Clowes 1997: 32). Both of these examples entail complex processes of worldmaking. For its part, the Browning poem compels readers to sift out from the Duke's elliptical, distorted version of events a divergent or rather more complete account of what happened, affording through these indirect means a blueprint for building the domain of factual (or at least probable) occurrences. The world that emerges through this process is one in which the Duke, despite or rather because of his own best efforts at spin or damage control, figures as an insanely jealous, homicidally possessive, and controlling spouse. Meanwhile, Enid's erotic fantasy demonstrates in another way the multifacetedness of storyworlds, which typically encompass not just worlds that are socially and institutionally defined as "given" but also private worlds (Ryan 1991) or subworlds (Werth 1999) consisting of characters' beliefs, desires, intentions, memories, and imaginative projections. Some of these subworlds may never be expressed outwardly to other characters, as is likely the case with Enid's fantasy – hence Clowes's use of a typeface that distinguishes this sequence from other conversational exchanges represented in the text.

But what would a more general account of how narratives evoke storyworlds look like? And how do narrative ways of worldmaking differ from other representational practices that involve the construction or reconstruction of worlds, in a broad sense? In other words, when it comes to world-creation, what distinguishes narrative representations from other contexts in which people design and manipulate symbol systems for the purpose of structuring, comprehending, and communicating aspects of experience? I explore these issues in my next section.

Narrative Ways of Worldmaking

To capture what is distinctive about narrative ways of worldmaking, this section begins with an overview of Goodman's (1978) broad account of "ways of worldmaking." The building of storyworlds involves specific procedures set off against this larger set of background conditions for world-creation. I start to outline these procedures by developing an account of narrative beginnings as prompts for worldmaking. This in turn sets up my next section, where I survey a range of approaches to world-creation in narrative contexts, moving from accounts that characterize the experience of narrative worlds in a relatively macrostructural or gestalt way toward more microstructural approaches that seek to anchor types of inferences about storyworlds (including their temporal and spatial dimensions) in particular kinds of textual designs.

In his study *Ways of Worldmaking*, the philosopher Nelson Goodman develops ideas that afford context for my own analysis. Adopting a pluralist instead of a reductionist stance, Goodman argues that "many different world-versions are of independent interest and importance, without any requirement or presumption of reducibility to a single base" (Goodman 1978: 4), for example, the world-version propounded in physics. As Goodman puts it, "[t]he pluralists' acceptance of [world-versions] other than physics implies no relaxation of rigor but a recognition that standards different from yet no less exacting than those applied in science are appropriate for appraising what is conveyed in perceptual or pictorial or literary versions" (1978: 5). More generally, Goodman asks,

> In just what sense are there many worlds? What distinguishes genuine from spurious worlds? What are worlds made of? How are they made? What role do symbols play in the making? And how is worldmaking related to knowing? (Goodman 1978: 1)

Arguing that worldmaking "as we know it always starts from worlds already on hand; the making is a remaking," Goodman goes on to identify five procedures for constructing worlds out of other worlds: composition and decomposition; weighting; ordering; deletion and supplementation; and deformation (1978: 7–16). Brief definitions and examples of each procedure follow:

- **Composition and decomposition**: "on the one hand ... dividing wholes into parts and partitioning kinds into subspecies, analyzing complexes into component features, drawing distinctions; on the other hand . . . composing wholes and kinds out of parts and members and subclasses, combining features into complexes, and making connections" (1978: 7). Ethnographic investigation of an indigenous population, for example, may uncover the presence of several subcultures where only one had been recognized previously; conversely, the formation of new "hybrid" disciplines or subdisciplines (algebraic geometry, biochemistry, information design) results in new, more complex world-versions.

- **Weighting**: "Some relevant kinds of the one world, rather than being absent from the other, are present as irrelevant kinds; some differences among worlds are not so much in entities comprised as in emphasis or accent, and these differences are no less consequential" (1978: 11). From a macrohistorical perspective, the shift from a religious to a secular-scientific world-version entailed a reweighting of the particulars of the phenomenal world, which came to occupy a focus of attention formerly reserved for the noumenal or spiritual realm.
- **Ordering**: "modes of organization [patterns, measurements, ways of periodizing time, etc.] are not 'found in the world' but *built into a world*" (1978: 14). As suggested in chapter 4, taxonomies of plants, animals, or other entities are in effect world-versions built on a hierarchical systems of categories that may be more or less finely grained (and more or less densely populated), depending on whether one has expert or only a layperson's knowledge of a given domain. My world-version currently contains names for (and concepts of) only a few common types of insects, in contrast with the world-version of an entomologist.
- **Deletion and supplementation**: "the making of one world out of another usually involves some extensive weeding out and filling – actual excision of some old and supply of some new material" (1978: 14). I might study entomology, and supplement my world-version with new knowledge and new beings; alternatively, if because of climate change an insect species becomes extinct, the entomologist's world-version will undergo compulsory excision.
- **Deformation**: "reshapings or deformations that may according to point of view be considered either corrections or distortions" (1978: 16). Here one may think of arguments for a new scientific theory in favor of an older one (e.g., the geocentric vs. the heliocentric

models of the solar system) from the perspective of those who are parties to the debate.

As my examples of each worldmaking procedure indicate, there is nothing distinctively story-like about the worlds over which Goodman's account ranges, though there is nothing about the analysis that excludes storyworlds, either. Narrative worlds, too, might be made through processes of composition and decomposition: think of allegories fusing literal and symbolic worlds, or decomposition in texts such as *The Canterbury Tales*, where the narrative ramifies into a frame tale that constitutes the main diegetic level and embedded or hypodiegetic levels created when characters within that frame tell stories of their own. Weighting may also be a generative factor: consider postmodern rewrites that evoke new world-versions by reweighting events in their precursor narratives, as when Jean Rhys's *Wide Sargasso Sea* generates a new storyworld on the basis of Charlotte Brontë's *Jane Eyre* by using as a metric for evaluating events not Jane Eyre's or Edward Rochester's perspective (as refracted through Jane's telling) but rather Antoinette Cosway's. So too with ordering: narrative worlds can be made when new time-scales are deployed, as when Alain Robbe-Grillet as a practitioner of the *nouveau roman* in France produced novel worlds by drastically slowing the pace of narration (Robbe-Grillet [1957, 1959] 1965), or when the average shot length in Hollywood films diminished over time to produce more rapid cuts between scenes (Morrison forthcoming). Deletion and supplementation likewise find their place in the building of storyworlds. I may tailor my recounting of my own life experiences to adjust for differences among groups of interlocutors, going into more detail among close friends and less detail when asked a question during a job interview. And as for deformation, the film version of *Ghost World* can be viewed as a reshaping of the graphic novel version, and more generally any adaptation of a prior text in another medium for storytelling will result in alterations of the sort that Goodman includes under this rubric (cf. Genette [1982] 1997).

In short, Goodman's is a broad, generic account of worldmaking procedures, operative in both non-narrative and narrative contexts. The basis for distinctively narrative ways of worldmaking must thus be sought in other, more specific procedures set off against this larger set of background conditions for world-creation. In my next subsection, I discuss how story openings trigger particular kinds of worldmaking strategies that cut across storytelling media and narrative genres, but that are also inflected by the specific constraints and affordances of various kinds of narrative practices.

Narrative beginnings as prompts for worldmaking: taking up residence in storyworlds

Story openings prompt interpreters to take up residence (more or less comfortably) in the world being evoked by a given text. Openings from different story genres can be compared and contrasted along this dimension, underscoring how part of the meaning of "genre" consists of distinctive protocols for worldmaking – though again, the approach being outlined in this book predicts that a common core of worldmaking procedures, specific to the narrative text type, cuts across such generic differences. Likewise, the model predicts that distinctively narrative processes of world-creation obtain in various media for storytelling. Here the issue is how the analyst, when comparing and contrasting a variety of narrative openings, might distinguish generically narrative from medium-, genre-, and even text-specific worldmaking procedures.

Consider the beginning of "Hills Like White Elephants":

[1] The hills across the valley of the Ebro were long and white. [2] On this side there was no shade and no trees and the station was between two lines of rails in the sun. [3] Close against the side of the station there was the warm shadow of the building and a curtain, made of strings of bamboo beads, hung across the open door into the bar, to keep out flies. [4] The American and the girl with him sat at a table in the shade, outside the building. [5] It was very hot and the express from Barcelona would come in forty minutes. [6] It stopped at this junction for two minutes and went to Madrid.

[7] "What should we drink?" the girl asked. [8] She had taken off her hat and put it on the table. (Hemingway [1927] 1987: 211)

How do these eight sentences evoke (a fragment of) a narrative world? What specific textual cues allow readers to draw inferences about the structure, inhabitants, and spatiotemporal situation of this world? Further, how does the worldmaking process here differ from that triggered by the following seven-sentence paragraph at the beginning of Richard Morgan's science fiction novel *Altered Carbon*?

[1a] Chemically alert, I inventoried the hardware on the scarred wooden table for the fiftieth time that night. [2a] Sarah's Heckler and Koch shard pistol glinted dully at me in the low light, the butt gaping open for its clip. [3a] It was an assassin's weapon, compact and utterly silent. [4a] The magazines lay next to it. [5a] She had wrapped insulating tape around each one to distinguish the ammunition: green for sleep, black for the spider-venom load. [6a] Most of the clips were black-wrapped. [7a] Sarah had used up a lot of green on the security guards at Gemini Biosys last night. (Morgan 2002: 3, emphases added)

As Paul Werth points out (1999: 56), story openings that, like Hemingway's and Morgan's, include noun phrases with definite articles and demonstrative pronouns (*the* American and *the* girl, *that* night) can be aligned with what the philosopher David Lewis (1979) termed the process of *accommodation*. At issue is the way a text can economically evoke the storyworld (or "text world" in Werth's terms) to which readers of a fictional text must imaginatively relocate if they are to interpret referring expressions (*a curtain, the open door, the hardware, the scarred wooden table, the spider-venom load*, etc.) and deictic expressions (*on this side, last night*) properly[4] – mapping them onto the world evoked by the text rather than the world(s) that the text producer and text interpreter occupy when producing or decoding these textual signals. Thus, readers of Morgan's text assume that the scarred wooden table in sentence 1a occupies the world inhabited by the earlier experiencing-I but not (necessarily) the world of the older narrating-I looking back retrospectively on this scene. Likewise, in sentence 7a the phrase *last night* has to be interpreted in light of what some narratologists have termed the story-NOW, rather than the discourse-NOW: *last night* refers to the night prior to the one in which Sarah and the experiencing-I sit together at the table, not the night prior to the moment occupied by the narrating-I at the time of the telling.

But if readers rely on similar sorts of textual cues to accommodate to Hemingway's and Morgan's story openings, this being part of what it means to interpret both texts as members of text-type category *narrative*, the process of accommodation unfolds differently in each case – in ways that can be correlated with the generic differences between the texts. Marie-Laure Ryan's (1991) account of "fictional recentering," and her related notion of the principle of minimal departure, can be used to explore the differences involved. In Ryan's account, developed under the auspices of a possible-worlds approach to narrative, the storyworld evoked by a fictional narrative can be described as an alternative possible world to which interpreters are openly prompted to relocate, such that, for the duration of the fictional experience, "the realm of possibilities is . . . recentered around the sphere which the narrator presents as the actual world" (Ryan 1991: 22). The world evoked by the text may be more or less accessible to the world(s) in which that narrative is produced and interpreted, providing the basis for a typology of genres (1991: 31–47).

As compared with the reference world of a news report, for instance, the storyworld evoked by a science fiction novel about a super-race with telekinetic powers – or for that matter, a world in which Heckler and Koch shard pistols can shoot spider-venom loads – is less accessible to (less compatible with the defining properties of) the world of the here and now. Yet if no textual or paratextual indicators block their default interpretive stance, readers or film viewers will abide by what Ryan terms the principle of minimal departure, which states that "when readers construct fictional worlds, they fill in the gaps . . . in the text by assuming the similarity of the fictional worlds to their own experiential reality" (2005b: 447). Thus readers of Hemingway's story assume that the interlocutors are human beings rather than murderous aliens who have bodysnatched male and female earthlings in order to dupe the waitress and the other people at the bar. Even more crucially, perhaps, readers assume that the Ebro in the story is the same Ebro that exists in the actual world and runs through a particular valley in Spain. By contrast, in the case of Morgan's text readers are prompted, not only by the book's opening paragraphs but also by the futuristic design on its cover, as well as its placement in the science fiction section of the library or local bookstore, to engage in strategies for worldmaking that are not fully continuous with those used to make sense of their everyday experience. In this world (set 500 years in the future), different kinds of ammunition for the same gun have either a narcotizing effect or a lethal deadliness (sentence 2a); what is more, the use of chemical stimulants to enhance alertness is so common that it can be mentioned elliptically in a subordinate clause, as in sentence (1a). Yet the principle of minimal departure continues to apply. Unless cued to do otherwise, readers will assume that Sarah's use of the sleep-inducing ammunition instead of the spider-venom variety reflects her commitment to killing only when necessary – not, say, a perverse fixation on putting people to sleep, or a mere random tic on her part.

Hemingway's and Morgan's texts show how a common stock of procedures for narrative worldmaking can be inflected differently when different genres are involved. By the same token, worldmaking procedures for in narrative contexts are also affected by differences of medium. Consider the opening of Monica's story:

MONICA:	(1)	So that's why I say..UFO or the devil got after our <u>black</u> <u>asses</u>,
	(2)	for showing out.
	(3)	> I don't know what was <
	(4)	but we walkin up the <u>hill</u>,
	(5)	<u>this</u> ↑<u>way</u>, comin up through here.
INTERVIEWER 1:	(6)	Yeah.
MONICA:	(7)	And..I'm like on <u>this</u> side and Renee's right here.

In this context, procedures for worldmaking are affected by a different system of affordances and constraints than the system that impinges on written narrative texts, whatever their genre. On the one hand, properties associated with written discourse, particularly its deliberate or "worked-over" nature in contrast with the relative spontaneity of spoken discourse (Chafe 1994), allow producers of literary narrative to situate participants in quite richly detailed storyworlds – of the sort already evoked in a single paragraph from each of the two texts cited above. The increased span of time separating the production of the narrative from its interpretation, and for that matter the longer span of time allowed for interpretation of literary narratives, facilitates denser concentrations of detail than would be typical for face-to-face storytelling (Herman 2004). Yet contexts of face-to-face narration are enabling when it comes to other worldmaking procedures – procedures that are, conversely, subject to constraints imposed by the nature of written communication.

Producers of fictional narratives (in whatever genre) have to rely on the process of accommodation and the principle of minimal departure to prompt readers to relocate to the distinct space-time coordinates of the world evoked by a written text. In contrast, because she is telling her story on-site, or where the events being recounted are purported to have occurred, by using deictic expressions such as *this way* and *here* in line 5 and *this side* and *right here* in line 7 Monica can prompt her interlocutors to draw on information available in the present interactional context – specifically, information about the layout of the scene and its terrain – to build a model of the overall spatial configuration of the storyworld she is attempting to evoke. In this way, in the case of spatial deictics – expressions like *here* and *there* – face-to-face storytelling affords more options for anchoring texts in contexts of interaction than do literary narratives. To help their interlocutors assign referents to such expressions, storytellers can cue their interlocutors to draw analogies between the spatial configuration of the storyworld and that of the world in which the narrative is being told and interpreted. Thus, in using the deictic expressions in lines 5 and 7, Monica prompts her interlocutors to project a storyworld-external space onto a storyworld-internal space, and vice versa. Arguably, these hybrid or blended locations are richer than those that readers can access through the process of accommodation triggered by spatial deictics in a written, literary narrative such as Hemingway's or Morgan's. As is characteristic for literary narratives, accommodation in these texts results not in a blending of spatiotemporal coordinates but rather a deictic *shift* (see Segal 1995, Zubin and Hewitt 1995, and below) from the here and now orienting the act of interpretation to that orienting participants in the storyworld.[5]

In Clowes's *Ghost World*, meanwhile, still other medium-specific affordances and constraints (along with particular textual and paratextual cues) impinge on the process of narrative worldmaking. Exploiting the visual dimension of graphic storytelling, the cover of the novel features uncaptioned images of the two main characters that serve immediately to orient readers within the storyworld evoked by the text. The cover signals the complex life-situation of protagonists who are struggling to make the transition from adolescence to adulthood: Rebecca is shown blowing a bubble with her chewing gum, while Enid is portrayed with serious-looking thick-framed glasses that she perhaps wears to appear older than she actually is. The front matter of the volume continues to shape readers' inferences about what kind of storyworld they are about to enter, drawing on the verbal as well as the visual information track to do so. One panel represents what can be assumed in retrospect to be Enid's bookshelf, with a heterogeneous set of texts ranging from *2000 Insults* to *Encyclopedia of Unusual Sex Practices*, *Oedipus Rex*, and *Scooby*

Doo, to Nora Brown's novel *Henry Orient* (the basis for a 1964 comedy starring Peter Sellars), to a CD by the French pop singer France Gall – suggesting not only Enid's eclectic tastes but also the bewilderingly diverse narratives circulating in the culture and converging on the two characters as they try to navigate surrounding social expectations, family and educational contexts, and their own evolving relationship. Two other images (without accompanying text) included in the front matter show Enid and Rebecca at a younger age standing in front of a cemetery marker – again, in retrospect, readers can assume that this is Enid's mother's grave – and then the two characters in dressed in their caps and gowns for high-school graduation, with Enid making an obscene gesture at something (the entire graduation scene?) toward which she and Rebecca are facing.

Accordingly, by the time readers get to the first page of chapter 1 of the novel, the visual and verbal cues already provided up to this point provide crucial context for narrative worldmaking. True, local links between neighboring panels assist with basic aspects of the world-creation process, as when, in the first panel, Enid asks "Why do you have this?" and is then seen holding a copy of *Sassy* magazine in the next panel. Here the image of the magazine is a correlative, in a different semiotic medium, of the particular features of the landscape to which Monica points when she uses forms like *this way* and *this side* to launch her own story. But more than this, when Enid critiques Rebecca's purchase of the magazine by asserting that "These stupid girls think they're so hip, but they're just a bunch of trendy stuck-up pre-school bitches who think they're 'cutting edge' because they know who 'Sonic Youth' is!" (Clowes 1997: 9), this remark carries world-creating implications because of the context already afforded by the cover and the front matter. Whereas in another storyworld an utterance of this sort might be interpreted as a digression about a character's pet peeves, given Enid's life experiences and the contents of her bookshelf her comment can be construed as one that bears on Enid's and Rebecca's central concerns, the questions that they seek to answer and that thereby drive the narrative forward: namely, how to position themselves relative to more or less dominant social norms and practices, including those that seek to pass themselves off as countercultural trends but that in actual fact contribute to the masking and thus perpetuation of the status quo.

My most general point about the opening of *Ghost World* is that Clowes exploits the medium-specific resources of graphic storytelling to facilitate readers' relocation to this narrative world. Clowes relies on both images and words to enable this process of accommodation, or rather transportation, which can also be accomplished through particular kinds of verbal expressions, as in written fiction, or a combination of verbal and gestural productions, as in face-to-face storytelling. Yet in my previous paragraph I have also begun to touch on other, more complex dimensions of narrative worldmaking – dimensions that arise from a temporally extended experience of and not just one's initial migration to a storyworld. The approaches reviewed in my next subsection seek to shed light, from various perspectives, on this more temporally extended process of experiencing narrative worlds.

Narrative Worlds: A Survey of Approaches

Having discussed how story openings trigger particular kinds of worldmaking strategies that cut across storytelling media and narrative genres, but that are also inflected by the specific constraints and affordances of various kinds and modes of narrative practice, I now survey a range of approaches to the scope and nature of narrative worlds. I start with accounts that characterize the experience of narrative worlds in a relatively macrostructural or gestalt way and then move toward more microstructural approaches that seek to anchor types of inferences about storyworlds (including their temporal and spatial dimensions) in particular kinds of textual designs. My next section builds on this work to show how narratological approaches to time and space can be recontextualized – better understood – as part of a broader inquiry into narrative ways of worldmaking, and in particular the WHERE and WHEN components of the worldbuilding process.

Thus far I have focused on how story openings trigger worldmaking procedures that are shared by all instances of narrative as a text-type category, but that can take on different inflections depending on genre- and medium-specific factors that also contribute to the process of world-creation. In this section, I pull back for a broader overview of research on the procedures used to create and update worlds in narrative contexts. The richness and variety of this scholarship suggest the centrality of worldmaking to the experience of narrative viewed as a cognitive structure and resource for interaction as well as a kind of text.

As I argued in *Story Logic* (Herman 2002a: 9–22) and have already suggested above, the power of narrative to create worlds goes a long way towards explaining its immersiveness, its ability to transport interpreters into places and times they must occupy for the purposes of narrative comprehension (Gerrig 1993; Ryan 2001a; Young 1987). Again, it would be difficult to account for the immersive potential of stories by appeal to structuralist notions of *story* or *fabula*, that is, strictly in terms of events and existents arranged into a plot by the narrative presentation. Interpreters of narrative do not merely reconstruct a sequence of events and a set of existents, but imaginatively (emotionally, viscerally) inhabit a world in which, besides happening and existing, things matter, agitate, exalt, repulse, provide grounds for laughter and grief, and so on – both for narrative agents and for interpreters working to make sense of their circumstances and (inter)actions.

Transportation to narrative worlds

A good starting point for any account of the immersive power of storyworlds is Richard Gerrig's 1993 study, *Experiencing Narrative Worlds*. Gerrig uses the metaphor of transportation to characterize how readers make sense of the storyworlds evoked through print texts, whether fictional or nonfictional. Gerrig (1993: 10–11) identifies six key elements of the source concept of transportation and discusses how each element can be projected onto corresponding features of the target domain, namely, the process by which readers interpret representations of narrative worlds:

1 Someone ("the traveler") is transported.
2 by some means of transportation.
3 as a result of performing certain actions.
4 The traveler goes some distance from his or her world of origin.
5 which makes some aspects of the world of origin inaccessible.
6 The traveler returns to the world of origin, somewhat changed by the journey.

In contrast to models for narrative analysis such as Labov's (1972), which purport to find direct, fixed mappings from particular kinds of formal structures to specific narrative functions,[6] Gerrig's cognitive-psychological account emphasizes the mental operations that enable worldmaking rather than the specific textual triggers that induce interpreters to perform those operations. As Gerrig puts it, "[i]f we define the experience of narrative worlds with respect to an endpoint (the operation of whatever set of mental processes transports the reader) rather than with respect to a starting point (a text with some formal features), we can see that no a priori limits can be put on the types of language structures that might prompt the construction of narrative worlds" (1993: 4). In this respect, Gerrig's approach bears a family resemblance to Walton's (1990) work on fiction as a game of make-believe, according to which written texts, images on screen, physical objects, and other sorts of triggers of fictional experiences can all be assimilated to the category of "props" in the game that enables and sustains the make-believe world. Gerrig's premise is that worldmaking processes are the same across fictional and nonfictional texts; Walton's, that the process of getting caught up in make-believe worlds is the same irrespective of medium.

Possible-worlds theory and fictional recentering

Complementing Gerrig's metaphor of transportation is Ryan's (1991, 2005b) account of fictional recentering – an account that helps specify not just the relation between the world of origin and the target world, but also the structure of the target world itself. Thus, in tandem with Doležel (1998), Pavel (1986), and other theorists (e.g., Margolin 1990b; Martin 2004; Ronen 1994), Ryan draws on ideas from analytic philosophy and modal logic to argue that narrative universes are recognizable because of a shared modal structure; this structure consists of a central world that counts as actual and various satellite worlds that can be accessed through counterfactual constructions voiced by a narrator or by the characters, and also through what the characters think, dream, read, etc. Of course, not every narrative faithfully exemplifies this structure; indeed, as McHale (1987) has shown, a hallmark of postmodern fiction is its refusal to adhere to ontological boundaries and hierarchies of precisely this sort. Yet in the case of metaleptic narratives such as Borges's "Tlön, Uqbar, Orbis Tertius" (Borges 1964: 3–18), where a world initially construed as a far-flung satellite ultimately merges with the baseline reality of the story, their ontological subversiveness can be registered because of how such texts deviate from the default template for worldmaking. By contrast, Hemingway's story conforms to that standard template. The current scene of interaction between Jig and the unnamed male character constitutes the base structure or point of reference for this narrative universe, with the man momentarily opening a window onto a satellite world when (for example) he uses a counterfactual or as-if construction to frame an angry rejoinder to Jig's dismissive comment that he is someone who would never have seen a white elephant: " 'I might have [seen a white elephant]. . . . Just because you say I wouldn't have doesn't prove anything'" (p. 211). Likewise, in *Ghost World*, the structure of the narrative largely conforms to the standard case of fictional recentering – though, in addition to the (self-mocking) representation of Clowes in the panel mentioned in chapter 3, in the novel's closing pages Enid catches a glimpse of (and touches the still wet paint used by) the artist who has been writing the phrase "ghost world" as graffiti on walls and fences in the storyworld. Here, the reader might infer, Enid comes close to encountering the creator of the storyworld that bounds her reality, and thereby metaleptically breaking the limiting frame of that world. Meanwhile, in the case of *UFO or the Devil*, Monica presents her story as a factual account of her and Renee's encounter with a supernatural being. Readers are thus prompted not to recenter to a fictional world but rather to relocate to what Monica presents as another, earlier time-frame within the actual world, which she constructs as encompassing supernatural events as well as those bound by the normal laws of space, time, physical causality, etc.

In short, the existence of base worlds surrounded by satellites affords structure for all narrative sense-making, even in the case of narratives that engage in innovative strategies of worldmaking by subverting or obscuring this standard hierarchy of worlds. True, as discussed in my previous paragraph, differences among narrative genres (and between fictional versus nonfictional accounts) can be correlated with different sorts of relationships among the worlds contained in narrative universes. But the system of possibilities within which such worldmaking operations take place remains constant across all narrative kinds, and helps identify those kinds as instances of narrative in the first place. At issue are the possible worlds that orbit around what is presented as what Ryan calls the "text actual world" (TAW), or world assumed as actual within the narrative. Narratives typically feature a range of private worlds or subworlds (cf. Werth 1999: 210–58) inhabited or at least imagined by characters; these satellite worlds include knowledge-worlds, obligation-worlds, wish-worlds, pretend worlds, and so on. Further, the plot of any narrative can be redefined as "the trace left by the movement of these worlds within the textual universe. [For] participants, the goal of the narrative game . . . is to make TAW coincide with as many as possible of their [private worlds] . . . The moves of the game are the actions through which characters attempt to alter relations between worlds" (Ryan 1991: 119–20).

Thus, in Hemingway's story, it is not just that satellite worlds come into view as Jig and the male character discuss possible courses of action in response to the unstated "given" of Jig's pregnancy. Rather, the conflict that drives the plot emerges from the two characters' different strategies for bringing the TAW into alignment with their private worlds, particularly their wish-worlds and intention-worlds – the male character seeking to do so by encouraging Jig to go through with an abortion, Jig by gaining some recognition from the man that having the child would not necessarily be inimical to their relationship. Note, too, that the different kinds of worlds that can be interpreted as TAWs account, in turn, for differences among narrative kinds. In contrast with "Hills" and *Ghost World*, in *UFO or the Devil* supernatural beings are part of the TAW, producing two planes of existence in the manner characteristic of what Pavel (1986) would describe as worlds with "salient" ontologies. The title of Clowes's text might initially trigger the inference that his, too, is a salient fictional world in Pavel's sense; but what emerges as ghostly over the course of the novel is Enid's and Rebecca's past life as kids in school, a life now giving way to the complexity and ambiguity of the situations they face as they enter adulthood. In the case of Monica's story, once the orienting assumption of a dual or salient ontology has been made, then interpretation of the narrative in terms of relations among subworlds and the TAW can proceed. Thus key conflicts in Monica's narrative turn on clashes between her subworlds (e.g., wish- and intention-worlds) and the TAW – for example, her and Renee's desire to escape a supernatural creature to whom she attributes baleful intentions, or her intention to convey the authenticity as well as the frightening import of her experiences to her friend's grandmother, who, however, dismisses them as merely imaginary.

Deictic shift theory, text worlds, and contextual frames

Gerrig's (1993) scheme purposely underspecifies the means of transportation to narrative worlds because its main concern is with the mental operations supporting the experience of those worlds rather than the range of textual triggers that can activate the operations in question. Ryan's possible-worlds approach is somewhat more textcentric; for example, it accommodates the study of how textual markers (e.g., modal auxiliary verbs) can signal relations among the TAW and various satellite worlds – as when Hemingway's male character protests Jig's suggestion that he is not the sort of person who would ever have seen a white elephant. But other research provides the basis for still finer-grained analyses of how specific textual cues afford structure for world creation. The point is not to try to delimit in advance what kinds of language structures might prompt or allow for the construction of narrative worlds, but rather to indicate reasonably robust patterns in interpreters' use of particular classes of textual cues as scaffolding for world-construction.

For instance, Segal's (1995) account of deictic shift theory helps illuminate the cognitive reorientation (and associated discourse-processing strategies) required for an interpreter's successful relocation to a narrative world; it also suggests that over longer, more sustained experiences of narrative worlds, interpreters may need to make successive adjustments in their position relative to the situations and events being recounted. As Segal puts it,

> when one reads [or views, or hears] a narrative as it is meant to be read [seen, heard], he or she is often required to take a cognitive stance within the world of the narrative. A location within the world of the narrative serves as the center from which the sentences are interpreted. In particular, deictic terms such as *here* and *now* refer to this conceptual location. It is thus the *deictic center*. DST [Deictic Shift Theory] is a theory that states that the deictic center often shifts from the environmental situation in which the text is encountered, to a locus within a mental model representing the world of the discourse. (1995: 15; cf. Zubin and Hewitt 1995)

Thus, over the course of any of my chief illustrative narratives, inter-preters must track several shifts to different deictic centers – on pain of misconstruing what is going on the story, i.e., not carrying out the instructions for world-building included in the narratives' verbal texture. In "Hills," for example, and as discussed above in connection with Lewis's idea of "accommodation," an initial deictic shift is required for the reader to take up the cognitive vantage-point in terms of which the preposition *across*, in sentence 1, and the prepositional phrase *On this side*, in sentence 2, can be parsed. Immediately after the open-ing paragraph, the deictic center shifts again, this time to the male character's vantage-point as he observes Jig from up close; this is the cognitive stance from which the sentence "She had taken off her hat and put it on the table" must be interpreted. Note that here the use of the past perfect tense (*had taken off her hat*) implies a return of the male character's focus of attention to Jig's position within the current scene, as well as a perception of how her appearance has altered over time – that is, since the last time the male character observed Jig closely. Later in the story, the perspective point from which the storyworld must be cognitively regarded, so that the relevant sentences can be properly construed, shifts to Jig. Thus, in the following passage, the deictic center from which the relevant spatial prepositions must be parsed has shifted; in the second and third sentences of the passage it is Jig doing the look-ing, not the male character:

> The girl stood up and walked to the end of the station. Across, on the other side, were fields of grain and trees along the banks of the Ebro. Far away, beyond the rivers, were mountains. (Hemingway [1927] 1987: 213)

Likewise, a sentence found near the end of the story ("They were all waiting reasonably for the train" [p. 214]) must be interpreted as encoding the male character's cognitive stance toward events, or else construction of the narrative world will be skewed toward the wrong deictic center.

Other microstructural approaches to narrative worlds include the text-world theory developed by Paul Werth and the account of contextual frames outlined by Catherine Emmott. For Werth (1999: 180–209), to construct a mental model of the world evoked by a text, interpreters of verbal narratives rely on deictic and referential elements that Werth calls *world-building elements*. By contrast, the foregrounded part of the text, or what it is about, consists of *function-advancing propositions*. Werth identifies a number of tests that he argues to be diagnostic of function-advancing as opposed to merely world-building textual features: for example, simple past-tense indicative verbs in English versus past-progressive constructions, or more generally expressions that link participants to particularized actions and events versus the text world in which those actions and events are embedded. Thus, in Monica's story, the opening lines set up a foreground–background relation between the continuous activity of walking and discrete acts of looking that mark the inception of both a disruptive, disequilibrium-causing event and the impact of that event on Monica's and Renee's experiential awareness. Likewise, in lines 15–17, the activity of walking again serves as a back-drop for a specific perceptual act and the new state of the storyworld that that act reveals: namely, the change in the ball's position along a vertical axis in space.

MONICA:	(3)	> I don't know what was <
	(4)	but we walkin up the <u>hill</u>,
	(5)	this ↑<u>way</u>, comin up through here.
INTERVIEWER 1:	(6)	Yeah.
MONICA:	(7)	And..I'm like on <u>this</u> side and Renee's right here.
	(8)	And we <u>walkin</u>
	(9)	and I look over the <u>bank</u>* ... {.2}
	(10)	and I see this ... {.3} < <u>BI:G BALL</u> >.
	[....]	
	(15)	And I'm still <u>walkin</u> you know*
	(16)	Then I look back over my side ag<u>ain</u>,
	(17)	and it has °<u>risen up</u>*° ... {2.0}

But by the same token Werth's account raises the question of whether a sharp line can always be drawn between world-building and function-advancing aspects of narrative. For example, in the Hemingway para-graph excerpted above, does sentence 4 stand out from the preceding sentences as foregrounded incipit against world-building background, or is sentence 7 the true incipit, and if so why: the selection of a focal participant within the scene, the use of a speech report, the repres-entation of a punctual event of asking rather than a durative process of sitting at a table in the shade, or all of these factors working in concert? If the latter is the case, then which factor is most crucial and why?

For her part, Emmott (1997) focuses on how readers recruit from mental representations or *contextual frames* to assign referents to pronouns across more or less extended stretches of narrative discourse. Emmott focuses specifically on the processes by which readers use textual cues to bind characters into or out of such mentally constructed contexts, which thereby underpin subsequent interpretations of character-indexing pronouns. Thus, in the opening of Hemingway's story, a noun phrase (*the girl*) binds Jig into what Emmott would term a *primed* contextual frame – first in sentence 4 and then again in sentence 7. Her presence in that frame allows readers to assign a referent to the pronoun *She* in sentence 8. Similarly, a noun phrase in sentence 5, *the express from Barcelona*, allows readers to identify the referent of *It* in sentence 6, differentiating this referring expression from the vacuous *It* in the expression *It was very hot* in sentence 5. Further, Emmott's account sheds light on strategic referential vagueness of the sort found in "Hills." In particular, the recurrence of the neuter pronoun *it* (cf. also the demonstrative pronoun *that*) across the subsequent lines of the story suggests how the characters themselves exploit the vagueness of the term's referential scope – and also how this discourse strategy emanates from a refusal to name and thereby come to terms with a central fact about their relationship:

> "The beer's nice and cool," the man said.
> "*It's* lovely," the girl said.
> "*It's* really an awfully simple operation, Jig," the man said. "*It's* not really an operation at all." [. . .]
> "We'll be fine afterwards. Just like we were before."
> "What makes you think so?"
> "*That's* the only thing that bothers us. *It's* the only thing that's made us unhappy." (Hemingway [1927] 1987: 212, emphases added)

But how might Emmott's language-based account of contextual frames be adapted to account for worldmaking procedures in other storytelling media, including multimodal narratives like Clowes's novel and Zwigoff's film adaptation of it – that is, narratives that draw on more than one semiotic channel as they prompt interpreters to build a storyworld?[7] Note that, in the case of graphic narratives, even where explicit verbal indicators about the temporal position of events are absent, the rendering of a character's appearance or the setting can suggest the position of a given scene or occurrence on an overarching time-line, how it fits within a particular context, in Emmott's sense of that term. Likewise, visual cues can help interpreters differentiate between the main or framing diegetic level and the subordinate or framed (= hypodiegetic) levels produced when characters become narrators in their own right. Hence in sequences C and D from *Ghost World* the rectangular boxes that represent Enid's utterances at the primary narrative level that she shares with Rebecca during their late-night phone call are set off from the rounded speech balloons used to report Enid's and Naomi's (earlier) utterances within the embedded or hypodiegetic narrative that Enid is subsequently recounting to Rebecca on the phone. Further, prior to and during these sequences, Enid's appearance changes in ways that allow readers to identify different time-frames or contexts. When she begins her call with Rebecca Enid is wearing the (dominatrix's) mask that she purchased earlier that day at the adult book store. Then, as she tells Rebecca about the experience of purchasing the mask, Enid assumes the appearance she had earlier that day with Josh. Later in the phone call, Enid removes the mask and she also appears in a mask-less state in the images that correspond to the encounter with Naomi that she also tells Rebecca about during their call. But the shirt that Enid is shown wearing in the second panel of sequence D is different than the one she is wearing when she purchases the mask with Josh – suggesting that these embedded narratives focus on events that transpire on different days.

Here we can use Emmott's term *enactor* to characterize how inter-preters monitor different versions of participants encountered in nar-rative flashbacks or embedded stories like Enid's. Readers of verbal narratives rely on mental representations or contexts to keep track of the current enactor, since flashbacks are not always explicitly signaled by changes in verbal texture. In graphic storytelling, however, visual as well as verbal cues (the appearance of a character or what he or she is wearing, the color and texture of the background in a given frame, the contrasting shapes of speech balloons, the contents of a represented speech act, etc.) can activate contexts pertinent for deter-mining when a given enactor or character-version is taking part in the narrated events.

Configuring Narrative Worlds: The WHAT, WHERE, and WHEN Dimensions of Storyworlds

Those coming to narrative theory for the first time are sometimes left with the "So what?" question when faced with something like Genette's ([1972] 1980) account of narrative temporality – in the absence of any larger concern with how flashbacks and flash-forwards can "thicken" one's sense of the history of a narrative world, or how fluctuations in the speed of narration provide a basis for distinguishing between focal and backgrounded elements in that world. However, by starting with world-creation as a basic cognitive and communicative function served by storytelling, and then working backward to the formal structures that support this root function of narrative, it is easier to motivate – to provide warrant for – fine-grained analyses of the spatial and temporal dimensions of storyworlds.

As indicated in my previous section, approaches such as deictic shift theory, possible-worlds theory, and contextual frame theory already take into account how time and space enter into the process of world-creation, that is, the WHERE and WHEN dimensions of narrative worlds. An approach based on shifting deictic centers allows for study of how narrative worlds are structured around cognitive vantage-points that may change over the course of an unfolding story; the approach thus underscores how one of the challenges of narrative interpretation is tracking which vantage-point constitutes the cognitive filter at what point in the developing action. Revealing interconnections between perspective, time, and space, the approach also allows for comparison between narratives in which the orienting perspective point remains relatively stable and fixed (like Monica's) and those marked by more or less rapid shifts of cognitive stance (like *Ghost World*). Similarly, accounts based on possible worlds are intrinsically concerned with time and space: characters' situation vis-à-vis the spatial layout of the TAW (and proximity to or distance from other characters) affects their ability to bring that world into conformity with their wishes, intentions, and felt obligations, even as the shifting relations among such private worlds or subworlds and the TAW provide a way to measure time's passing as events become etched into the history of the narrated domain. Likewise, based on the assumption that characters will be bound into and out of particular contexts over time, and that such contexts will be distributed spatially as well as temporally, Emmott's contextual frame theory points to the nexus of the WHAT, WHERE, and WHEN factors in narrative worldmaking.

In the remainder of this section I review other research focusing on issues of narrative time and space, and suggest how this work can be reconceptualized as an attempt to specify procedures for narrative worldmaking.

The temporal dimension of storyworlds

In the terms being outlined in the present chapter, Genette's ([1972] 1980) influential account of time in narrative can be viewed as a heuristic framework for studying the WHEN component of world-creation. In other words, when Genette distinguishes between simultaneous, retrospective, prospective, and "intercalated" modes of narration (as in the epistolary novel, where the act of narration postdates some events but precedes others), these narrative modes can be interpreted in light of the different kinds of structure that they afford for worldmaking. Retrospective narration accommodates the full scope of a storyworld's history, allowing a narrator to signal connections between earlier and later events through proleptic foreshadowings of (for example) the eventual impact of a character's actions on his or her cohorts. Simultaneous narration, in which events are presented in tandem with the interpreter's effort to comprehend the contours and boundaries of the narrated domain, does not allow for such anticipations-in-hindsight; rather, inferences about the impact of events on the storyworld remain tentative, probabilistic, open-ended. Hemingway's text interestingly combines features of these two modes insofar as it is told retrospectively but with a dearth of narratorial commentary that inhibits drawing connections among earlier and later events or prospection into the future of this narrative world. In this respect, "Hills" contrasts with both *Ghost World* and *UFO or the Devil*. As discussed in my previous subsection, Clowes's novel features embedded narratives told by the characters, who thereby connect past events to the current moment of telling, as well as images of Enid and Rebecca from earlier time-frames. For her part, Monica prospects forward into an already past future when in lines 56–60 of her narrative she notes that, after the encounter she reports, she never again ventured out into the woods at night.

Likewise, Genette's categories of duration, order (on which I have already begun to comment), and frequency can be explicated more productively if they are linked to the broader issue of narrative worldmaking. Duration can be computed as a ratio between how long events take to unfold in the world of the story and how much text is devoted to their narration; in this model, speeds can range from descriptive pause (where there is a span of text coupled with an absence of storyworld events), to scene (where there is an assumed equivalency between the span of text included and the duration of the events that it is used to recount), to summary (where in comparison to scene there is a shorter textual span relative to the duration of events), to ellipsis (where there is no textual span even though one or more events can be assumed to have transpired). This aspect of the temporal system thus constitutes a metric of value or at least attentional prominence: in extended narratives the shift from rapidly surveyed backstory or expositional material to a slower, scenic mode of presentation can signal aspects of the storyworld valued (or at any rate noticed) by a narrator (cf. Sternberg 1978). Meanwhile, as suggested by my discussion of retrospective versus simultaneous narration above, order can be analyzed by matching the sequence in which events are narrated against the sequence in which they can be assumed to have occurred, yielding chronological narration, analepses or flashbacks, and prolepses or flashforwards, together with various sub-categories of these nonchronological modes. How does the storyworld evoked by a narrative with a richly analeptic or proleptic structure (*The Sound and the Fury* or *The Prime of Miss Jean Brodie*, respectively) contrast with that evoked by a narrative that largely confines itself to the present, as Hemingway's text does?[8] How is a narrative world "thickened" by forays backward and forward in time, and what processing strategies are triggered by such temporal agglutination? Finally, frequency can be calculated by measuring how many times an event is narrated against how many times it can be assumed to have occurred in the storyworld. Again, more than just a range of formal possibilities, frequency affords ways of allocating attention to and evaluating events in narrative worlds – with repetitive narration foregrounding some event or set of events, iterative narration providing a summative gloss on multiple storyworld incidents, and singulative narration being the baseline metric in this context.

The spatial dimension of storyworlds

Though their concern with space is less longstanding than their interest in temporality, narrative theorists have in recent years increasingly studied WHERE-related factors of world-creation. This work was given impetus by Bakhtin's concept of the chronotope, defined as "a formally constitutive category of literature . . . [in which] spatial and temporal indicators are fused" in a manner which is originally associated with a particular genre, but which is subsequently taken up in later texts in ways that lead to generic intermixing and the co-presence of phenomena hailing from different phases of "the historico-literary process" ([1937–8] 1981: 84–5). Zoran (1984) built on Bakhtin's account to develop a three-level framework for studying the space-time nexus in narrative. This framework includes the topological level (a map of the narrated world that can be reconstructed from all the elements of the text); the chronotopic level (a domain in which space and time jointly constitute vectors of movement, broadly defined); and the textual level (where space is structured by the semiotic medium of the narrative text, as when the linear nature of verbal language organizes spatial relationships into a temporal continuum). Still more recently, theorists of space in narrative have borrowed from psychological and psycholinguistic work on spatial cognition, as well as cognitive-linguistic research on how abilities and dispositions bound up with embodied human experience find reflexes in the structure and interpretation of language. Buchholz and Jahn have suggested that this recent work harmonizes with Iurii Lotman's earlier account of the value-saturation of spatial oppositions, whereby distinctions such as near/far, high/low, etc. are correlated with judgments such as good/bad, valuable/worthless, etc. (2005: 554).

These and other developments can again be contextualized via notions of narrative worldmaking, in this case its WHERE dimension. For example, in *Story Logic*, I draw on some of the relevant research to suggest how particular textual cues prompt interpreters to *spatialize* storyworlds, that is, to build up mental representations of narrated domains as evolving configurations of participants, objects, and places (Herman 2002a: 263–99). In a text like Hemingway's, this approach can be used to examine how shifts between foregrounded and backgrounded objects and regions in the text, as well as the directions of movement traced by the main participants in the scene (Jig, the man, and the waitress), enable readers to segment the narrative into smaller episodes, each situated in a particular space-time region of the narrative world. The approach also sheds light on other, related questions, such as how Hemingway uses particular sub-spaces (the hills across the valley, the bar, Jig's and the man's table) to stage aspects of the characters' conflict, and also how this constellation of sub-spaces coheres into a world – what net effect the process of moving from one space to the next generates.

Likewise, in *UFO or the Devil* Monica recounts detailed trajectories of movement through the storyworld, locating herself (more precisely, her younger, experiencing self) within an orientational grid defined by two cross-cutting axes. Monica locates Renee at her side (line 7), along an axis that runs perpendicular to their path of motion through the storyworld. Along a second main axis runs the vector leading from Monica's house, the starting-point of the girls' journey, to Renee's grandmother's house. Throughout the narrative, Monica uses verbs and participles associated with motion (*we walking up the hill . . . we walkin . . . I'm still walkin . . . we just walkin . . . take off runnin . . . we run all the way to her grandmother's*) to trace the girls' movement along this second vector, and also to correlate their speed of motion with their emotional response to events: the more scared they are, the faster they move through space.

Further, Monica's use of internal focalization affords an expressive resource by which the narrative locates the self's experiences in space as well as in time. Perceptual verbs, spatial prepositions and adverbs, and other forms used in lines 9, 16, 27, 29, 35, 37, and 40 – e.g., *look over the bank, look back over my side again, it's right behind us, we still lookin back* – encode a particular perceptual position. These forms indicate that Monica and Renee are, for the duration of the reported action, in front of the big ball, looking back as the apparition keeps pace with them despite their best efforts to outrun it. The narrative thus enacts the situated, embodied nature of all perception, both in the lines just mentioned and also more globally, given that what can be seen is determined by the vantage-point of the experiencing-I over the course of the story. In this way, *UFO or the Devil* suggests not only that what can be seen, what is known about the world, alters with the spatial coordinates of the embodied self that is doing the looking; more than this, it suggests that a self is in part constituted by what it sees, when, and where – with narrative being one of the principal means for tracing this perceptual flux.

Worlds Disrupted: Narrativity and Noncanonical Events

Pointing ahead to the next chapter, this final section addresses another key sub-element of what I have characterized as the third basic element of narrative: namely, the way stories prototypically represent not just a narrative world but also world disruption, that is, events introducing disequilibrium or noncanonical situations into that world – as experienced by human or human-like agents.

As already suggested in my preliminary discussion in chapter 1 as well as in chapter 4, narrative prototypically involves more than particularized temporal sequences unfolding within more or less richly detailed storyworlds. In line with Propp's ([1928] 1968) account of disruptive events as the motor of narrative, and with Todorov's (1968) argument that narratives trace (at least part of) a path leading from an initial state of equilibrium, through a phase of disequilibrium, to an endpoint at which a different sort of equilibrium is restored, work by Bruner (1990, 1991) suggests just how narrative worldmaking differs from other representational practices that entail the construction or reconstruction of worlds. Narratives do not merely evoke worlds more or less distant from or proximate to the world of the here and now, through procedures of the sort discussed above. More than this, stories place an accent on unexpected or noncanonical events – events that disrupt the normal order of things for human or human-like agents engaged in goal-directed activities and projects within a given world, and that are experienced as such by those agents.

As the previous formulation suggests, what counts as normal or canonical will vary from world to world, narrative to narrative – as will, therefore, what counts as disruptive, disequilibrium-causing, noncanonical. Bruner's (1991) notion of canonicity and breach – his argument that "to be worth telling, a tale must be about how an implicit canonical script has been breached, violated, or deviated from in a manner to do violence to . . . [its] 'legitimacy' " (1991: 11) – allows for such variability, since what is expected in one cultural, subcultural, or situational setting may be atypical in another. Further, differences among kinds of narratives can be correlated with the way they engage with different sorts and degrees of noncanonicity. In Monica's tale of the supernatural, narrative affords a means for navigating the breach between (1) expectations based on the assumed physical regularities of nature (big, glowing balls, in the general course of events, do not appear out of thin air and chase people at night) and (2) what transpires when Monica and Renee make their frightening journey through the dark woods. The story also enables Monica to come to terms with how she herself is changed – irreversibly – by this experience. In *Ghost World*, by contrast, the laws of nature are never in question; at issue, rather, are the social scripts to which Enid, Rebecca, and the other characters in the storyworld orient as a basis for action and interaction – scripts bearing on gender and family roles, as well as sexual relationships, responsibilities associated with adulthood versus adolescence, etc. The novel as a whole traces events leading up to the divergent life-courses of the two main characters, caused in part by Rebecca's willingness to accommodate to dominant social scripts versus Enid's resistance to those same scripts.[9] The text also suggests how narrative furnishes resources for managing clashes between competing sets of scripts, for example, those associated with transformative experiences and transitions between life-stages. Hence the loss-of-virginity story that Enid tells to Naomi and retells to Rebecca in sequences C and D, as well as a panel on the penultimate page of the novel that shows Enid walking in the opposite direction from schoolchildren heading back to school in the autumn. For its part, Hemingway's text focuses on Jig's and the male character's conflicting responses to the unexpected event of Jig's becoming pregnant. As "Hills" suggests, narrative provides a means not only for representing the disruption of a normal order of things, but also for registering and cross-comparing the merits of various strategies for adjusting to such altered circumstances.

Despite the very different narrative worlds they evoke, what remains constant across my main illustrative examples is a focus on taking the measure of time, process, change – on recording and evaluating how a storyworld is no longer the same in the aftermath of events that have a consequential, life-changing impact on agents living and acting within that world. As suggested in chapter 4, descriptions, too, can represent processes unfolding in time. But narratives characteristically concern themselves not just with the processual but more specifically with disruption – transgressions of the expected or at least normal order of events that might or might not result from time's passing.[10] Noteworthy and thus narratable disruptions, then, are anchored in the contingent rather than the necessary, what might eventuate from a given set of circumstances rather than what is logically entailed by them.

To capture this distinction between mere process and narratable disruption, some narrative scholars have developed the concept of *tellability* – sometimes distinguished from *narrativity*. Tellability has been defined as that which makes an event or configuration of events (relevantly) reportable – that is, tellable or narratable – in a given communicative situation (Herman 2002a: 100–5; Labov 1972; Labov and Waletzky 1967; Norrick 2007; Prince [1987] 2003; Ryan 1991, 2005c). By contrast, narrativity has been defined as a property by virtue of which a given text or discourse is more or less readily interpreted *as* a story (Fludernik 1996; Herman 2002a: 100–5; Prince 1999, [1987] 2003, 2005; Sternberg 1990, 2001). The idea here is that a given story can be more or less tellable in different sets of circumstances, and also that different representations that can be included in the category "narrative" may be more or less tellable or reportable, depending on the occasion of telling. Chapter 3 of this book explores similar issues, characterizing narrative as a mode of representation that has to be interpreted in light of a particular discourse context or storytelling occasion, and examining how judgments about the meaning of a narrative are a function of particular communicative situations, which are in turn shaped by the process of telling and interpreting stories. But in another sense, the approach outlined in this book suggests that issues of tellability and narrativity may not be separable in the way that previous scholars of story have argued – or at least that the concept of tellability may need to be divided to cover two different meanings, namely, "salient in some communicative context" and "salient in the context of some storyworld" (cf. Herman 2007a).

In evoking a storyworld, the degree to which a representation foregrounds a more or less marked (and thus noteworthy or tellable) disruption of the canonical or expected order of events is itself one of the factors or properties explaining how readily the representation can be interpreted as an instance of the text-type category *narrative*, versus, say, *description*. Thus, rather than being an optional feature of representations that would still be narratively configured without it, (some degree of) reportability or tellability is built into the nature of narrative at the level of worldmaking. Once a world has been evoked and interpreters have relocated to it, orienting themselves to its canonical scripts or "givens," the procedures specific to narrative worldmaking require that the world be one in which those givens are called into question, jeopardized by events that are more or less radically noncanonical, more or less antithetic to the normal order of things. However, the innumerably many kinds of worlds that can be evoked by narratives, together with the many degrees of disruptiveness that the same sort of event might possess in different contexts, suggests the futility of attempting to fix in advance what makes something tellable, what constitutes a narratable disruption in the order of a world.

In my final chapter, I turn to the fourth basic element of narrative, already hinted at in the present section: namely, the felt, lived *experience* of disruptive events – their impact on real or imagined consciousnesses affected by a storyworld-in-flux. In short, narrative ways of worldmaking depend crucially not just on disruptiveness as such but moreover on events that are experienced *as* disruptive for some mind or constellation of minds.[11]

6

The Nexus of Narrative and Mind

(iv) **What it's like**. *Narrative representations convey the* experience *of living through storyworlds-in-flux, highlighting the pressure of events on real or imagined consciousnesses affected by the occurrences at issue. Thus – with one important proviso – it can be argued that narrative is centrally concerned with* qualia, *a term used by philosophers of mind to refer to the sense of "what it is like" for someone or something to have a particular experience. The proviso is that recent research on narrative bears importantly on debates concerning the nature of consciousness itself.*

The Consciousness Factor

This chapter draws on ideas from the philosophy of mind, among other areas within the umbrella discipline of cognitive science, to flesh out the notion of an experiencing consciousness. The chapter thus seeks to explain why I characterize the representation of what it's like to experience disruptive events in a storyworld as one of the basic elements of narrative.

In this chapter, I explore a fourth basic element of narrative – another critical property of the representational practices that are more or less amenable to being understood in narrative terms, depending on their structure and the contexts in which they unfold. At issue is the way stories highlight the impact of events on the mind or minds experiencing those events within a storyworld. Narrative, I argue, is a mode of representation tailor-made for gauging the felt quality of lived experiences. Accordingly, the less a given representation registers the pressure of an experienced world on one or more human or human-like consciousnesses, the less central or prototypical an instance of the category "narrative" that representation will be – all other things being equal.[1] To put the same point another way, to the extent that a representation embodies the elements of **situatedness**, **event sequencing**, and **worldmaking/world disruption** but backgrounds or suppresses **what it's like**, that representation will be pushed closer to the edge than the center of the category space of "narrative," where forms such as "chronicle" or "report" verge on the fuzzy border separating narratives from descriptions, as discussed in chapters 1 and 4.

That said, like the other basic elements of narrative discussed in this book, what it's like should be viewed not as a failsafe guarantee of the presence of narrative, but rather as a marker of texts that circulate in communicative contexts in the manner that is characteristic of – or prototypical for – narratives. Also, like the factors of particularity and disruptiveness, what might be called the consciousness factor operates in a gradient or more-or-less manner, resulting in more or less prototypical instances of the category *narrative* – with the caveat that judgments about what counts as prototypical are themselves subject to change across different contexts (see chapter 4). Furthermore, the very notions of mind and consciousness demand closer scrutiny in this connection. Indeed, as I go on to discuss below, recent scholarship on narrative not only stands to benefit from but also itself bears importantly on conceptions of mind developed in the fields included within the umbrella discipline of cognitive science, including philosophy, psychology, and linguistics (cf. Herman 2007b).

Before I move on to a more detailed discussion of the nexus of narrative and mind in the remainder of this chapter, I address in my next section an important preliminary question: namely, whether my emphasis on consciousness as a key factor of narrativity is perhaps a byproduct of my focus on a particular class (or corpus) of narratives that I am using, tacitly, as a yardstick for my analysis of stories in general.

Consciousness across Narrative Genres

For Fludernik (1996, 2003), it is not plot but experientiality – that is, the evocation of an experiencing human or human-like consciousness on which narrated situations and events are represented as impinging – that constitutes narrativity, or what makes narrative narrative. Yet if one admits degrees of narrativity, then other factors besides consciousness must be invoked to account for the extent to which a given story will be construed as being prototypically narrative. My previous chapters have sought to characterize the other features at issue, suggesting that capturing what it's like to experience storyworld events constitutes a critical property of but not a sufficient condition for narrative. But by the same token, the consciousness factor can be argued to be criterial for narrative in general rather than for particular kinds of narratives (e.g., psychological novels).

A key difference between narrative genres is the extent to which they foreground the factor of consciousness – highlight the impact of events on an experiencing mind – in the storyworlds that they evoke. In psychological fiction like the novels of the later Henry James, for example, the filtering consciousness of the experiencing protagonist takes center stage, to the point where the term "novel of consciousness" has been applied to texts such as *The Ambassadors* and *Wings of the Dove* (cf. Jahn 2007). By contrast, in some action-adventure films, for instance, or in some of the more radical experiments of Robbe-Grillet ([1957, 1959] 1965) and other practitioners of the *nouveau roman*, the consciousness factor can be assigned a more subordinate position within the overall structure of a representation that nonetheless remains recognizably narrative in nature. Indeed, one of the hallmarks of the *nouveau roman* is the way it tests the very limits of narrativity, exploring the threshold past which events cease to be narratable, precisely by suppressing or at least occluding the consciousness factor in its representation of unfolding situations and events (Richardson 2006: 7–8; cf. Warhol 2005: 222–3).

However, in alluding to Henry James's well-documented use of a center of consciousness, "reflector," or filtering perceptual agent in his later novels (cf. Teahan 1995), I have broached what F. K. Stanzel ([1979] 1984) characterized as a distinctively modernist narrative technique – namely, figural narration. Figural narration, which as Stanzel noted began to appear in high concentrations only in the late nineteenth and early twentieth centuries, in texts by writers such as Henry James, Franz Kafka, James Joyce, and Virginia Woolf, contrasts with the two other "narrative situations" identified by Stanzel: namely, first-person narration and distanced third-person or "authorial" narration. In figural narration, there is in effect a blending of first-person and third-person narration: a third-person or heterodiegetic narrator recounts events filtered through the perspective or focalizing perceptions of a reflector figure, that is, a particularized center of consciousness. Stanzel's approach raises a broader question: is it the case that in emphasizing the consciousness factor in narrative (in general) my account is skewed toward written, literary narratives published only during the past hundred years or so? More specifically, is the explicit concern with consciousness a historically contingent byproduct of the rise of psychological fiction, such that in interpreting it as a core factor or feature of narrativity I am conflating one type of narrative with narrative *tout court*, illicitly extrapolating from one kind of literary fiction until its generic profile becomes identified as the signature of narrative itself? To address these issues, I propose to revisit some of the ideas of Monika Fludernik, whose work I have drawn from in making the claim that the impact of narrated situations and events on an experiencing consciousness constitutes a core property of narrative (see Fludernik 1996: 12–13, 28–30, 49–50; Fludernik 2003).

In Fludernik's account, the factor chiefly responsible for making narratives interpretable *as* narratives is human experientiality, or "the evocation of consciousness [in terms of] cognitive schema of embodiedness that relate to human existence and human concerns" (Fludernik 1996: 168).[2] In fuller terms:

> [The model presented in Fludernik (1996)] constitutes narrativity not – as is traditionally the case – in reference to *plot* or *story*, but in reference to what I have called *experientiality*. This term . . . describes the typical quality of natural narratives in which surprising events impinge on the protagonist (usually coterminous with the narrator) and are resolved by his (or her) reaction(s) – a sequence that provides an illustrative "point" to the story and links the telling to its immediate discourse context. . . . By introducing the concept of experientiality, I was concerned to characterize the purpose and function of the storytelling as a process that captures the narrator's past experience, reproduces it in a vivid manner,

and then evaluates and resolves it in terms of the protagonist's reactions and of the narrator's often explicit linking of the meaning of this experience with the current discourse context. (Fludernik 2003: 245)

However, as Alber notes, Fludernik's account of experientiality as constitutive of stories raises the question of how to distinguish between narrative and lyric (Alber 2002: 68–9), or for that matter why "inarticulate screams of horror" should not count as narratives. Alber also points out that for Fludernik the boundary between narrative and lyric is permeable, implying that degrees of narrativity can be assigned to representations that share with lyric poems the core feature of experientiality but that exhibit other features more prototypically associated with narrative. In other words, if one posits experientiality as constitutive of narrative but also admits degrees of narrativity, then other factors besides consciousness must be invoked to account for the relative ease or difficulty of processing a given text or representation as narrative in nature. In the present study, I have tried to characterize the other features at issue, suggesting that capturing what it's like to experience storyworld events constitutes a critical property of but not a sufficient condition for narrative. But just how critical to narrative – that is, to narrative in general rather than to particular kinds of narratives – is the consciousness factor anyway?

Partly as an attempt to answer this question, I outlined in a previous study (Herman 2002a) an account of narrative genres as "preference-rule systems," or systems that involve graded judgments about what is more or less typical (or "preferred") for a given situation or case. My approach builds on Frawley's definition of a preference rule as "a statement in probabilistic form of the relative strength of two or more items for interpretation relative to some property or properties" (1992: 57). For example, with respect to the property of "punctuality," the linguistic items *sip*, *drink*, and *chug* can be arranged along a scale (*sip* > *drink* > *chug*) to indicate which of these verbs would be preferred when it comes to coding a process as punctual versus durative or ongoing. Likewise, and in accordance with Halliday's (1994) functional account of grammar as an instrument for construing the world in terms of types of processes, genres can be defined as sets of preference rules bearing on how processes unfolding in the storyworld should be coded or represented (e.g., as mental, behavioral, verbal, or other). Such preference-rule systems in turn create default assumptions about the roles that protagonists will play within storyworlds (e.g., experiencer, behaver, sayer, etc.) (cf. Herman 2002a: 140–69). In the genre of psychological fiction, for instance, the preference is to code processes in the storyworld as mental ones, thereby selecting "experiencer" as the default role-assignment for protagonists in this kind of narrative. By contrast, in the tip-of-the-iceberg mode of narration used in Hemingway's "Hills," explicit characterization of mental processes is backgrounded in favor of accounts of behavioral and verbal processes, such that Jig and the male character are coded predominantly as behavers and sayers. From this perspective, Hemingway's text could be interpreted as a form of narrative worldmaking sometimes termed *behaviorist narration* (Prince [1987] 2003) – though as I discuss later on in this chapter "Hills" does in fact prompt interpreters to frame inferences about the nature and quality of the characters' conscious experiences. Indeed, a strictly behaviorist narrative would arguably be a contradiction in terms (cf. Herman forthcoming a; Palmer 2003); for if a representation completely eliminated or occluded the consciousness factor it would fall outside the (elastic) text-type category of "narrative."

The foregoing remarks suggest that the factor of consciousness will be more or less accentuated depending on the narrative genre in question; it is not the case that, for every narrative genre, the default role-assignment for the protagonist will be that of "experiencer." But here the reciprocal relation between contexts and prototypes, discussed in chapter 4, becomes salient once again. Genres can described as contexts that define the degree to which the consciousness factor must be foregrounded for a story to count as a prototypical instance (or "standard case") of that narrative kind. What it's like, in other words, is likely to be coded in a more explicit way in a Henry James novel, or for that matter in a tale of the supernatural like Monica's, than in a narrative that, like Hemingway's, seeks to innovate upon the literary system precisely by omitting or suppressing narratorial reports of characters' attitudes, dispositions, and emotional states. But different degrees of explicitness or detail in the representation of consciousness should not be confused with the option *either* to evoke what it is like for human or human-like agents to undergo experiences in storyworlds *or else* to factor out that dimension altogether. Rather, my argument is that the absence of the element of what it's like from a text or a representation is tantamount to zero-degree narrativity – even if one or more of the elements of situatedness, event sequencing, and worldmaking/world disruption is in play. For example, the more the element of what it's like is factored out to produce a skeletal albeit chronologically ordered list of the events associated with a political coup, the greater the distance between that representation and exemplars of *narrative* – and the closer the representation will come to exemplars of *description*. Conversely, the presence of what it's like coupled with a complete absence of event sequencing (as in Alber's example of inarticulate screams of horror) likewise results in the expulsion of a text or representation beyond the frontiers of narrative.

But how might the consciousness factor itself be further specified – in a manner that, rather than privileging how the element of what it's like tends to function in a particular narrative genre, instead gets at the fundamental imbrication of mind and story, the nexus of narrative and mind thanks to which a given text or discourse can be interpreted as narratively organized in the first place? My next section draws on ideas from the cognitive sciences, which encompass fields ranging from psychology and linguistics to Artificial Intelligence and the philosophy of mind, to explore this issue. I also return to my main case studies, among other illustrative instances, to examine some particular manifestations of mind in narrative contexts.[3]

Experiencing Minds: What It's Like, Qualia, Raw Feels

It is productive to recontextualize Fludernik's conception of experientiality by drawing on Nagel's (1974) account of consciousness as a sense of "what it is like" to be someone or something. Philosophers of mind have developed the notion of "qualia" to discuss this what-it's-like dimension of consciousness; qualia are felt, subjective properties of mental states, such as those I experience when I see the white color of my cat's fur, or feel the bite of cold air on my face when I step outside on a winter evening. With this section revisiting my main case studies and exploring how qualia form a basis or rather condition for narrative, in my next section I test out the merits of the converse approach, considering whether narrative might be viewed as a basis or condition for conscious experience itself.

Ways of characterizing what it's like

As already suggested in my previous section, Fludernik seeks to develop an approach to the problem of narrativity, or what constitutes narrative, that moves away from the older, Aristotelian emphasis on plot and instead accentuates experientiality, which she describes as "the quasi-mimetic evocation of 'real-life' experience" (1996: 12). Having characterized experientiality as the key condition for narrativity, Fludernik goes on to write that in the constitution of experientiality, "[t]he most crucial factor is that of the protagonist's emotional and physical reaction to [events as they impinge on her situations and activities] . . . since humans are conscious thinking beings, (narrative) experientiality always implies – and sometimes emphatically foregrounds – the protagonist's consciousness" (1996: 30). In this subsection, though I do not treat the element of what it's like as more fundamental to narrative than the other basic elements discussed in previous chapters, I suggest how it can be productive to explore this fourth basic element by drawing on recent research on the nature of consciousness – and by integrating that research with previous work in narrative theory that likewise takes consciousness into account. The research at issue suggests not only that that narrative is centrally concerned with *qualia*, a term used by philosophers of mind to refer to the sense of what it's like for someone or something to have a particular experience, but also that narrative bears importantly on debates concerning the nature of consciousness itself.

As Davies (1999) points out, conscious mental states, including sensations (the feel of the fur on my cat, Tinker), perceptions (the whiteness of Tinker's fur, or the sound of her complaining meows when she is hungry), and "occurrent thoughts" (thoughts about how I'll soon need to purchase more cat food for Tinker, and where I'll need to go to get it) are a pervasive yet puzzling aspect of our mental lives. The puzzling part of consciousness is how – and why – such awareness could be the product of the physical processes, the firing of neurons and other electrochemical activities, that take place in the human brain. What surfaces here is the so-called "explanatory gap" in cognitive science (Levine 1983), already mentioned in chapter 4. At issue is the gap between what we know about physical brain states and the condition of conscious awareness, the phenomenology of our mental lives, that may or may not be supervenient on those states. To put the same point another way, there is a gap between current understandings of the complex forms of neuronal activity in the brain and what Nagel (1974) has influentially characterized as the what-it's-like dimension of conscious experience – the dimension whereby there is something that it is like be a certain creature or system, whether a bat, a human, or (potentially) an intelligent machine or robot. To restrict myself to the human case, how could the structure of the brain, so far as neuroscience understands it, give rise to the sensation I have when I pet Tinker, or perceive her white fur, or hear her hungry meow? And why should I have such sensations? In other words, in what way am I advantaged (say, from the standpoint of evolution) by my having consciousness?

To be sure, an extensive literature has grown up around this problem, or cluster of problems, in the philosophy of mind; it is beyond the scope of the present study to review the complete history of the debate or the full range of positions adopted by participants in the ongoing discussion.[4] Instead, my treatment here will focus specifically on the what-it's-like dimension of consciousness and on how accounts of that dimension are pertinent for my own argument that the consciousness factor can be characterized as a basic element of narrative. I begin with an overview of research on a key concept developed by philosophers of mind and others to capture this what-it's-like dimension, namely, the idea of qualia or states of felt, subjective (or first-person) awareness attendant upon consciousness. I then move to a discussion of the concept's relevance for an analysis of the main case studies I have been focusing on in this book. In this part of my analysis, I explore the representation of qualia in narrative contexts, which I argue to be recognizable as such partly because of how stories orient themselves around the what-it's-like properties of experiencing consciousnesses in storyworlds. Then, in my final section, I explore grounds for making the converse claim, which is a more radical, controversial, and speculative one: namely, that we cannot even have a notion of the felt quality of experience without narrative.

Qualifying qualia

As Levin notes, in the philosophy of mind "[t]he terms *quale* and *qualia* (pl.) are most commonly used to characterize the qualitative, experiential, or felt properties of mental states" (1999: 688). Or, as Dennett puts it, " '[q]ualia' is an unfamiliar term for something that could not be more familiar to each of us: *the ways things seem to us*" (1997: 619).

At issue, as Dennett writes, is the "particular, personal, subjective . . . quality" of one's conscious experiences at a given moment (1997: 619) – in Nagel's (1974) terms, the sense or feeling of what it is like to be someone or something having a given experience. Talk about qualia, then, stems from the intuition that conscious experiences have ineliminably subjective properties, a distinctive sense or feeling of what it is like for someone or something to experience them.

To spell out the notion of qualia, Searle (1997) offers the following account of the sensation of pain; he contextualizes his account by relating qualia both to the notion of the intrinsically first-person nature of conscious awareness (see my next section) and to the idea of the explanatory gap, that is, the problem of moving from the neuroscience of brain structures and processes to the what-it's-like dimension of consciousness:

> My pain has a certain qualitative feel and is accessible to me in a way that is not accessible to you. Now how *could* these private, subjective, qualitative phenomena be caused by ordinary physical processes such as electrochemical neuron firings at the synapses of neurons? There is a special qualitative feel to each type of conscious state, and we are not in agreement about how to fit these subjective feelings into our overall view of the world as consisting of objective reality. Such states and events are sometimes called "qualia," and the problem of accounting for them within our overall worldview is called the problem of qualia. . . . all conscious phenomena are qualitative, subjective experiences, and hence are qualia. There are not two types of phenomena, consciousness and qualia. There is just consciousness, which is a series of qualitative states. (1997: 8–9)

However, Searle's is just one take on the problem of qualia, and the idea continues to be debated among scholars who have adopted a range of positions on their status. Physicalists such as Dennett (1991, 1997) argue for the possibility of reducing qualia to brain states. From this perspective, conscious experience only seems to have an irreducibly subjective or first-person character, and is in fact susceptible to description and explanation in the "third-person" terms afforded by scientific discourse (cf. Blackmore 2005; Hutto 2000: 100–3).[5] By contrast, antireductionists such as Jackson (1982) and Levine (1983) emphasize what they see as an unbridgeable (explanatory) gap between accounts of brain physiology and the phenomenology of conscious experience. Proponents of this view follow Nagel (1974) in underscoring the irreducibly subjective or first-person nature of consciousness. Meanwhile, functionalists argue that qualia are "multiply physically realizable," such that they could in principle be emulated on a computer system, for example, and are therefore not specific to an individual brain (see Tye 2003: section 4).

For his part, Lodge (2002) has pursued yet another way – a way that has special relevance for the present chapter. For Lodge, "literature is a record of human consciousness, the richest and most comprehensive we have" (2002: 10). In particular, Lodge suggests that narrative fiction, and more specifically the use of free indirect discourse/thought, makes it possible to combine "the realism of assessment that belongs to third-person narration with the realism of presentation that comes from first-person narration" (2002: 45). From this perspective, narrative fiction provides a sort of dialectical synthesis of the third-person orientation of scientific discourse, including discourse on the nature of mind, and the first-person orientation of consciousness itself. As I discuss in my next subsection, however, qualia figure importantly not just in narrative fiction, let alone the subset of fictional texts where free indirect discourse is used, but more generally in storytelling practices whenever and wherever they occur. Indeed, my argument is that such practices constitute a coherent class of representational (or worldmaking) procedures precisely because of their shared concern with the impact of situations and events on the minds experiencing them. Cutting across differences of narrative genre, communicative context, and storytelling media is a common focus on the what-it's-like dimension of experiencing minds, insofar as they are affected by what is going on in the narrated world.

What it's like in the case studies

To pick back up with an issue broached above, although Hemingway's fiction in general and "Hills Like White Elephants" in particular might be thought of as a "behaviorist" mode of narration, presenting only overt, surface behaviors of the characters and omitting narratorial commentary on more or less fugitive internal states (dispositions, thoughts, attitudes, memories, etc.), as the characters' conversation unfolds in the story a rich context of felt experience emerges.[6] Here one might reiterate Hemingway's statement concerning his own tip-of-the-iceberg method of composition: "I always try to write on the principle of the iceberg. . . . There is seven-eighths of it underwater for every part that shows" (quoted in Johnston 1987: 31). This statement suggests that

Hemingway's chosen strategy is to prompt readers to draw inferences about what it's like for the characters to experience events unfolding in the storyworld, rather than providing direct characterizations of the qualia or, as they are also called, the "raw feels" (van Gulick 2004: section 2.2) of these fictional minds. But consider the following passage from the story:

> The girl looked across at the hills.
> "They're lovely hills," she said. "They don't really look like white elephants. I just meant the coloring of their skin through the trees."
> "Should we have another drink?"
> "All right."
> The warm wind blew the bead curtain against the table.
> "The beer's nice and cool," the man said.
> "It's lovely," the girl said. (Hemingway [1927] 1987: 212)

How the hills appear to Jig, the warmth of the wind, the sight (and presumably sound) of the bead curtain's being blown against the table by the breeze, and the taste of the cool beer: all of these qualia or raw feels are encoded in the text and situated in the dynamic unfolding of the characters' experiences, in a manner that helps distinguish Hemingway's narrative worldmaking from other strategies for world-construction (lists, syllogistic arguments, statistical analyses, etc.), which do not place a premium on representing what it's like to live through the events in the world being evoked, as discussed in my previous chapter. Grounding the representation of the characters' interchange in what it's like for them to experience this scene of talk (Herman 2006b), passages such as the one just excerpted cue readers to adopt a particular interpretive stance toward the text as a whole. Specifically, readers are prompted to project from the explicit information given about the characters' words and actions a dense constellation of raw feels, whether they are explicitly mentioned or merely implied. What emerges is a pattern of felt, conscious experience by virtue of which narrative modes of representation can be recognized as such.

Likewise, qualia figure importantly in Monica's story, where the older narrating-I uses prosodic resources of spoken discourse to underscore the impact of events on her younger, experiencing self during the encounter with the big, glowing orange ball – thereby indexing her own narrative orientation toward the unfolding interaction and cuing her interlocutors to maintain the same orientation toward her ongoing worldmaking efforts. Thus, in line 17 the slowed-down, emphatic pronunciation of the verb phrase *risen up*, together with the two-second pause separating this phrase from Monica's next utterance, suggests a re-enactment in the present of her past experience of witnessing the apparition and of registering the extent to which it defied her expectations about how the world works.

(15)   And I'm still <u>walkin</u> you know*
(16)   Then I look back over my side a<u>gain</u>,
(17)   and it has °<u>risen</u> <u>up</u>*° ... {2.0}
(18)   And I'm like "(↗)SHI::T." ... {.5} you know.

Here Monica's use of the present-tense form of the perfective construction – *has risen up* – reinforces this re-enactment in the present of the qualia of an earlier time-frame.

The semantic content of these lines dovetails with their prosodic profile, emphasizing the intensity of Monica's experience of the ball's frighteningly anomalous movements, which she relives performatively in the here and now. Similarly, in lines 38 and 39, Monica again uses prosodic resources to highlight the impact on her earlier self of the ball's expectation-violating manner of progress through space:

(37)   It's just a-<u>bouncin</u> behind /us/
(38)   it's <u>no:t</u>.. > touchin the <u>ground</u>, <
(39)   it's bouncin in the <u>air</u>. ... {.5}

The elongated pronunciation of *not*, the rushed-through production of *touchin the ground*, and the use of heightened volume and pitch for *not*, *ground*, and *air* all reinforce the contrast between the expected and the actual mode of movement; even the rapid rate of delivery in line 38 serves this purpose, helping to accentuate the semantic content of the subsequent line. The sound properties of spoken discourse therefore constitute a key resource for representing what it's like, allowing first-person narrators like Monica to reconstitute the qualia defining the felt, subjective character of the storyworlds that they seek to evoke in the here and now of communicative interaction. More than this, prosody allows storytellers in face-to-face interaction to establish a performative link between different phases of the self whose coherence and continuity derive in part from this ongoing process of re-performance – a process that more traumatic experiences, by splitting off the past from the present, can disrupt.

In *Ghost World*, Clowes exploits word–image combinations to evoke qualia in his own storytelling medium. Thus, in the second panel in sequence A, the utterance attributed to Rebecca in the speech balloon, together with her facial expression and hand-to-her-mouth posture of surprise, suggests what it's like for Rebecca to experience the shock of first seeing Enid's new hairstyle (the subsequent narration reveals that she has dyed it green, though that color is not part of the three-tone color scheme [blue, white, and black] of the text as whole and so is not displayed anywhere in Clowes's panels). In the doubly embedded narrative presented in sequences C and D, Clowes uses Rebecca for similar purposes. Thus, in the first panel of sequence D, in the hypo-hypodiegetic narrative here underway (Enid is telling to Rebecca during a late-night phone conversation the story of how she told her own loss-of-virginity story to Naomi, their common acquaintance), what it's like for these characters emerges from Rebecca's posture and engrossed demeanor together with Enid's re-narration of her own reaction to the letter she receives from her first sexual partner ("I couldn't *believe* it!"). As with Monica's narrative, Enid's re-enactment of how these events impinged on her and Rebecca's earlier, experiencing selves links together the different phases of these selves – selves whose continuity over time derives in part from just this (ongoing) process of re-performance. Meanwhile, to revisit from a different perspective an aspect of *Ghost World* discussed in chapter 3 in connection with the idea of positioning, in sequence B, readers are likely to use the design of the first two panels as a basis for assessing the status of the image represented in the third panel. Specifically, they are likely to infer that this image of the former bass player is part of what it's like for Rebecca to experience this locus within the unfolding storyworld – given her physical position and the orientation of her torso and gaze in the preceding panel. More precisely, this image evokes the quale corresponding to how the bass player appears to Rebecca at this moment in the history of the emerging storyworld.

However, it is not just that the example narratives ground themselves in raw feels, that is, evoke what it was like to live through a storyworld-in-flux. What is more, my case studies suggest that narrative allows for more or less direct, explicit reflection on – for critical and reflexive engagement with – competing accounts of the world-as-experienced. Arguably, narrative is unique in this respect: stories, and stories alone, afford an environment in which versions of what it was like to experience situations and events can be juxtaposed, comparatively evaluated, and then factored into further accounts of the world (or *a* world). Along the same lines, in Hemingway's text the question of qualia enters directly into the plot: the conflict at the heart of the story concerns what an experience (more specifically, the experience of having an abortion) will or would be like for the person who undergoes that procedure. In other words, "Hills" portrays an interaction in which one of the participants seeks to manage and minimize the felt experience of events from his interlocutor's vantage-point. To draw again on the terms of positioning theory discussed in chapter 3, in the storyline that the male character seeks to project, the subjectively experienced character of storyworld events – the qualia associated with them – is at odds with what Jig herself senses they are or will be like. Jig, being of another mind, therefore rejects the male character's other-positioning strategies. Similarly, at the very end of the story, the male character tries to emplot their current interaction as one in which Jig, after going through a brief period of feeling "unwell," recovers her equilibrium. Jig rejects this storyline, which is based on an attempt to position her in terms of the polarity feeling worse/feeling better; but she does not necessarily project a storyline of her own vis-à-vis their recent interaction:

"Do you feel better?" he asked.
"I feel fine," she said. "There's nothing wrong with me. I feel fine."
(Hemingway [1927] 1987: 214)

Jig thus rejects the presupposition of the male character's question, but does not engage in a self-positioning act that might lend a sense of closure to their recent dispute – or to the narrative itself.

Similarly, *UFO or the Devil* does not just register the impact of events on experiencing minds but moreover uses narrative to stage a dispute between competing accounts of the world-as-experienced. Two moments of conflict constitute kernel events of the story: (1) Monica and Renee's tense encounter with the glowing orange ball, and (2) Monica's dispute with Renee's grandmother concerning what was at stake in that encounter. These kernel events, furthermore, are tightly interlinked. By constructing herself as an accountably frightened experiencer in her narrative about event (1), Monica provides crucial context for the interpretation of event (2). In essence, the second event is a dispute in which one of the participants again seeks to gain narrative control over the felt experience of the first event from her interlocutor's vantage-point. In other words, in the storyline proposed by Renee's grandmother, the first event lacks the experiential profile that Monica herself imputes to that kernel event, in part by configuring it *as* an event in the present story. And once more, as my phrasing here indicates, the positioning logic discussed in chapter 3 directly intersects with these characters' felt experience of events – the qualia that define what it is like for them to have or undergo experiences from a particular vantage-point on the storyworld. Rejecting the grandmother's other-positioning strategies, Monica refuses to become the self she would have to be – to experience the mode of felt, subjective awareness she would have to experience – were she to take up the position entailed by the grandmother's storyline.

Resituating raw feels

In the foregoing paragraphs I have suggested that qualia, raw feels, or the what-it's-like dimension of conscious awareness play a crucial role in – indeed, help define the scope and nature of – storytelling practices across media and genres. Furthermore, I have argued that, more than just representing qualia, narrative as a mode of representation uniquely allows for the comparison of versions of what it was like to experience particular situations and events. This last line of argument, which is based in part on previous studies exploring the nexus of narrative and mind (Herman 2007b; see also Herman forthcoming a), and which suggests that narrative not only reflects but helps shape the sense of what it is like to live through worlds-in-flux, provides a convenient transition to the final section of this chapter.

As noted in chapter 3, a *discursive* approach to narrative and mind can be contrasted with a *cognitivist* approach. In the cognitivist approach, discourse (print texts, conversational interaction, graphic novels, films, etc.) can be viewed as a window onto underlying mental processes that form a kind of bedrock layer for psychological inquiry. By contrast, the discursive approach studies how the mind is oriented to and accounted for – that is, constructed – in systematic, norm-governed ways by participants in these and other modes of discourse production, e.g., through processes of positioning. A key question in this context is whether the notion of qualia or raw feels can be reconciled with a discursive conception of mind – an understanding of mind as not just revealed but also constituted via the collaborative processes by which discourse is produced and interpreted.

Thus, in one of the earlier studies just mentioned (Herman forthcoming a), I argue that in the case of "Hills Like White Elephants" there are grounds for replacing Hemingway's own surface-and-depth metaphor of the iceberg with a more "lateralized" or distributed model, in which memories, emotions, and qualia – in short, the mind – are spread out as a distributional flow in what the characters do and say (as well as what they do not do and do not say), in the material environment that constitutes part of their interaction, in the method of narration used to present their verbal and nonverbal activities, and in readers' own engagement with all of these representational structures. From this perspective, rather than being lodged in a "privileged and insulated inner arena" that is separated off from the body and the world – to quote Clark's (1998: 508) characterization of the focal object of early work in cognitive science – the experiential profile of events emerges from the participants' use of verbal as well as nonverbal acts, in a richly material setting, to engage in the discursive construction of mind. My final section traces out some of the implications of this discursive approach for research on the link between storytelling and qualia, narrative and what it's like. More specifically, I move from exploring the issue with which I've been concerned up to now – how, by evoking what it's like for one or more minds to experience events, a text or discourse meets a threshold condition for narrativity – to examining a second issue, which is in a sense the converse of the first. The second issue is whether narrative affords a basis or context for the having of (an) experience in the first place.

Storied Minds: Narrative Foundations of Consciousness?

Contributing to debates within the philosophy of mind about the status of qualia or raw feels, Searle (1992), in contrast with eliminativist physicalists such as Dennett (1991, 1997), suggests that raw feels are real but irreducibly subjective. Insofar as qualia thus have a "first-person ontology," we cannot inspect them in the way we can inspect objects in the world. In this final section, I discuss how narrative's essential concern with experiencing consciousnesses might bear on these issues. More generally, underscoring an emphasis of this book as a whole, I stress how coming to terms with the basic elements of narrative will require a synthesis of ideas and methods from multiple disciplines – not just the philosophy of mind, but psychology, linguistics, ethnography, and other fields across the arts and sciences.

Significantly, many of the arguments about qualia in the philosophy of mind are couched in the form of stories or story-like thought experiments. Thus Jackson's (1982) "knowledge argument" centers around Mary, the neuroscientist, who encounters a qualitative difference between what she knows through her study of the physiology of brains experiencing color, on the one hand, and, on the other, the subjective, phenomenological knowledge of color that she herself acquires when she is finally let out of her windowless, colorless laboratory. Meanwhile, Chalmers (1996) uses an imagined race of zombies (humanoid beings exactly like us except that they have no conscious experiences) to argue against both strict physicalist and functionalist critiques of the concept of qualia (cf. Kirk 2003). Zombies hard-wired just like us but lacking raw feels, neuroscientists without a life beyond the lab: in these contexts, storytelling constitutes not just a repository of qualia, but furthermore a resource for exploring their nature and functions. The broader issue is whether, not just in the domain of philosophical argumentation but also in people's everyday engagement with the world, narrative affords scaffolding for consciousness itself. In other words, what are the grounds for making the strong claim that narrative not only represents what it is like for experiencing minds to live through events in storyworlds, but furthermore constitutes a basis for having – for knowing – a mind at all, whether it is one's own or another's?

Relevant here is Searle's emphasis on what he terms the first-person ontology of conscious mental states: "[c]onscious mental states and processes have a special feature not processed by other natural phenomena, namely, subjectivity. . . . in consequence of its subjectivity, [an experienced] pain is not equally accessible to any observer. Its existence, we might say, is a first-person existence" (1992: 94) In other words, "the ontology of the mental is an irreducibly first-person ontology," and "the real world . . . contains an ineliminably subjective element" (1992: 95). Searle goes on to write:

> If I try to observe the consciousness of another, what I observe is not his subjectivity but simply his conscious behavior, his structure, and the causal relations between structure and behavior. . . . the standard model of observation simply doesn't work for conscious subjectivity. It doesn't work for other people's consciousness, and it doesn't work for one's own. For that reason, the idea that there might be a special method of investigating consciousness, namely "introspection," which is supposed to be a kind of inner observation, was doomed to failure from the start, and it is not surprising that introspective psychology proved bankrupt. (1992: 97)

The problem here, as Searle notes, is that there is "no way for us to picture subjectivity as part of our world view because, so to speak, the subjectivity in question is the picturing" (1992: 98). What these formulations suggest is that there is no way to step outside consciousness and observe it as it really is, since consciousness simply *is* the (act or process of) observing, i.e., the qualia associated with observing or experiencing the world from a particular, irreducibly subjective or first-person vantage-point. Two further implications follow from these claims. First, I cannot observe the raw feels bound up with my own observational acts; strictly speaking, therefore, (my) consciousness cannot be represented but only experienced. Conscious states are not inner, mental objects that I can inspect in the same way I inspect other kinds of objects like stones, adjustable wrenches, or contact lenses; instead, they are structures of experience, or rather ways of experiencing.[7] Second, not only is my relation to my own consciousness necessarily mediated because of its subjective profile, but, further, I would seem to be cut off – absolutely, ontologically – from the consciousness of another. I can experience, though not observe or inspect, only my own raw feels; by contrast, I have no access to the qualia (uniquely) associated with a different first-person vantage-point, another mind.

How does narrative connect up with this constellation of issues – with the first-person ontology of consciousness, and its bearing on questions about knowing or accessing one's own or others' minds? For his part, Strawson (2004) criticizes what he sees as an overextension of narrative as a paradigm for inquiry (or explanatory scheme) by theorists such as Bruner (1987, 1990), MacIntyre (1984), Ricoeur (1990), Schechtman (1997), and Taylor (1989). Strawson critiques both what he characterizes as the psychological narrativity thesis, which holds that the self is narratively structured, and what he terms the ethical narrativity thesis, which states "that experiencing or conceiving one's life as a narrative is a good thing; a richly Narrative outlook is essential to a well-lived life" (2004: 428). Strawson draws a distinction between types of people he calls Diachronics and Episodics, and argues that the tendency to narrativize one's experiences displayed by some Diachronics is just that – a tendency that must be situated within a range of non-pathological human tendencies only some of which involve chaining together experiences into a time-line that stretches back into the past and extends forward into the future. Aligning himself squarely with the Episodics, Strawson notes his own lack of concern with temporally remote events:

> it's clear to me that events in my remoter past didn't happen to me* [where the asterisk denotes "that which I now experience myself to be when I'm apprehending myself specifically as an inner mental presence or self" (p. 433)]. But what does this amount to? It certainly doesn't mean that I don't have any autobiographical memories of these past experiences. I do. Nor does it mean that my autobiographical memories don't have what philosophers call a "from-the-inside" character. Some of them do. And they are certainly the experiences of the human being that I am. It does not, however, follow from this that I experience them as having happened to me*, or indeed that they did happen to me*. They certainly do not present as things that happened to me*, and I think I'm strictly, literally correct in thinking that they did not happen to me*. . . . the from-the-inside character of a memory can detach completely from any sense that one is the subject of the remembered experience. (Strawson 2004: 433–4)

In this account, however, Strawson's chief concern is with (models of) the constitution of the self over time. It is a different question whether, at any given stage in the history of the self's engagement with the world, narrative affords a basis for the conscious experiences that the self (the I* in Strawson's terms) takes itself to be having. Likewise, to what extent do human beings rely on narrative to make sense of the ongoing experiences, the conscious mental states, of others – such that those experiences can be factored into their own understanding of the way the world is and how they should orient themselves to it?

Here it is worth emphasizing the similarity of structure or isomorphism between the temporally and perspectivally situated nature of
raw feels, on the one hand, and narrative as a resource for worldmaking,
on the other hand. Stories, thanks to the way they are anchored in a
particular vantage-point on the storyworlds that they evoke, and
thanks to their essentially durative or temporally extended profile, do
not merely convey semantic content but furthermore encode in their
very structure a way of experiencing events. To put the same point in
other terms, narrative, unlike other modes of representation such as
deductive arguments, stress equations, or the periodic table of the elements, is uniquely suited to capturing what the world is like from the
situated perspective of an experiencing mind. In turn, the isomorphism
between the structure of narrative and the structure of consciousness
may suggest a way beyond the paradox identified by Searle. Narrative,
as an extensive and longstanding body of narratological research suggests, does concern itself with representing the consciousness of characters (see, among others, Cohn 1978; Fludernik 1993; Herman 2007c;
Leech and Short [1981] 2007: 150–67, 255–81; Palmer 2004; Toolan [1988]
2001: 119–42; Zunshine 2006). But more than just representing minds,
stories emulate through their temporal and perspectival configuration
the what-it's-like dimension of conscious awareness itself. As Searle
notes, consciousness cannot be pictured but is rather the process of
picturing itself. But to this claim we can add another: narrative affords
a discourse environment optimally suited for the world-picturing process, since that environment shares crucial elements of structure with
raw feels. Hence stories point beyond what might be called the closure
of consciousness, that is, the impossibility of inspecting the very mech-
anisms by which inspection, as such, is made possible. Enacting and
not just representing ways of experiencing – the what-it's-like dimension of an encounter with a supernatural being, a difficult transition
from adolescence to adulthood, or a painful conversational exchange
that points up the willful obtuseness of a selfish and manipulative
romantic partner – stories capture and sustain our interest because
of how their structure maps on to the mind's own engagement with
the world.

The foregoing remarks suggest that, given the first-person ontology
of conscious mental states, narrative bears crucially on one's relation
with one's own as well as others' minds. For one thing, the having of
raw feels unfolds as a world-picturing process with which stories are

isomorphic. The link between how narratives are structured and the phenomenology of conscious awareness points to an indissoluble nexus between narrative and mind – irrespective of whether the constitution of the self over time entails a process of narrativization, whereby temporally remote experiences can be connected together to form a story-line stretching between me* (in Strawson's sense) and all that has affected me in the past or will affect me in the future. Furthermore, this same link between storytelling and consciousness goes to the heart of the problem of other minds. Thus, building on and refining Bruner's (1990) ideas, Hutto (2006a, 2007, 2008; cf. Gallagher 2006) has proposed what he terms the "Narrative Practice Hypothesis," according to which interpreting and producing narratives is the means by which humans "become skilled at the practice of predicting, explaining and explicating actions by appeal to reasons of the sort that minimally have belief/desire pairings at their core" (2007: 44). Accordingly, whenever a person's actions call for an explanation, it takes a "folk psychological narrative" to construct an account based on that person's belief-set, contextual circumstances, and assumed desires given his or her beliefs and the circumstances in question (2007: 45; cf. Herman 2003a).

Further, Hutto hypothesizes that it is through childhood engagement with narratives built around such belief-desire schemata that humans learn the forms and norms of folk psychology, or people's everyday understanding of how thinking works, the rough-and-ready heuristics to which they resort in thinking about thinking itself. We use these heuristics to impute intentions and plans to others, to evaluate the bases of our own conduct, to make predictions about future reactions to events, and to draw correlations between situations and occurrences and the raw feels associated with them. Developmentally, Hutto suggests, children acquire the ability to use such heuristics

> by engaging in story-telling practices, with the support of others [e.g., parents, older siblings, etc.]. The stories about those who act for reasons – i.e., folk psychological narratives – are the foci of this practice. . . . By participating in this kind of narrative practice children become familiar with the way the core propositional attitudes, minimally belief and desire, behave with respect to each other and their familiar partners: emotions, perceptions, etc. (Hutto 2007: 53; cf. Hutto 2008)

To extrapolate from Hutto's account, which focuses specifically on how folk-psychological narratives allow beliefs (what does X believe?)

and desires (what does X want?) to be paired together in ways that account for people's actions: narrative can be viewed as the fundamental resource used to construct explanations of others' behavior in terms of assumptions or hypotheses about their minds.[8]

Such explanations take the form of provisional, tentative ascriptions to others of motivations, beliefs, goals, and other mental states, including the what-it's-like dimension of experiencing the taste of a freshly sliced tomato, the sight of a dramatic sunset, or the pain of a twisted ankle. And in parallel with ideas discussed in my previous subsection, narrative allows for critical and reflexive engagement with competing accounts based on different strategies for ascription. Just as stories, and stories alone, afford an environment in which versions of what it was like to experience situations and events can be comparatively evaluated, likewise narrative provides a discourse context in which different accounts of someone's mind can be proposed, tested against other versions, and modified or abandoned as necessary – based on the goodness-of-fit between the ascribed mental states and the whole pattern of the person's experiences, conduct, and demeanor. Monica, for example, embeds Renee's grandmother's folk-psychological narrative within her own narration, thereby stigmatizing it as one that misconstrues her and Renee's minds. Likewise, in sequence B from *Ghost World*, Clowes uses the resources of multimodal narration to juxtapose Rebecca's and Enid's accounts of the mental states and dispositions that explain Enid's conduct and demeanor toward men – with Rebecca ascribing to Enid a generalized contempt for men based on excessively high standards, and Enid responding by mentioning a counterexample and then angrily ascribing to Rebecca a counter-model of her (Rebecca's) mind as too accepting, insufficiently discerning when it comes to potential romantic partners.

Which come first: the experiences-in-worlds that give rise to stories or the storytelling processes by which worlds are made? The present subsection is designed to provoke further discussion about rather than settle once and for all such deep questions concerning the nexus of narrative and mind. At the very least, my hope is that my remarks here – like this book as a whole – will convince readers of the need to engage further with these and other questions that are crucially important for narrative inquiry. In addition, through the interdisciplinary approach outlined in this and my other chapters, I hope to have demonstrated that no one area of study can come to terms with the multidimensional complexity of stories and storytelling. In developing my account of basic elements of narrative, one of my overarching aims has thus been to foster more dialogue about stories among people who, from all academic fields and indeed all walks of life, create, engage with, and analyze narrative in its many guises, from everyday storytelling in face-to-face interaction, to oral history and autobiography, to films, graphic novels, and narratives associated with digital environments, to the multitude of stories found in the world's narrative literature. Further dialogue of this kind is a prerequisite for taking the measure of stories not just as a means of artistic expression or a resource for communication but also a fundamental human endowment.

Appendix

Literary Narrative: Ernest Hemingway's "Hills Like White Elephants" (1927)

Synopsis of the Narrative

Hemingway's brief story – it has fewer than 1,500 words – focuses on a conversation between an unnamed male character and Jig, the woman who has been impregnated by the male character (one can assume). The story is set on a hot day at a train station in Spain, in a valley through which the Ebro river flows. As they wait for the train to Madrid, the two characters briefly discuss the appearance of the landscape surrounding them (specifically, Jig mentions that the hills across the valley look like white elephants), then order drinks and engage in a sometimes tense conversational exchange about the possibility of Jig's having an abortion. When the story ends, with the characters expecting the train to arrive momentarily, it remains unclear what course of action they will pursue – although the closing lines perhaps suggest that Jig has acceded to the male character's suggestion that she get the abortion, or at least decided that any further discussion of the matter with him would be fruitless.

Page numbers inserted in brackets in the text correspond to those in Hemingway ([1927] 1987).

[p. 211] The hills across the valley of the Ebro were long and white. On this side there was no shade and no trees and the station was between two lines of rails in the sun. Close against the side of the station there was the warm shadow of the building and a curtain, made of strings of bamboo beads, hung across the open door into the bar, to keep out flies. The American and the girl with him sat at a table in the shade, outside the building. It was very hot and the express from Barcelona would come in forty minutes. It stopped at this junction for two minutes and went to Madrid.

"What should we drink?" the girl asked. She had taken off her hat and put it on the table.

"It's pretty hot," the man said.

"Let's drink beer."

"*Dos cervezas,*" the man said into the curtain.

"Big ones?" a woman asked from the doorway.

"Yes. Two big ones."

The woman brought two glasses of beer and two felt pads. She put the felt pads and the beer glass on the table and looked at the man and the girl. The girl was looking off at the line of hills. They were white in the sun and the country was brown and dry.

"They look like white elephants," she said.

"I've never seen one," the man drank his beer.

"No, you wouldn't have."

"I might have," the man said. "Just because you say I wouldn't have doesn't prove anything."

The girl looked at the bead curtain. "They've painted something on it," she said. "What does it say?"

"Anis del Toro. It's a drink."

"Could we try it?"

[p. 212] The man called "Listen" through the curtain. The woman came out from the bar.

"Four reales." "We want two Anis del Toro."

"With water?"

"Do you want it with water?"

"I don't know," the girl said. "Is it good with water?"

"It's all right."

"You want them with water?" asked the woman.

"Yes, with water."

"It tastes like liquorice" the girl said and put the glass down.

"That's the way with everything."

"Yes," said the girl. "Everything tastes of liquorice. Especially all the things you've waited so long for, like absinthe."

"Oh, cut it out."

"You started it" the girl said. "I was being amused. I was having a fine time."

"Well, let's try and have a fine time."

"All right. I was trying. I said the mountains looked like white elephants. Wasn't that bright?"

"That was bright."

"I wanted to try this new drink. That's all we do, isn't it – look at things and try new drinks?"

"I guess so."

The girl looked across at the hills.

"They're lovely hills," she said. "They don't really look like white elephants. I just meant the coloring of their skin through the trees."

"Should we have another drink?"

"All right."

The warm wind blew the bead curtain against the table.

"The beer's nice and cool," the man said.

"It's lovely," the girl said.

"It's really an awfully simple operation, Jig," the man said. "It's not really an operation at all."

The girl looked at the ground the table legs rested on.

"I know you wouldn't mind it, Jig. It's really not anything. It's just to let the air in."

The girl did not say anything.

"I'll go with you and I'll stay with you all the time. They just let the air in and then it's all perfectly natural."

"Then what will we do afterwards?"

"We'll be fine afterwards. Just like we were before."

"What makes you think so?"

"That's the only thing that bothers us. It's the only thing that's made us unhappy."

[p. 213] The girl looked at the bead curtain, put her hand out and took hold of two of the strings of beads.

"And you think then we'll be all right and be happy."

"I know we will. You don't have to be afraid. I've known lots of people that have done it."

"So have I," said the girl. "And afterwards they were all so happy."

"Well," the man said, "if you don't want to you don't have to. I wouldn't have you do it if you didn't want to. But I know it's perfectly simple."

"And you really want to?"

"I think it's the best thing to do. But I don't want you to do it if you don't really want to."

"And if I do it you'll be happy and things will be like they were and you'll love me?"

"I love you now. You know I love you."

"I know. But if I do it, then it will be nice again if I say things are like white elephants, and you'll like it?"

"I'll love it. I love it now but I just can't think about it. You know how I get when I worry."

"If I do it you won't ever worry?"

"I won't worry about that because it's perfectly simple."

"Then I'll do it. Because I don't care about me."

"What do you mean?"

"I don't care about me."

"Well, I care about you."

"Oh, yes. But I don't care about me. And I'll do it and then everything will be fine."

"I don't want you to do it if you feel that way."

The girl stood up and walked to the end of the station. Across, on the other side, were fields of grain and trees along the banks of the Ebro. Far away, beyond the river, were mountains. The shadow of a cloud moved across the field of grain and she saw the river through the trees.

"And we could have all this," she said. "And we could have everything and every day we make it more impossible."

"What did you say?"

"I said we could have everything."

"We can have everything."

"No, we can't."

"We can have the whole world."

"No, we can't."

"We can go everywhere."

"No, we can't. It isn't ours any more."

"It's ours."

"No, it isn't. And once they take it away, you never get it back."

"But they haven't taken it away."

"We'll wait and see."

[p. 214] "Come on back in the shade," he said. "You mustn't feel that way."

"I don't feel any way," the girl said. "I just know things."

"I don't want you to do anything that you don't want to do –"

"Nor that isn't good for me," she said. "I know. Could we have another beer?"

"All right. But you've got to realize –"

"I realize," the girl said. "Can't we maybe stop talking?"

They sat down at the table and the girl looked across at the hills on the dry side of the valley and the man looked at her and at the table.

"You've got to realize," he said, "that I don't want you to do it if you don't want to. I'm perfectly willing to go through with it if it means anything to you."

"Doesn't it mean anything to you? We could get along."

"Of course it does. But I don't want anybody but you. I don't want anyone else. And I know it's perfectly simple."

"Yes, you know it's perfectly simple."

"It's all right for you to say that, but I do know it."

"Would you do something for me now?"

"I'd do anything for you."

"Would you please please please please please please please stop talking?"

He did not say anything but looked at the bags against the wall of the station. There were labels on them from all the hotels where they had spent nights.

"But I don't want you to," he said, "I don't care anything about it."

"I'll scream," the girl said.

The woman came out through the curtains with two glasses of beer and put them down on the damp felt pads. "The train comes in five minutes," she said.

"What did she say?" asked the girl.

"That the train is coming in five minutes."

The girl smiled brightly at the woman, to thank her.

"I'd better take the bags over to the other side of the station," the man said. She smiled at him.

"All right. Then come back and we'll finish the beer."

He picked up the two heavy bags and carried them around the station to the other tracks. He looked up the tracks but could not see the train. Coming back, he walked through the bar-room, where people waiting for the train were drinking. He drank an Anis at the bar and looked at the people. They were all waiting reasonably for the train.

He went out through the bead curtain. She was sitting at the table and smiled at him.

"Do you feel better?" he asked.

"I feel fine," she said. "There's nothing wrong with me. I feel fine."

Narrative Told during Face-to-Face Communication: *UFO or the Devil* (2002)

Synopsis of the Narrative

This story, which I've titled *UFO or the Devil*, was told by Monica, a pseudonym for a 41-year-old African American female, to two white female fieldworkers in their mid-twenties engaged in a research project on the dialects spoken in western North Carolina.

The narrative was recorded on July 2, 2002, in Texana, North Carolina, near where the events recounted are purported to have occurred (see Figures 1 and 2 below for maps).[1] Below I provide both a sketch of Texana and a transcript of the narrative, but it should be noted at the outset that the interview during which Monica told this story was not a structured, sociolinguistic interview per se. Rather, the fieldworkers happened to encounter Monica while visiting her sister, whom they had already interviewed on several occasions. After establishing a rapport with Monica, they then retrieved their recording equipment from their car and continued what had become by that point a relatively informal conversational interaction.

The fieldworkers initially prompted Monica with questions about her family background and her experiences in places she had lived, but once the interaction got underway it was largely Monica who directed the flow of the discourse, apart from a few follow-up questions by her interlocutors. Thus the story that I have titled *UFO or the Devil* (based on a phrase used by Monica in the first line) was told as part of a larger sequence of narratives through which Monica cumulatively presents a portrait of herself.[2] In this self-portrait, Monica emerges as someone who was profoundly shaped by experiences in her family and community settings; who has explored multiple educational and career options, while living in several urban centers in addition to the more rural environs of Texana; and who is now in a position to look back at these formative experiences and gauge their impact on her current

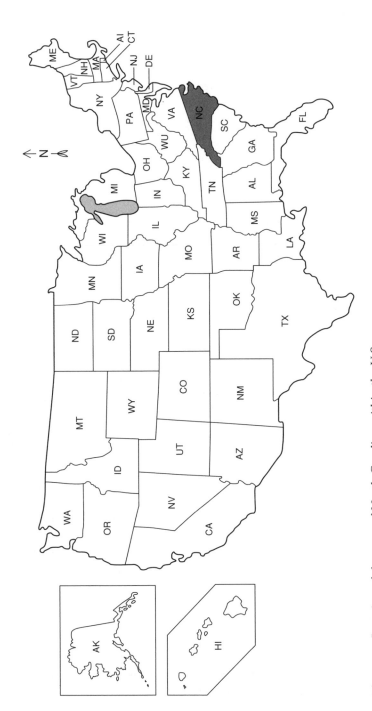

Figure 1 Location of the state of North Carolina within the U.S. Mapping software provided courtesy of John Adamson, Management Information Specialist, Texas AgriLife Extension, Texas A&M University System. <http://monarch.tamu.edu/~maps2/>.

Figure 2   Location of Cherokee County within North Carolina
Mapping software provided courtesy of John Adamson, Management
Information Specialist, Texas AgriLife Extension, Texas A&M University
System. <http://monarch.tamu.edu/~maps2/>.

sense of self. As the transcript reveals, the narrative that I have excerpted
from this much more extended interaction (the total duration of the
tape-recording is more than 145 minutes) concerns not only Monica's
and her friend's encounter with what Monica characterizes as a supernatural apparition – a big, glowing orange ball that rises up in the air
and pursues them menacingly – but also Monica's and Renee's subsequent encounter with Renee's grandmother, who disputes whether
the girls' experience with the big ball really occurred.

Background on Texana

Located in Cherokee County, which is otherwise nearly totally white,[3]
Texana is a community consisting almost exclusively of African Amer-
icans; indeed, with about 150 residents, only 10 of whom are white,

Texana is the largest black Applachian community in western North Carolina (Mallinson 2006: 69, 78). It is situated about one mile from Murphy, North Carolina, as well as other small white communities, and interactions among residents of Texana and these neighboring communities are sometimes tense (Mallinson 2006: 78). Indeed, as Mallinson discusses (2006: 71–6; cf. Mallinson 2008), the ethnic profile of members of the Texana community is considerably more complicated than this initial characterization would suggest. As Mallinson notes, "Texana residents are descendants of African, Cherokee, Ulster Scots-Irish, and Irish-European ancestors – which is the case for many black Appalachians, particularly those whose ancestors were slaves" (2006: 71). In consequence, feeling that the ethnic categories listed on questionnaires and surveys are unable to capture their complex heritage, most Texanans self-identify as black, since this designation refers to skin color rather than a pariticular ethnic or racial background (2006: 75).

The complex ethnic situation in Texana bears importantly on the way Monica uses her narrative to position herself and others – to invoke a concept that I discuss more fully in chapter 3 of this book. From the start of her narrative, Monica indexes herself as a member of the enclave African American (or at least non-white) community based in Texana and positioned contrastively against the surrounding, predominantly white population of Cherokee County. (As my discussion in chapter 3 suggests, this formulation captures only part of the positioning logic at work in the narrative.) Prior to the time of the interview, Monica had written features for a local newspaper during black history month, and she had also spoken openly about how racism and sexism had prevented her from advancing in the medical field despite her completion of a training course for emergency medical technicians (Mallinson 2006: 89, 97). More generally, as Mallinson remarked in a personal communication, "From what I learned about [Monica], race is very salient to her . . . she told us a lot of stories about gender/racial prejudice that she faced in her life, how racist Cherokee County is, how she felt growing up in Texana and what happened after she moved to Dayton, Atlanta, etc."

In the following transcript, I have segmented the narrative into numbered clauses for the purposes of analysis; I have also listed the transcription conventions used to annotate the story. Further, readers can access a sound file containing a recording of Monica's story at the following URL: <http://www.ohiostatepress.org/journals/narrative/

herman-audio.htm>. Indeed, given the importance of prosody in Monica's narrative, readers may wish to wish to consult this online resource as they assess my subsequent analysis rather than rely solely on my own attempt to capture relevant prosodic details in the transcript.

Transcription Conventions

*Adapted from Jefferson 1984; Ochs et al. 1992; Schegloff, "Transcription" [n.d];
and Tannen 1993.*

... { }	represents a measurable pause, more than 0.1 seconds; approximate durations given in curved brackets (... {.3} = a pause lasting 0.3 seconds)
..	represents a slight break in timing
-	a hyphen after a word or part of a word indicates a self-interruption or "restart" by the current speaker
*	indicates a rising intonational contour, not necessarily a question
.	indicates a falling, or final, intonation contour, not necessarily the end of a sentence
,	indicates "continuing" intonation ("more to come"), not necessarily the end of a clause
:	indicates the prolongation of a sound just preceding it; more than one colon indicates a sound of even longer duration
_	underlining indicates stress or emphasis, either through increased loudness or heightened pitch. UPPER CASE letters indicate extremely loud talk, and <u>UNDERLINING</u> is added for even louder speech productions
° °	Two degree signs indicate that the talk between them is noticeably quieter than the surrounding discourse
↑ ↓	The up and down arrows mark rises and and falls of pitch; up arrows indicate sharper rises in pitch than those marked with underlining in stressed or emphasized words
(↘)	indicates downward change of pitch within the boundaries of a word; inserted before the syllable in which the change occurs
(↗)	indicates upward change of pitch within the boundaries of a word; inserted before the syllable in which the change occurs

> <   indicate that the talk between these symbols is compressed or
      rushed relative to the surrounding discourse
< >   indicate that the talk between these symbols is markedly slower
      than the surrounding discourse
[indicates overlap between different speakers' utterances
=   indicates an utterance continued across another speaker's over-
      lapping utterance
/ /   enclose transcriptions that are not certain
( )   enclose nonverbal forms of expression, e.g. laughter unaccom-
      panied by words
[....] in short extracts indicates omitted lines

MONICA:	(1)	So that's why I say..UFO or the devil got after our <u>black</u> <u>asses</u>,
	(2)	for showing out.
	(3)	> I don't know what was <
	(4)	but we walkin up the <u>hill</u>,
	(5)	<u>this</u> ↑<u>way</u>, comin up through here.
INTERVIEWER 1:	(6)	Yeah.
MONICA:	(7)	And..I'm like on <u>this</u> side and Renee's right here.
	(8)	And we <u>walkin</u>
	(9)	and I look over the <u>bank</u>* ... {.2}
	(10)	and I see this ... {.3} < <u>BI:G</u> <u>BALL</u> >.
	(11)	It's <u>glowin</u>, ... {.2}
	(12)	and it's <u>orange</u>. ... {.3}
	(13)	And I'm just like ... {1.0}
	(14)	°"nah..you know just-° nah it ain't <u>nothin</u>" you know.
	(15)	And I'm still <u>walkin</u> you know*
	(16)	Then I look back over my side ag<u>ain</u>,
	(17)	and it has °<u>risen</u> <u>up</u>*° ... {2.0}
	(18)	And I'm like "(↗)SHI::T." ... {.5} you know.
	(19)	So but <u>Re(↗)nee</u>- I still ain't say nothin to her
	(20)	and I'm not sure she see it or <u>not</u>, ... {.2}
	(21)	so I'm still not <u>sayin</u> anything
	(22)	we just °<u>walkin</u>.° ... {1.0}
	(23)	Then I look over the bank <u>again</u>
	(24)	and I don't <u>see</u> it,

(25)   and then I'm like °"well, you know."° ... {.3}

(26)   But <u>then</u> ... {.2}for some reason I feel some heat
        > or somethin other <

(27)   and I < <u>look</u> <u>back</u> >

(28)   me and Renee did at the same time

(29)   it's right <u>behind</u> us. ... {1.0}

(30)   We like- ... {.2} /we were scared and-/..

(31)   "<u>AAAHHH</u>" you know=

                                              [

INTERVIEWER 2:   (32)   (laughs)

MONICA: (33)   > =at the same time. <

(34)   So we take off <u>runnin</u> as <u>fast</u> as we can,

(35)   and we still lookin <u>back</u>

(36)   and every time we look back it's with us. ... {.5}

(37)   It's just a-<u>bouncin</u> behind /us/

(38)   it's <u>no:t</u>.. > touchin the <u>ground</u>, <

(39)   it's bouncin in the <u>air</u>. ... {.5}

(40)   °Just like this ... {.2} behind us°

(41)   as we <u>run</u>. ... {1.0}

(42)   We run <u>all</u> the way to her grandmother's

(43)   and we <u>open</u> the door

(44)   and we just fall out in the floor,

(45)   and we're cryin and we scre:amin

(46)   and < we just can't <u>breathe</u>. > ... {.3}

(47)   We that <u>scared</u>..

(48)   "What's <u>wrong</u> with you all" you know

(49)   and   we   <u>tell</u>   them..you   know..what   had
        <u>happened</u>.

(50)   And then her grandmother tell us

(51)   it's some ↓ <u>mineral</u>.. this or ↓ <u>that</u>

(52)   they just form

(53)   bah bah ↓ <u>bah</u> ↓ <u>bah</u>

(54)   and ... {.3} the way we ↓ <u>ran</u>..it's the ↓ <u>heat</u>

(55)   and..you know ... {.3}Bull(↘)shit.

(56)   You know..but so I never knew in my LIFE ...
        {.2} ab<u>out</u> that

(57)   but we didn't <u>do</u> that anymore. ... {1.0}

INTERVIEWER 1:   (58)   Right.

MONICA: (59)   When dark goddamn came

(60)   our ass was at <u>home</u>.

Excerpted Panels from *Ghost World* (1997),
a Graphic Novel by Daniel Clowes

Synopsis of the Narrative

Focusing on two teenage girls trying to navigate the transition from high-school to post-high-school life, *Ghost World* stands out contrastively against the backdrop afforded by the tradition of superhero comics, for example. Far from possessing superhuman powers, Enid Coleslaw[4] and Rebecca Doppelmeyer struggle with familial and romantic relationships, resist the stereotypes their peers try to impose on them, and are bought face to face, on more than one occasion, with the fragility and tenuousness of their own friendship. In this way, closer in spirit to the female *Bildungsroman* than to action-adventure narratives, *Ghost World*, which was originally published as installments in the underground comics tradition and subsequently assembled into a novel, overlays a graphic format on content that helped extend the scope and range of comics storytelling generally: the acquisition of gendered identities, the aftermath of fractured families, the attempt to find a path to adulthood that is not tantamount to conformism, and so on.

The novel as a whole traces events leading up to the divergent life-courses of the two main characters, caused in part by Rebecca's willingness to accommodate to dominant social scripts versus Enid's resistance to those same scripts. Zwigoff's film adaptation of the novel accentuates even more the increasingly divergent paths of the main characters. In the movie, Rebecca nags Enid to get a job so that they can get an apartment together and, in a moment suggesting incipient conformism on Rebecca's part, expresses particular admiration for a fold-out ironing board built into the wall of the apartment that she has leased.

Ghost World also examines more or less entrenched cultural expectations about male versus female roles – interrogated for example in the scene in which Enid and Josh (Enid and Seymour in the film version) visit an adult bookstore/sex toy shop and Enid openly mocks what is on offer there. Relatedly, the novel explores Enid's and Rebecca's difficulty in finding suitable or even tolerable romantic partners, the focus of Sequence B below. In Zwigoff's 2001 film version, this difficulty helps explain why Enid gravitates toward Seymour, a character more than twice her age but similarly suspicious of dominant social norms and values – at least for most of the film.

Sequence A

Sequence B

Sequences C and D.   These two sequences are part of the same chapter of *Ghost World* but are separated by intervening material not reproduced here.

Sequences C and D   *(cont'd)*

Screenshots from Terry Zwigoff's Film
Adaptation of *Ghost World* (2001)

Screenshot 1 Just after Rebecca has said that the "blond guy . . . like gives me a total boner," and Enid responds, "He's like the biggest idiot of all time," the person in question walks by and says "You guys up for some Reggae tonight?" Enid then points her thumb in his direction and gives Rebecca a "told-you-so" look.

Screenshot 2 At the bar where Seymour, frustrated that he can't hear the blues musician whose playing he came to see, says, "I can't believe these people. They could at least turn off their stupid sports game till he's done playing." In the middle background is the woman with whom Enid tries to fix Seymour up, but who seems as put off by Seymour's lecture on ragtime versus blues as he is by her comment that the band Blues Hammer (see Screenshot 7) plays "authentic blues" and is "so great."

Screenshot 3 The blues artist whose performance Seymour and Enid come to the bar to hear.

Screenshot 4 One of the patrons in the bar where Seymour complains about the "sports game" and the noise level that prevents him from hearing the blues guitarist who he hopes will autograph a rare copy of one of his albums.

Screenshot 5 Another patron in the bar. As Enid sizes up her surroundings, her glance falls on this person, who burps ostentatiously after taking a drink from his beer, as well as another male patron who stares lewdly at the waitress after he has tipped her, and a third in sunglasses that give him a somewhat menacing appearance (see Screenshot 6). Then Enid looks at Seymour sitting at the table with the female patron with whom he proves to have nothing in common.

Screenshot 6 Two other male patrons on whom Enid's gaze falls as she takes stock of the men near her in the bar. (The waitress, having served beer to the patron on the right, moves away toward the camera in the foreground.)

Screenshot 7 The band Blues Hammer begins its first set, the lead singer/lead guitarist having started by shouting out over the microphone: "Alright, people. Are you ready to boogie? 'Cause we gonna play some authentic way down in the Delta blues. Get ready to rock your world!"

Glossary

The following is a glossary of key terms for narrative study. If a term is set in SMALL CAPS within a definition, that term (or a cognate) has its own glossary entry. Further, readers should consult the index for pointers to discussions (elsewhere in the volume) of terms not listed here.

Glossary definitions that refer to "the Labovian model" allude to the research on storytelling in face-to-face interaction (more specifically, interview situations) that was pioneered by Labov and Waletzky (1967) and further developed in later work by Labov (1972) and many other narrative scholars. See chapters 1 and 2 of this book (and also Bamberg 1997a) for further discussion of the possibilities and limitations of this approach to narrative analysis.

For additional information about the keywords included in this glossary as well as other relevant terms and concepts, readers are encouraged to consult other recently published guides to the field. The following works provide foundations for further study:

Abbott, H. P. ([2002] 2008). *The Cambridge Introduction to Narrative*. 2nd edn. Cambridge: Cambridge University Press.
Herman, D. (ed.) (2007). *The Cambridge Companion to Narrative*. Cambridge: Cambridge University Press.
Herman, D., M. Jahn, and M.-L. Ryan (eds.) (2005). *Routledge Encyclopedia of Narrative Theory*. London: Routledge.
Herman, L., and B. Vervaeck (2005). *Handbook of Narrative Analysis*. Lincoln: University of Nebraska Press.
Jahn, M. (2005). *Narratology: A Guide to the Theory of Narrative* <http://www.uni-koeln.de/~ame02/pppn.htm>.
Keen, S. (2004). *Narrative Form*. London: Palgrave Macmillan.
Leech, G., and M. Short ([1981] 2007). *Style in Fiction: A Linguistic Introduction to English Fictional Prose*. 2nd edn. Harlow: Pearson/Longman.

Lothe, J. (2000). *Narrative in Fiction and Film: An Introduction.* Oxford: Oxford University Press.

Phelan, J., and P. J. Rabinowitz (eds.) (2005). *A Companion to Narrative Theory.* Oxford: Blackwell.

Prince, G. ([1987] 2003). *A Dictionary of Narratology.* 2nd edn. Lincoln: University of Nebraska Press.

Riessman, C. K. (1993). *Narrative Analysis.* Thousand Oaks, CA: Sage.

Riessman, C. K. (2007). *Narrative Methods for the Human Sciences.* Thousand Oaks, CA: Sage.

Rimmon-Kenan, S. ([1983] 2002). *Narrative Fiction: Contemporary Poetics.* 2nd edn. London: Routledge.

Ryan, M.-L. (ed.) (2004). *Narrative across Media: The Languages of Storytelling.* Lincoln: University of Nebraska Press.

Scholes, R., J. Phelan, and R. Kellogg (2006). "Narrative Theory, 1966–2006: A Narrative." In *The Nature of Narrative* (pp. 283–336). Oxford: Oxford University Press.

Toolan, M. ([1988] 2001). *Narrative: A Critical Linguistic Introduction.* 2nd edn. London: Routledge.

ABSTRACT   In the Labovian model, the abstract is a pre-announcement of the gist of a story about to be told, used to clear the floor for the more or less extended turn at talk required to convey the narrative.

ACTANT   A term used by structuralist NARRATOLOGISTS to designate general roles fulfilled by particularized actors or characters. One such role is Opponent, which is fulfilled by characters as diverse as the big ball in *UFO or the Devil* and the Devil himself in *Paradise Lost.*

ADDRESSEE. See AUDIENCE; PARTICIPATION FRAMEWORK

ADDRESSOR. See NARRATOR; PRODUCTION FORMAT

AGENCY   At the level of the STORY, agency concerns characters' ability to bring about deliberately initiated EVENTS, or actions, within a STORYWORLD. But agency is also a pertinent concern at the level of storytelling or NARRATION, affecting who gets to tell what kind of story in what contexts. FEMINIST NARRATOLOGY explores differences in the sorts of agency available to male versus female characters and NARRATORS.

ANACHRONY   Nonchronological NARRATION, where EVENTS are told in an ORDER other than that in which they can be presumed to have occurred in the STORYWORLD.

ANALEPSIS   The equivalent of a flashback in film. Analepsis occurs when EVENTS that occur in the ORDER ABC are told in the order BCA or BAC.

AUDIENCE   As discussed in chapter 3, in the narrative communication model developed by structuralist NARRATOLOGISTS and refined by rhetorical theorists of narrative, the audience can be defined as real or imagined addressees of (multi-layered) acts of NARRATION. This model distinguishes among actual authors, IMPLIED AUTHORS, and NARRATORS on the production side of the storytelling process, and, on the interpretation side, the corresponding roles of actual readers, (types of) IMPLIED READERS, and NARRATEES (the audience implicitly or explicitly addressed by the narrator in the text). In this account of how narrative communication takes place, an implied author might communicate something to an implied reader by having a narrator tell a particular kind of story in a particular way to a specific narratee – as in *Ghost World* when, during a late-night phone call with Rebecca, Enid engages in UNRELIABLE NARRATION and misreports what she actually told Naomi on an earlier occasion (see the discussion in chapter 3).

AUTODIEGETIC NARRATION   First-person or HOMODIEGETIC narration in which the NARRATOR is also the main character in the STORYWORLD (as in *UFO or the Devil*).

BACKSTORY   A type of EXPOSITION often involving ANALEPSIS or flashback; a filling in of the circumstances and events that have led to the present moment in a STORYWORLD, and that illuminate the larger implications of actual or potential behaviors by characters occupying a particular narrative "now."

CHARACTER. See AGENCY; MIMESIS

CLASSICAL NARRATOLOGY. See POSTCLASSICAL NARRATOLOGY

CODA   In the Labovian model, the coda serves a "bridging" function at the end of a story told in face-to-face interaction, returning the focus of attention from the world of the story to the world of the here and now, in which the current discourse is unfolding.

COGNITIVE NARRATOLOGY   A strand within POSTCLASSICAL NARRATOLOGY that focuses on mind-relevant dimensions of storytelling practices, wherever – and by whatever means – those practices occur.

COMPLICATING ACTION   In the Labovian model, this is the interest-bearing element of the narrative, involving unexpected or non-canonical, and thus TELLABLE, situations and events.

CONFLICT   A state or process whose most general form can be captured in the following terms: an initial state of equilibrium in a STORYWORLD is upset by a more or less disruptive EVENT or chain of events. I argue in this book that NARRATIVE more or less explicitly foregrounds such unexpected, noncanonical events; however, storyworlds-in-flux need not involve conflict in the narrower sense – that is, in the sense of clashes among the beliefs, desires, and intentions of two or more characters in a narrative, or between dissonant aspects of a single character.

CONSCIOUSNESS REPRESENTATION   The representation of characters' (or narrators') minds in narrative discourse. Topics of study in this area include the structural possibilities for representing conscious experience – that is, the system of available mind-revealing techniques – as well as the evolution or emergence of such techniques over time, and the interconnections among those techniques and broader conceptions of mind circulating in the culture or in more specialized discourses. See also EXPERIENTIALITY; QUALIA

CONSONANT NARRATION   Dorrit Cohn's (1978) term for a mode of NARRATION in which a narrator's presentation of events in the storyworld merges with a character's vantage-point on those events. In the case of first-person or HOMODIEGETIC narration, Cohn refers to consonant self-narration. In the case of third-person or HETERODIEGETIC narration, consonant narration is the equivalent of what Stanzel calls the figural NARRATIVE SITUATION. In either case, it corresponds to what Genette terms internal FOCALIZATION. See also DISSONANT NARRATION

COUNTER NARRATIVES. See HEGEMONY

DEIXIS   Deictic terms like *I*, *here*, and *now* are expressions whose meaning changes depending on who is uttering them in what discourse context.

DESCRIPTION   A kind of text or discourse (i.e., a TEXT TYPE) core instances of which ascribe properties to situations, objects, and events, whether statically (as in *That cat is elegant*) or dynamically (as in *Tuesdays and Thursdays I eat cereal for breakfast and on other days I eat toast and jelly*).

DIALECT REPRESENTATION   The representation of a speech variety used by one or more characters in a narrative text; such speech representations can be used to position and identify characters within regional, class-based, ethnic, and gender-related coordinates, suggesting alterity or otherness.

DIEGESIS   In one sense, the term *diegesis* corresponds to what NARRATOLOGISTS call STORY; in this usage, it refers to the STORYWORLD evoked by the narrative text and inhabited by the characters. In a second usage, *diegesis* (along with cognate terms such as *diegetic*) refers to one pole on the continuum stretching between modes of speech presentation in narrative texts. In this second usage, techniques for presenting speech that are relatively diegetic are those in which a NARRATOR's mediation is evident, as in INDIRECT DISCOURSE. By contrast, modes that are relatively MIMETIC background the narrator's mediating role, as in DIRECT DISCOURSE or free direct discourse, where speech tags like *she said* are omitted to produce the sense of unfiltered access to characters' utterances.

DIRECT DISCOURSE   A technique for representing characters' speech. In DD, a NARRATOR reproduces a character's utterance in a manner that (one can assume) mirrors the way it was performed in the STORYWORLD.

DISCOURSE   In NARRATOLOGY, the "discourse" level of narrative (in French, *discours*) corresponds to what Russian Formalist theorists called the *sjuzhet*; it contrasts with the "STORY" (*histoire*) level. In this usage, *discourse* refers to the disposition of the SEMIOTIC cues used by interpreters to reconstruct a STORYWORLD.

DISSONANT NARRATION   Dorrit Cohn's (1978) term for a mode of NARRATION in which a narrator's presentation of events in the storyworld differs from a character's vantage-point on those events. In the case of first-person or HOMODIEGETIC narration, Cohn refers to dissonant self-narration. In the case of third-person or HETERODIEGETIC narration, dissonant narration is the equivalent of what Stanzel calls the authorial NARRATIVE SITUATION and what Genette calls zero FOCALIZATION. See also CONSONANT NARRATION

DURATION   The ratio between how long situations and events take to unfold in the STORYWORLD and how much text is devoted to their NARRATION. Variations in this ratio correspond to different narrative speeds; in order of increasing speed, these are PAUSE, STRETCH, SCENE, SUMMARY, and ELLIPSIS.

ELLIPSIS   The omission of STORYWORLD events during the process of NARRATION; in ellipsis, narrative speed reaches infinity.

EMPLOTMENT   The process by which situations and events are linked together to produce a PLOT. Arguably, the more overtly or reflexively a narrative emplots the events it recounts, and thereby draws attention to its status as a constructed artifact, the less immersed interpreters will be in the STORYWORLD evoked by the text. See also PLOT

EPISODE   A bounded, internally coherent sequence of situations and EVENTS that can be chained together with other such narrative units to form larger narrative structures.

EVALUATION   In the Labovian model, evaluation refers to the expressive resources used by storytellers to signal the point of a narrative, or why it is worth telling in the first place. Evaluation, in this sense, helps ward off the question that every storyteller dreads: "So what?"

EVENT   A change of state, creating a more or less salient and lasting alteration in the STORYWORLD. Events can be subdivided into temporally extended processes, deliberately initiated actions, and happenings not brought about intentionally by any AGENT.

EXPERIENCING-I   In retrospective first-person or HOMODIEGETIC (or AUTODIEGETIC) NARRATION, the younger self who lived through the experiences recounted by the older, NARRATING-I.

EXPERIENTIALITY   Term used by Fludernik to denote "the evocation of consciousness [in terms of] cognitive schema of embodiedness that relate to human existence and human concerns" (1996: 168). Chapter 6 of this study builds on Fludernik's work to highlight the impact of storyworld events on experiencing minds as a basic element of narrative – that is, as a critical property of NARRATIVE (or condition for NARRATIVITY). However, the chapter uses other terms (*the consciousness factor, qualia, what it's like, raw feels,* etc.) in part to avoid the inference that the other basic elements discussed in this book (**situatedness, event sequencing,** and **worldmaking/world disruption**) can be subordinated to **what it's like** as somehow less fundamental – as Fludernik's model prima facie implies (cf. Alber 2002).

EXPLANATION   A TEXT TYPE contrasted with those of NARRATIVE and DESCRIPTION in chapter 4. Different kinds of practices fall within the domain of explanation, including both qualitative explanations based on a single case study and quantitative explanations based on statistical analyses of the frequency with which a given phenomenon occurs. In the classical Covering Law Model of explanation developed in the philosophy of science, particular phenomena are explained when they can be characterized as instances of more general covering laws (e.g., water freezes at 0 degrees Celsius; substance X is water and it is below 0 degrees today; so that explains why substance X froze).

EXPOSITION   A presentation, sometimes given in the form of BACKSTORY, of the circumstances and EVENTS that form a context or background for understanding the main action in a narrative.

EXTRADIEGETIC NARRATOR   A NARRATOR who does not inhabit the STORYWORLD evoked by a narrative. Narrators can be extradiegetic-HOMODIEGETIC, like the older Pip who narrates his life experiences in Charles Dickens's *Great Expectations*, or extradiegetic-HETERODIEGETIC, like Hemingway's narrator in "Hills."

FEMINIST NARRATOLOGY   A strand of POSTCLASSICAL NARRATOLOGY that explores how issues of gender bear on the production and interpretation of stories.

FICTION   Positively, fiction can be defined as type of discourse or communicative practice in which participants are transported, through a more or less immersive experience, to a STORYWORLD assumed to be imaginary rather than actual. Negatively, fiction can be defined as a type of discourse or communicative practice for which questions of truth-value do not apply in the way that they do for factual discourse. Thus, whereas journalists and police detectives attempt to verify a witness's account of events by comparing the account with those given by other witnesses, it would be a category mistake to try to ascertain the truth status of the specific events represented in Charlotte Brontë's *Jane Eyre* (i.e., whether the events actually happened) by comparing the novel with newspaper articles or historical records originating from the same period. Likewise, a subsequent fictional text that rewrites the novel, such as Jean Rhys's *Wide Sargasso Sea*, cannot validate or invalidate Brontë's text, but rather constitutes another, autonomous, fiction.

FOCALIZATION   Genette's ([1972] 1980) term for modes of perspective taking in narrative discourse. In internal focalization, the viewpoint is restricted to a particular observer or REFLECTOR, whereas in zero focalization the viewpoint is not anchored in a localized position. Further, internal focalization can be fixed, variable, or multiple. In "Hills," the focalization is variable, shifting between the vantage-points of Jig and the male character.

FREE INDIRECT DISCOURSE   A technique for representing characters' speech. Couched as a report given by a NARRATOR, FID also contains expressivity markers (for example, DIALECT REPRESENTATIONS) that point to the speech patterns of a particular character.

FREQUENCY   The ratio between the number of times something is told and the number of times it can be assumed to have occurred in the STORYWORLD. In singulative NARRATION, there is a one-to-one match between how many times an EVENT occurred and how many times it is told; in iterative narration, something that happened more than once is told once; and in repetitive narration, the number of times something is told exceeds the frequency with which it occurred in the STORYWORLD.

GAPS   Lacunae or omissions in what is told or in the process of telling. Omissions in the telling constitute ELLIPSES; those in the told underscore the radical incompleteness of fictional worlds. (How many siblings did Captain Kirk of *Star Trek* have? In *The Incredible Hulk* comics, where was Bruce Banner's maternal grandfather born?).

HEGEMONY   The dominance of a particular view or group over other views or groups, often through a process of manufactured consent, whereby those in a subordinate role are induced to participate in their own domination. A key question for narrative study is how stories can both shore up hegemony, in the form of "master narratives," but also critique such domination, by way of "counter narratives" that contest entrenched accounts of how the world is (cf. Bamberg and Andrews 2004).

HETERODIEGETIC NARRATOR   A NARRATOR who has not participated in the circumstances and events about which he or she tells a story.

HOMODIEGETIC NARRATOR   A NARRATOR who has participated (more or less centrally) in the circumstances and events about which he or she tells a story. At the limit, homodiegetic narration shades off into AUTODIEGETIC narration.

HYPODIEGETIC NARRATIVE   A story within a story. In *UFO or the Devil*, the story about the big ball recounted by the younger Monica and Renee to Renee's grandmother (shortly after their encounter with the apparition) is a hypodiegetic narrative.

IDEOLOGY. See HEGEMONY

IMPLIED AUTHOR   In the account developed by Booth ([1961] 1983), the implied author is a role or persona assumed by an actual author. That role can be described as a set of norms and values that actual authors adopt for the purpose of producing a given narrative. For rhetorical theorists, interpreting a narrative entails searching the text for clues about these norms and values, which in turn enable the AUDIENCE to detect favored versus disfavored character traits, modes and degrees of UNRELIABLE NARRATION, etc.

IMPLIED READER   The intended addressee or AUDIENCE of the IMPLIED AUTHOR; another term for what rhetorical narrative theorists of narrative call the authorial audience. The implied reader of Hemingway's

"Hills" will know for example that Madrid is a city in Spain – though an actual reader unschooled in geography may not know these details.

INDIRECT DISCOURSE   A technique for representing characters' speech. In contrast to DIRECT DISCOURSE, in ID a NARRATOR reports in a more or less summary fashion characters' utterance(s), rather than reproducing them verbatim.

INTRADIEGETIC NARRATOR   A character NARRATOR, like Enid in *Ghost World* when she recounts to Rebecca how she previously told Naomi her loss-of-virginity story; in other words, a character in a STORYWORLD who in turn narrates a story within the story, that is, a HYPODIEGETIC NARRATIVE.

MASTER NARRATIVES. See HEGEMONY

MEDIUM   For Kress and van Leeuwen (2001), *media* can be viewed as means for the dissemination or production of what has been designed in a given MODE; thus media "are the material resources used in the production of semiotic products and events, including both the tools and the materials used" (2001: 22). See also MODE

METALEPSIS   A confusion or entanglement of narrative levels, as when characters situated in a story within a story (or HYPODIEGETIC NARRATIVE) migrate into the DIEGESIS or main narrative level. In Flann O'Brien's *At Swim-Two-Birds*, for example, the protagonist writes a novel whose characters then jump up one narrative level and attack the novelist who created them.

MIMESIS   An ancient Greek word meaning "imitation." In the study of FICTIONAL narrative, the concept of mimesis is relevant both for the analysis of character (the mimetic dimension of a character accounts for the tendency of the AUDIENCE to treat him or her as a real person) and for the analysis of speech representation (in contrast with more DIEGETIC techniques for representing characters' utterances, such as INDIRECT DISCOURSE, more mimetic techniques, such as DIRECT DISCOURSE, background the NARRATOR's mediating role).

MODE   For Kress and van Leeuwen (2001), modes are semiotic channels (or environments) that can be viewed as a resources for the *design* of a representation formulated within a particular type of discourse, which is in turn embedded in a specific kind of communicative interaction. See also MEDIUM

MONOMODAL NARRATION   Forms of narrative practice that exploit a single semiotic channel (e.g., print text, telephone conversations, sign language) to evoke a STORYWORLD.

MULTIMODAL NARRATION   Forms of narrative practice that exploit more than one semiotic channel (e.g., words and images, or utterances and gestures) to evoke a STORYWORLD.

NARRATED MONOLOGUE   Cohn's (1978) term for the mode of thought representation that is equivalent to FREE INDIRECT DISCOURSE in the realm of speech representation.

NARRATEE   The AUDIENCE of the NARRATOR, like Naomi in *Ghost World* when Enid tells her how she lost her virginity, or Renee's grandmother in *UFO or the Devil*. Insofar as the narratee is an AUDIENCE role more or less explicitly inscribed in a narrative text, it is distinct from both the actual reader and the IMPLIED READER.

NARRATING-I   In retrospective first-person or HOMODIEGETIC (or AUTODIEGETIC) NARRATION, the older, narrating self who tells about the situations and events experienced by the younger, experiencing-I.

NARRATION   The process by which a NARRATIVE is conveyed; depending on the SEMIOTIC medium used, this process can involve complex combinations of cues in different channels (visual, auditory, tactile, etc.), yielding MULTIMODAL versus MONOMODAL NARRATION. Also, some theorists of narrative make narration the third term in a tripartite model that includes the STORY level, the DISCOURSE or text level on the basis of which the story can be reconstructed, and the narration as the communicative act that produces the discourse.

NARRATIVE   Analyzing stories into four basic elements – **situatedness, event sequencing, worldmaking/world disruption,** and **what it's like** – this book defines narrative as (i) a mode of representation that is situated in – must be interpreted in light of – a specific discourse context or occasion for telling. This mode of representation (ii) focuses on a structured time-course of particularized EVENTS. In addition, the events represented (iii) introduce some kind of disruption or disequilibrium into a STORYWORLD, whether that world is presented as actual or fictional, realistic or fantastic, remembered or dreamed, etc. The representation also (iv) conveys what it is like to live through this storyworld-in-flux, highlighting the pressure of events on (in other words, the QUALIA of) real or imagined consciousnesses undergoing the disruptive experience at issue. See also STORY

NARRATIVE DISCOURSE. See DISCOURSE

NARRATIVE SITUATIONS   The Austrian narrative theorist Franz Karl Stanzel ([1979] 1984), developing a nomenclature that has been especially influential in German-language traditions of narrative inquiry, distinguished among three main narrative situations: first-person, third-person or authorial, and figural, which combines a third-person narrative voice with a REFLECTOR figure or particularized center of consciousness.

NARRATIVITY   That which makes a story a story; a property that a text or discourse will have in greater proportion the more readily it lends itself to being interpreted as a NARRATIVE, i.e., the more prototypically narrative it is. As discussed in chapters 1 and 4, however, what constitutes an expected or prototypical form of narrative practice can vary, depending on the communicative circumstances involved.

NARRATOLOGY   An approach to narrative inquiry developed during the heyday of STRUCTURALISM in France. Instead of working to develop interpretations of individual narratives, narratologists focused on how to describe narrative viewed as a SEMIOTIC system – that is, as a system by virtue of which people are able to produce and understand stories.

NARRATOR   The AGENT who produces a NARRATIVE. Some story analysts distinguish among AUTODIEGETIC, EXTRADIEGETIC, HETERODIEGETIC, HOMODIEGETIC, and INTRADIEGETIC narrators.

ORDER   A way of describing the relation between two temporal sequences: the sequence of events that can be assumed to have unfolded in the STORYWORLD, and the unfolding of the DISCOURSE used to recount that sequence. When these two sequences are aligned, the result is chronological narration. ANACHRONY results when the sequences are dis-aligned, yielding ANALEPSES (or flashbacks), PROLEPSES (or flashforwards), and sometimes complex combinations and embeddings of the two.

ORIENTATION   In the Labovian model, the term *orientation* refers to the part of the narrative in which storytellers provide information about the context in which the COMPLICATING ACTION occurs, including time, place, characters, etc.

PARATEXT   Materials accompanying a text, such as a title, authorial attribution, date of publication, preface, epigram, afterword, etc. These materials afford resources for interpretation, allowing readers to channel and delimit their inferential activities by situating texts within generic (or TEXT-TYPE) categories, historical epochs, authors' oeuvres, sociopolitical controversies, and so on.

PARTICIPATION FRAMEWORKS   As discussed in chapter 3, in place of older, dyadic models of communication, based on the "global folk categories" of *speaker* and *hearer*, Goffman decomposes these supposedly primitive terms "into smaller, analytically coherent elements" (1981: 129) that he groups into PRODUCTION FORMATS (cf. speaker) and participation frameworks (cf. hearer). Participation frameworks encompass a range of possible participant statuses, including those of *addressee*, unaddressed but ratified participant (= *bystander*), or unaddressed and unratified participant (= *eavesdropper*).

PAUSE   The slowest possible narrative speed; a type of DURATION in which the NARRATOR'S DISCOURSE continues to unfold, even though the action has come to a standstill.

PERSPECTIVE/POINT OF VIEW   Issues of perspective and point of view are now most often treated under the heading of FOCALIZATION. Genette ([1972] 1980) drew a contrast between focalization and NARRATION to distinguish between who sees or perceives and who speaks in a narrative, respectively.

PLOT   Abbott (2007) distinguishes among three senses of the term *plot*: a type of story (as in "marriage plot"); the combination and sequencing of EVENTS that makes a story a story and not just an assemblage of events; and a sense similar to that of DISCOURSE, by which theorists emphasize how the plot rearranges and otherwise manipulates the events of the STORY. See also EMPLOTMENT

POSITIONING   In Harré and van Langenhove's account (1999: 1–31), one can position oneself or be positioned in discourse as powerful or powerless, admirable or blameworthy, etc. In turn, a position can be specified by characterizing how a speaker's contributions are taken as bearing on these and other "polarities of character" in the context of an overarching storyline – a narrative of self and other(s) being jointly elaborated (or disputed) by participants, via self-positioning and other-positioning speech acts.

POSTCLASSICAL NARRATOLOGY   Frameworks for narrative research (e.g., COGNITIVE NARRATOLOGY, FEMINIST NARRATOLOGY, and TRANSMEDIAL NARRATOLOGY) that build on the work of classical, structuralist NARRATOLOGISTS but supplement that earlier work with concepts and methods that were unavailable to story analysts such as Roland Barthes, Gérard Genette, A. J. Greimas, and Tzvetan Todorov during the heyday of STRUCTURALISM. See chapter 2 for a fuller discussion.

PRODUCTION FORMATS   As discussed in chapter 3, in place of older, dyadic models of communication, based on the "global folk categories" of *speaker* and *hearer*, Goffman decomposes these supposedly primitive terms "into smaller, analytically coherent elements" (1981: 129) that he groups into production formats (cf. speaker) and PARTICIPATION FRAMEWORKS (cf. hearer). Production formats encompass the roles of *author* (I design the words to be uttered), *animator* (I give voice to words authored by another or others), *principal* (I am the person for whose sake the words are uttered), and *figure* (I give voice to an utterance produced by me in some other context).

PROLEPSIS   The equivalent of a flashforward in film. Prolepsis occurs when events that occur in the order ABC are told in the order ACB or CAB.

PROSODY   In linguistics, a term used for speech characteristics such as intonation, rhythm, and the distribution and length of pauses, as well as volume, tempo, and voice quality.

PSYCHO-NARRATION   Cohn's (1978) term for the mode of thought representation that is equivalent to INDIRECT DISCOURSE in the realm of speech representation.

QUALIA   Term used by philosophers of mind to refer to the sense or feeling of *what it is like* (Nagel 1974) for someone or something to have a given experience.

QUOTED MONOLOGUE   Cohn's (1978) term for the mode of thought representation that is equivalent to DIRECT DISCOURSE in the realm of speech representation.

REFLECTOR   A term coined by the novelist Henry James to designate the center of consciousness through whose perceptions events are filtered in a narrative using third-person or HETERODIEGETIC narration. A paradigm case would be Gregor Samsa in Franz Kafka's *Metamorphosis*.

REMEDIATION   The inter-adaption of sign systems, whereby an artifact or representation originally produced in one medium is transposed into another. Remediation is thus a more general process than, say, film adaptation, since it encompasses everything from plastic action figures based on television series or comic books, to video games based on movies (or vice versa), to transcriptions based on audiorecorded or videorecorded communicative interactions.

RESOLUTION   In the Labovian model, the resolution of a story marks the point past which it no longer makes sense to ask "And then what happened?"

SCENE   Scenic presentation is a narrative speed or mode of DURATION in which one can assume a direct equivalence between how long it takes for things to happen in the STORYWORLD and how long it takes the NARRATOR to recount those happenings.

SEMIOTICS   The study of signs. C. S. Peirce divided signs into three main types: *icon*, where there is a resemblance between signifier and signified (as when big eyeglasses are placed in front of an optometrist's office); *index*, where there is a causal relation between signifier and signified (as when smoke signifies fire); and *symbol*, where there is a conventional relation between signifier and signified (as with verbal language).

SERIAL NARRATION   NARRATION across multiple EPISODES. Individual episodes in serial narratives can be relatively autonomous (*Star Trek, Law & Order*) or else thoroughly enmeshed in the larger history of a STORYWORLD that emerges incrementally, from episode to episode (*The Sopranos, Friday Night Lights*).

SHOT/REVERSE SHOT   A sequence of shots in a film that alternates between (a) the viewpoint assumed to correspond to a character's angle of vision and (b) a viewpoint from which that character's facial reactions can be seen.

STORY   In informal usage, *story* is a synonym for NARRATIVE. In NARRATOLOGY, the "story" level of narrative (in French, *histoire*) corresponds to what Russian Formalist theorists called the *fabula*; it contrasts with the "DISCOURSE" (*discours*) level. In this sense, *story* refers to the chronological sequence of situations and events that can be reconstructed on the basis of cues provided in a narrative text.

STORYWORLD   The world evoked by a NARRATIVE text or DISCOURSE; a global mental model of the situations and events being recounted. Reciprocally, narrative artifacts (texts, films, etc.) provide blueprints for the creation and modification of such mentally configured storyworlds.

STRETCH   A narrative speed or mode of DURATION faster than PAUSE but slower than SCENE, in which both narration and action progress but what is told transpires more rapidly than the telling.

STRUCTURALISM   An approach to literary and cultural analysis, especially prominent in the 1960s and 1970s, that used linguistics as a "pilot-science" to study diverse forms of cultural expression as rule-governed signifying practices or "languages" in their own right. NARRATOLOGY was an outgrowth of this general approach.

STYLISTICS   A field of study that draws on tools from linguistics to analyze how language is used (sometimes in transgressive or defamiliarizing ways) in literary works, including narratives.

SUMMARY   A narrative speed or mode of DURATION faster than SCENE but slower than ELLIPSIS; summaries are more or less compressed accounts of STORYWORLD occurrences.

TELLABILITY   To be tellable, situations and EVENTS must in some way stand out against the backdrop formed by everyday expectations and norms, and thus be worth reporting.

TEXT TYPE   A kind of text, such as NARRATIVE, DESCRIPTION, or EXPLANATION. As discussed in chapter 4, text types are broader in scope than literary *genres* (*Bildungsroman*, psychological novel, etc.); instead, they can be equated with the "primary speech genres" characterized by Bakhtin ([1953] 1986: 60) as relatively stable types of utterance that develop within particular spheres of language use.

TRANSMEDIAL NARRATOLOGY   A strand of POSTCLASSICAL NARRATOLOGY premised on the assumption that, although storytelling practices in different media share common features insofar as they are all instances of the narrative TEXT TYPE, those practices are nonetheless inflected by the constraints and affordances associated with a given MEDIUM (Herman 2004; Ryan 2004). Unlike classical NARRATOLOGY, transmedial narratology disputes the notion that the STORY level of a narrative remains wholly invariant across shifts of medium. However, it also assumes that stories do have "gists" that can be REMEDIATED more or less fully and recognizably – depending in part on the SEMIOTIC properties of the source and target media.

UNRELIABLE NARRATION   A mode of NARRATION in which the teller of a story cannot be taken at his or her word, compelling the AUDIENCE to "read between the lines" – in other words, to scan the text for clues about how the STORYWORLD really is, as opposed to how the NARRATOR says it is.

Notes

Preface

1 Bolter and Grusin (1999) characterize remediation in terms of factors bearing on inter-adaptations of sign systems (cf. Genette [1982] 1997), that is, how a representation designed in one such system can be adapted in another. For a more detailed analysis of the structure and functions of multimodal versus monomodal narration, see Herman (forthcoming c), which examines two kinds of multimodal storytelling: word–image combinations in superhero comics and utterance–gesture pairings in video-recorded personal-experience narratives.

Chapter 1

1 As indicated in the glossary, in common usage *narrative* and *story* are synonyms. However, in the specialized terminology used by some theorists of narrative, the "story" level of narrative (in French, *histoire*) corresponds to what Russian Formalist theorists called the *fabula*; it contrasts with the "discourse" (*discours*) level. In this sense, *story* refers to the chronological sequence of situations and events that can be reconstructed on the basis of cues provided in a narrative text. See chapters 2, 4, and 5 for fuller discussion.

2 Here the term *people* is shorthand for "embodied human or human-like individuals invested with felt, conscious awareness of the situations and events recounted in the narrative."

3 There have also been particularly productive interactions between the field of narrative inquiry and Artificial Intelligence research. See, e.g., Lönneker (2005), Mateas and Senger (2003), Meister (2003), and Salway et al. (2003).

4 I am indebted to Lambrou (2008) for her discussion of Eggins and Slade's (1997) use of Plum's model. See my next chapter for further discussion of the Labovian approach.

5   Here it should be noted that my own case study of face-to-face narration, Monica's telling of *UFO or the Devil* in the context of sociolinguistic field-work, is a narrative with this same profile. However, I bring to bear on Monica's narrative a range of ideas from multiple traditions of narrative inquiry. This analytic strategy is complementary to the one outlined in Georgakopoulou's study, namely, diversifying the range of storytelling practices to be included under the scope of narrative research.

6   Georgakopoulou likewise proposes to characterize stories as more or less prototypically narrative – in order to steer a course between the Scylla of "a closed set of must-have definitional criteria" for narrative and the Charybdis of "opening up the category of narrative to include everything" (2007: 37).

7   For more on the narrative foundations of human intelligence, see Bruner (1990, 1991), Herman (2003a, 2003b, 2007b), Herman and Childs (2003), and chapters 5 and 6 of this book.

8   As described in more detail in the Appendix (which includes maps), Texana is small community located in Cherokee County, North Carolina, in the western, mountainous part of this state situated in the southeast-ern region of the U.S. NSF Grant BCS-0236838 supported research on this narrative, and I am also greatly indebted to Christine Mallinson for her productive comments on earlier versions of my analysis of Monica's story, and also for her all-around collegiality and willingness to share insights about the Texana community and about Monica's position within that community. Thanks are also due to Tyler Kendall, whose work on the North Carolina Sociolinguistic Archive and Analysis Project (NC SLAAP) made it possible for me to extract and download the digitized sound file containing Monica's story. For more information about the scope and aims of NC SLAAP, see Kendall (2007).

9   For a critique of Bruner's distinction between paradigmatic and narrative reasoning, however, see Herman (1998). Also for an argument that Bruner engages in narrative imperialism (whereby the notion of story comes to encompass everything and thereby ceases to be useful), and for a balanced assessment of that argument, see, respectively, Strawson (2004) and Phelan (2005b). I discuss Strawson's position in more detail in chapter 6.

10   On the concept of "tellability," see Norrick (2007). On the distinction between the narrating-I, or the older self who tells, and the experiencing-I, or the younger self who undergoes the events being told about, see Lejeune (1989: 3–30).

11   Note that stories can contain other kinds of texts, as when a novel portrays two characters arguing with one another. Conversely, people engaging in a debate might use stories to support their positions. Hence, when talking about a text-type category, I am referring to what category the text as a

whole can most plausibly be slotted into, though I recognize that there will not necessarily be consensus about how to categorize a given text or artifact. See Chatman (1990), Herman (forthcoming b), and chapter 4 for further discussion.

12 Here and again in chapter 4 I have taken slight liberty with Mosher's terminology, inserting an extra syllable (for the sake of greater euphoniousness) in what he originally termed "descriptized narration."

13 As discussed in more detail in chapter 5, a storyworld can be defined as the world evoked by a narrative text or discourse. It is a global mental model of the situations and events being recounted – of who did what to and with whom, when, where, why, and in what manner. Reciprocally, narrative artifacts (texts, films, etc.) provide blueprints for the creation and modification of such mentally configured storyworlds.

14 For more on the concept of "qualia," see e.g. Dennett (1997), Levin (1999), Tye (2003), and chapter 6 of this volume.

15 As an anonymous reviewer of an earlier draft of this book noted, another strategy for analyzing narrative would be to draw on Wittgenstein's ([1953] 1958) concept of family resemblances. As the reviewer puts it, Wittgenstein makes the "interesting point that games are so diverse in character, like a family, that there may be *no single feature*, let alone four, that are shared by all games or all family members. Games are a looser constellation than that; might narrative(s) be like games?" But arguably – allowing for how different communicative contexts can generate different criteria for what counts as a prototypical story – there are in fact identifiable features associated with the narrative text type, realized more or less fully by different members of that text-type category. For instance, though some postmodern narratives may deliberately impede a reader's ability to reconstruct the time-line connecting the situations and events that they portray (Herman 2002a: 237–50), a representation that prevented events from being temporally ordered at all, and thus completely flouted the second basic element identified in this study, event sequencing, would fall outside the narrative text type altogether. Failing to meet this threshold condition for story, the representation might instead be categorized as, say, an unordered list.

16 My remarks about this first basic element of narrative, and my further discussion of it in chapter 3, should be compared with Tomasello's (1999, 2003) account of the process by which children acquire a language. Tomasello argues that language acquisition involves three components – linguistic expressions, concepts, and intended referents within joint attentional scenes – and not just the two identified by Saussure, namely, linguistic expressions and associated concepts (or signifiers and signifieds). In other words, Tomasello's is a usage-based account that emphasizes the importance

of reading for interlocutors' communicative intentions within frames of shared attention, where participants are jointly focused on objects in the world. As Tomasello puts it, "linguistic reference is a social act in which one person attempts to get another person to focus her attention on something in the world" (1999: 97). Hence children acquire language by coming to understand "adult communicative intentions as grounded inside a meaningful joint attentional scene" (1999: 108). Children then become skilled in the practice of using symbolic representations to communicate an intention to manipulate others' attentional focus, even as they learn to recognize that adults' communicative intentions are directed at the same end.

17   In some cases, however, descriptions do involve a time-sequence: recipes, for example, describe a specific sequence of cooking procedures. Hence the need for basic elements (iii) and (iv) – worldmaking/world disruption and what it's like – to capture what distinguishes narratives from other kinds of representations of temporal sequences. Again, see chapter 4 for further discussion.

Chapter 2

1   Below I provide a more detailed discussion of both "Labovian" and post-Labovian approaches to the study of narratives told during face-to-face interaction. For a fuller account of the widespread influence of Labov's model in particular, see Bamberg (1997a).

2   Relevant book series include *Frontiers of Narrative*, published by the University of Nebraska Press, *Narratologia*, published by Walter de Gruyter, *Studies in Narrative*, published by John Benjamins, and *Theory and Interpretation of Narrative*, published by the Ohio State University Press. Journals regularly featuring articles on narrative include, among others, *Ancient Narrative*, *Image (&) Narrative*, *Journal of Narrative Theory*, *Language and Literature*, *Narrative*, *Narrative Inquiry*, *New Literary History*, *Partial Answers*, *Poetics*, *Poetics Today*, and *Style*. In addition, a new journal titled *Storyworlds* will be launched in 2009 by the author.

3   For example, the symposium on "Narrative Intelligence," sponsored in November 1999 by the Association for the Advancement of Artificial Intelligence, assembled computer scientists, designers of computer games, philosophers, linguists, and theorists of literary narrative. AAAI built on this event by sponsoring, in November 2007, a follow-up symposium on "Intelligent Narrative Technologies" and approving, for spring 2009, a third symposium in this sequence. For its part, the 2004 interdisciplinary symposium on "The Travelling Concept of Narrative" held at the University

of Helsinki sought to connect humanistic and social-scientific trends in narrative research, as did the symposium on "Narratology beyond Literary Criticism" held at the University of Hamburg the previous year and the symposium on "Narratology in the Age of Interdisciplinary Narrative Research" held at the University of Wuppertal in 2007.

4   For a fuller discussion of this reciprocal influence, and of other aspects of what I am designating the classical tradition of narrative study, see Herman (2005a).

5   Further, as suggested in Herman (1999a), which outlines an account of postclassical narratology that I build on here, the more recent research does not just expose the limits but also exploits the possibilities of the older, structuralist models. A fitting analogy in this context is postclassical physics, which does not simply discard, classical Newtonian models but rather rethinks their conceptual underpinnings and re-examines their scope of applicability.

6   For more details, see Fludernik (2005: 48–51). As Fludernik also points out, working independently of the structuralist narratologists, F. K. Stanzel (cf. Stanzel [1979] 1984) developed an approach to the study of literary narrative that "was, and to some extent still is, the canonical narratological model in German-speaking countries and in parts of Eastern Europe" (p. 40). For a fuller comparison of Stanzel and Genette as major practitioners of (different variants of) classical narratology, see Herman and Vervaeck (2005a), chapters 1 and 2.

7   For a fuller account of rhetorical theories of narrative, see my next chapter.

8   For more detailed accounts, see Fludernik (2005), Herman (1999a), Herman and Vervaeck (2005b), Hyvärinen (2006), and Nünning (2003).

9   For an extended discussion of Ochs and Capps' (2001) powerful – indeed, revolutionary – account, see Herman (2002b).

10 It should also be pointed out that, early on, scholars such as Thomas Pavel (1976, 1985, 1986) and Gerald Prince (1973, 1980, 1982, 1983) authored path-breaking studies that drew on linguistic tools other than those used by the structuralist narratologists, thereby setting an important precedent for what I have termed postclassical approaches to narrative inquiry.

Chapter 3

1   Compare Roberts' (1999) three-part model of discourse in general (as opposed to narrative discourse in particular) as (1) a type of event, specifically a verbal exchange (i.e., language-based mode of interaction) involving human agents (cf. narration); (2) the linguistic content of that exchange (cf. text); and (3) the "structure of information that is presupposed

and/or conveyed by the interlocutors during the course of the discourse event in view of the explicit content of the exchange" (cf. story) (1999: 231).

2   The situation is even more complicated than my formulation here suggests. As Culler (1998: 25–8) notes in his exposition of Pratt's (1977) "speech-act theory of literary discourse," literary narratives like Hemingway's belong to a larger class of stories that can be termed "narrative display texts" whose relevance depends on their suitability for performance rather than the specific information or semantic content they might convey (Culler 1998: 26; Ochs and Capps 2001: 61). But what makes literary narratives special is the elaborate process of review, evaluation, and selection that causes readers to "assume that in literature complications of language ultimately have a communicative purpose and, instead of imagining that the speaker or writer is being uncooperative, as they might in other speech contexts, they struggle to interpret elements that flout principles of efficient communication in the interests of some further communicative goal" (Culler 1998: 27). Accordingly, the subversive effects of experiments like those of Robbe-Grillet and other avant-garde writers emerge against the backdrop afforded by a special kind of narrative occasion, in which readers work with the default assumption that all textual details are relevant to the overall communicative purpose of the narrative. Readers assume that the apparent irrelevance of Robbe-Grillet's extraordinarily detailed, prolix descriptions, for example, is itself relevant to the writer's own flouting of novelistic conventions. More generally, Pratt's approach provides independent support for my claim in this chapter (and in the book as a whole) that stories constitute a mode of representation that is situated in – must be interpreted in light of – a specific discourse context or occasion for telling.

3   A related idea is Gumperz's (1982: 130–52) concept of *contextualization cues.* Cues of this sort encompass all the (verbal as well as nonverbal) signals used by participants in discourse to prompt interlocutors to interpret what's going on as a specific kind of communicative interaction, thus helping to reduce the amount of inferential activity required to understand particular contributions to the ongoing discourse.

4   Garcia Landa (2004) also draws on Goffman's ideas to explore the structure and dynamics of narrative occasions.

5   As Hemingway put it, "I always try to write on the principle of the iceberg. ... There is seven-eighths of it underwater for every part that shows" (quoted in Johnston 1987: 31).

6   A more problematic case is Sebald's earlier novel, *The Emigrants* (Sebald [1992] 1996), which deliberately straddles the border between autobiography and first-person fictional narration.

7   See chapter 1, the Appendix, and Herman (2007b) for more information about this research project and also about Monica and her story.

8 As reported by Taylor (2001), "Enid Coleslaw" is an anagram for "Daniel Clowes." The use of this anagram suggests Clowes's identification with Enid in particular, and perhaps also provides clues about the norms and values associated with what rhetorical theorists of narrative would characterize as the implied author of *Ghost World* – that is, the communicative agent whom interpreters assume to be "responsible for the choices that create the narrative text as 'these words in this order' and that imbue the text with his or her values" (Phelan 2005a: 216). For fuller discussion, see the final section of this chapter.

9 For foundational work in this tradition, see Drew and Heritage (1992); Sacks (1992); Sacks, Schegloff, and Jefferson (1974); and Schegloff (1981). Schegloff (1997), meanwhile, argues that Labov's (1972) influential model for narrative analysis is based on one type of communicative situation – namely, personal experience narratives elicited during interviews – and should therefore not be viewed as a template for inquiry into stories of all sorts. See also notes 10 and 11, as well as my discussion in chapter 1 of Georgakopoulou's (2007) account of "small stories."

10 In the account proposed by Ochs and Capps (2001), one of the key dimensions of narrative is tellership, with the available possibilities ranging from one active teller to multiple active co-tellers. From this perspective, the marked situation to which Pratt refers (1977) would correspond to just one type of narrative occasion among others.

11 Here it is worth reiterating Schegloff's (1997) point that sociolinguistic interviews create a different kind of discourse environment for storytelling than other kinds of face-to-face communicative encounters. When stories are launched in interviews (depending on the exact circumstances and participants involved), co-narration can be a less typical or more marked communicative practice than it is in conversational interchanges among peers.

12 In this context, *the valley of the Ebro* can be characterized as a formulaic construction with a generic referential function, evoking a place generally known rather than a region or locale specific to this particular storyworld.

13 In Crystal's succinct formulation, *deixis* is a term used in linguistic theory "to subsume those features of language which refer directly to the personal, temporal or locational characteristics of the situation within which an utterance takes place, whose meaning is thus relative to that situation; e.g., *now/then, here/there, I/you, this/that*" (1997: 107).

14 Features such as this provide support for Lord's characterization of *Beowulf* as a work that is "transitional between oral and written" modes (1995: 105; cf. 212–37).

15 In Clover's account, Beowulf and Unferth's verbal duel closely matches the canonical form of the Norse *flyting*, which "consists of an exchange of

verbal provocations between hostile speakers in a predictable setting. The boasts and insults are traditional, and their arrangement and rhetorical form is highly stylized" (1980: 445–6). For a fuller discussion of this and other aspects of the Old English text, see Herman and Childs (2003).

16 Complementing the use of the Ramones song to refer to the popular (or rather punk) music scene, internal evidence suggests that the "Chuck" referred to by the woman on the TV screen is Chuck Woolery, host of the dating show *The Love Connection* (aired 1983–99). This allusion connects, in turn, with *Ghost World*'s focus on the difficulty of establishing and maintaining romantic and other relationships.

17 See Bamberg (1997b, 2004a, 2005) for work that draws on positioning theory to analyze three dimensions of narrative, which can be visualized as concentric circles spreading outward from the storyworld evoked by the act of telling a story in face-to-face interaction (cf. Moisinnac 2008): first, how the characters are positioned with respect to one another in the represented situations and events; second, how storytellers position themselves vis-à-vis their interlocutors in the context of the speech event through which the narrative is presented; and third, how the storyteller's discourse relates to more or less dominant storylines about the way the world is. I examine all of these dimensions as I use the idea of positioning to continue my exploration, in the current section, of the first basic element of narrative, situatedness.

18 As mentioned in the headnote to this section, discursive psychology is a subdomain of – or specific approach to – social psychology. Discursive psychologists draw a distinction between, on the one hand, "cognitivist approaches to language, where texts, sentences and descriptions are taken as depictions of an externally given world, or as realizations of underlying cognitive representations of that world" (Edwards and Potter 1992: 8), and, on the other hand, the discursive approach, which treats "discourse not as the product or expression of thoughts or mental states lying behind or beneath it, but as a domain of public accountability in which psychological states are made relevant" in particular contexts of talk (Edwards 2006: 41). See also chapter 6.

19 For perspectives on the opposition between master narratives and counternarratives, see Bamberg and Andrews (2004).

20 As also noted in the Glossary, the term *prosody* refers to speech characteristics such as intonation, rhythm, and the distribution and length of pauses, as well as volume, tempo, and voice quality.

21 For feminist (and other) critiques of Hemingway, see Benson (1990) and Wagner-Martin (1998).

22 To put this still another way, Clowes deploys a technique that modulates back and forth between what Stanzel ([1979] 1984) called the *authorial*

narrative situation, in which the narrator uses third-person narration to recount in a relatively distanced way events in which he or she is not a participant (cf. Henry Fielding's *Tom Jones* or George Eliot's *Middlemarch*), and the *figural* narrative situation, which again features third-person narration but filters the presentation of events through a center of consciousness or "reflector" located in the storyworld (cf. Franz Kafka's *The Trial* or Henry James's *The Ambassadors*).

23 I characterize the male character's remark about reggae as self-incriminating (at least from Enid's perspective) on the basis of internal evidence. Later in the novel, when Enid recounts to Rebecca the way she told her loss-of-virginity story to Naomi (see sequences C and D in the Appendix), Enid reports how she told Naomi that she first experienced sexual intercourse with Allen Weinstein, an "intense, moody hippie who smoked a *ton* of pot and listened to reggae (which was a drag) but *thank God* not The Grateful Dead" (p. 36). In the next panel, Enid's narration-within-the-narration continues: "I liked him because he always seemed too busy figuring out his counter-culture philosophy (which, of course, was total bullshit) to waste time with girls" (p. 36).

24 In a project currently under way (Herman 2008b), I use recent research on folk psychology, or the means by which people formulate accounts of their own and others' actions in terms of reasons for acting (Hutto 2008; Hutto and Ratcliffe 2007), to suggest grounds for moving away from the standard narrative communication model outlined in this section in favor of an alternative account that I abbreviate with the acronym CAPA. The proposed model consists of *Contexts* for acting, *Actions*, *Persons* who perform the actions, and *Ascriptions* of reasons for acting. Since my research is still in process, I will refrain here from going into further detail, apart from mentioning that CAPA features a reduced roster of explanatory entities (there is no hypostatized implied author or implied reader) and may offer a more unified picture of processes of narrative interpretation and everyday reasoning practices. That said, the narrative communication model described in the current section has been influential in the field of narrative studies, generating important scholarship on what this book characterizes as the basic element of situatedness.

25 Jakobson (1960) expands this schema to include a total of six communicative factors (addresser/sender, addressee/receiver, context, channel, code, and message) and suggests that the primary communicative function of a message will depend on which of these factors is its predominant focus or concern. Messages in which the sender predominates serve (primarily) an emotive or expressive function; receiver-centered messages, a conative or directive function; context-centered messages, a referential function; channel-centered messages, a phatic function (that is, they serve to provide

information about the status of the channel through which information is flowing, as when I use the back-channel tokens like *yeah . . . right . . . okay* to signal to my interlocutor on the phone that I'm still on the other end of the line); code-centered messages, a metalinguistic function (as when I say *In English the word* cat *refers to a four-legged animal that chases mice*); and messages that focus attention on the message itself, a poetic function.

26　For a critique of the very concept of narrator, as a communicative agent intermediate between authors and characters, see Walsh (2007: 69–85; cf. Banfield 1982).

27　The discourse marker *you know* has been variably interpreted as a "filler" by which speakers stall for more time to formulate an utterance (or signal their intention to continue a turn at talk), as a prompt for interlocutors to generate inferences about the significance of what is being said, and as a cue to generalize on the basis of a mention of a particular event or situation (see Schriffrin 1987: 267–311). In any case, the addressee orientation of *you know* underscores the extent to which the emotional profile of the events recounted in Monica's story emerges from collaborative discourse practices.

28　As Nieragden (2002: 686) notes, even within the category of autodiegetic narration Lanser (1981) has proposed a scale stretching from narrators who are the sole protagonists of the stories they tell (e.g., Holden Caulfield in Salinger's *The Catcher in the Rye*), to narrators who are witness-participants (Ishmael in Melville's *Moby-Dick*), to (often nameless) uninvolved eye-witnesses (the narrator in Capote's *In Cold Blood*).

29　These discriminations help reveal why Genette chose to use neologisms such as *homodiegetic* and *heterodiegetic* instead of older terms of art like *first-person* and *third-person*. Not only do these terms collectively form a nomenclatural system based on the root term *diegesis*; what is more, they help capture differences between texts or passages that would otherwise be lumped into the same category. Contrast, for example, the narrative functions of first-person reports by the author of an autobiography with those of first-person reports given by a character narrator like Enid in *Ghost World*.

30　It should be pointed out that, exploiting the visualizing potential of the medium, Clowes has included what can be construed as one unflattering self-portrait in the final panel on page 29 of the novel, which shows the "famous cartoonist" whom Enid calls "David Clowes" (but who is listed as "Dan Clowes – comic" in a panel two pages earlier). However, this image can be interpreted as a one-off representation of Clowes the actual author rather than as a case in which the narrating-I portrays his own participation in past events bracketed off from the here and now of the current moment of narration.

31   In what Stanzel ([1979] 1984) termed figural narration, however, it is
not always clear which statements are authenticated by the narrator and
which index the particularized, biased, and thus non-authoritative (or
relatively less authoritative) cognitive-perceptual activity of a character.
Insofar as figural narration involves third-person or heterodiegetic narration filtered through the vantage-point of a particularized center of
consciousness, this technique "creates an intermediary zone of relatively
authenticated fictional facts" (Margolin 2005b: 33; cf. Herman 2006b).

32   Here my simplified presentation passes over significant areas of dispute
regarding the nature of implied authors – and their status as explanatory
constructs (cf. Cohn 1999; Hansen 2007; Nünning 2005; Ryan 2001b). As Phelan
notes in his cogent overview of these debates (2005a: 38–48), whereas Booth
himself characterized the implied author as a persona adopted by an actual
author, subsequent theorists, more wary of giving scope to a communicative
agent to whom intentions can be (provisionally) attributed, have emphasized the role of the reader in assembling the implied author on the basis
of specific textual features (cf. Rimmon-Kenan [1983] 2002 and Chatman
1978, 1990). This shift of emphasis led in turn to Nünning's (1997) critique
of the concept on the grounds of vagueness and coherence: the implied
author seems to be both an agent involved in the production of the text and
an aspect of the reader's reception of the text (cf. Herman and Vervaeck
2005a: 17–18). In an attempt to avoid difficulties of this sort, Genette ([1983]
1988) proposed jettisoning the concept as (mostly) unnecessary for a theory
of narrative communication. See Booth (2005) for a lively account of his
original motivations for coining the term. For a critical genealogy of the
implied author as a bulwark against the anti-intentionalism of the Anglo-
American Formalist critics, see Herman (2008a); for a full history and
critique of the idea, see Kindt and Müller (2006). See also my next note,
as well as note 24 above.

33   Outlining strategies for resisting the anti-intentionalism of the New Critics,
Herman (2008a and 2008b) argues that ascriptions of communicative intention are fundamental to (even required for) narrative understanding, but
disputes the further claim that such ascriptions necessitate drawing inferences about an implied author. See also notes 32 and 24 above.

34   See Chatman (1978, 1990) for a fuller treatment of the concept of the implied
author vis-à-vis cinematic narratives.

35   See Phelan's (1989, 2005a) argument that characters can serve *mimetic* functions when they are represented in a way that underscores their status
as lifelike individuals, *synthetic* functions when a text foregrounds their
status as artificial constructs, and *thematic* functions when they serve
as representatives of relatively abstract ideas or themes that transcend
the particularities of individual persons. As my discussion suggests, at

a given point in the unfolding of a fictional account the authorial and
narrative audiences may be attending to different character functions at
one and the same time, so that I recognize Enid and Rebecca's status as
(theme-carrying) textual constructs while simultaneously feeling engaged
by their plights. Again, what narrative function a given character, circumstance, or incident realizes is inextricably interconnected with narrative
occasions, and vice versa.

36   See Labov (1972) and Prince (1983) for attempts to characterize the notion
of "narrative point," or the reason for a story's telling (cf. also Herman 2007a).

Chapter 4

1   In placing emphasis here and throughout this paragraph on the indis-
solubility of text and context, and as already noted in chapter 1, I am restat-
ing in other terms what Meir Sternberg has called the Proteus Principle:
"in different contexts . . . the same form may fulfill different functions
and different forms the same function" (1982: 148). Thus, to anticipate an
example discussed below: depending on context the clause *the house was
dark* may function both as a description of a house and as a narrative report
of the conscious experience of a character observing the house at a particular moment; conversely, either of these two communicative functions
could be fulfilled by a statement with a different form, such as *no light
emanated from the dwelling*. By analogy, my goal in this chapter (and in the
book as a whole) is not to try to isolate textual structures that serve as
failsafe guarantees of the presence of a story whenever and wherever those
structures occur. Rather, to reiterate, my aim is to diagnose critical properties of texts that can be interpreted as fulfilling a narrative function across
a range of contexts; to stipulate that the properties thus identified constitute
basic elements of narrative; and to specify the gradient or more-or-less manner in which those properties may be realized in a given case, resulting
in more or less prototypical instances of the category *narrative*. Further,
as I discuss later in this chapter, judgments about what counts as "prototypical" are themselves subject to change across different contexts.

2   Ryan (2005a) makes the important distinction between narrative viewed
as a cognitive construct or "mental script," on the one hand, and narrative
viewed as an embodied semiotic artifact (i.e., an actualized text), on the
other. In this chapter I extend Ryan's distinction, arguing for its applicability to descriptions and explanations as well as narratives. Meanwhile,
for more on the embedding of textual kinds in sociocultural, institutional,
and other forms of practice, see, e.g., Berkenkotter and Huckin (1995) and
Miller (1984).

3 To accommodate narrative representations in semiotic media other than verbal language, in the present analysis I draw on Chatman's definition of *text* as "any communication that temporally controls its reception by the audience" (1990: 7), i.e., "a time-regulating structure" (1990: 8). Also, anticipating the account developed here, Chatman defines genres as "special subclasses or combinations of text-types" (1990: 10).

4 As Görlach points out, however, not all text types are freely combinable with others: "Text types can be 'bound' or 'free,' as morphemes can: a 'dedication' always forms part of a larger unit, a book, and is therefore similar to a prefix in morphology; compare the status of a headline, a footnote, or even a reply as part of a conversation" (2004: 106). Chatman, for his part, uses the concept of "subserving" (or "being in the service of") to argue that "[m]ost texts utilize one overriding text-type, but it is generally subserved by other text-types" at the local level (1990: 2).

5 As discussed in chapter 1, Bruner (1990) characterizes narrative as a form of (or at least a primary vehicle for) explanation in the domain of folk psychology – that is, the domain of common-sense reasoning about others' as well as our own minds. Hutto (2007, 2008) extends and refines Bruner's work, developing an approach to folk psychology that Hutto characterizes as the Narrative Practice Hypothesis. See chapter 6 for a fuller account.

6 As should become evident from my discussion below, judgments having to do with what constitutes a prototypical instance (i.e., an exemplar or standard case) of a given category are just as cognitively fundamental as judgments having to do with what constitutes the "basic" or mid-level stratum within a hierarchical system of categories. In other words, in this context the word *basic* is being used in a specialized sense – as a technical term denoting the level in a hierarchy of categories that serves as a cognitive reference point for understanding categories (and instances of those categories) at other, more general or more specific levels.

7 On the concept of deictic shift, see Zubin and Hewitt (1995).

8 Then again, as discussed below and again in my next chapter, an important tradition of research (cf. Bremond 1980; Kafalenos 2006; Propp [1928] 1968; Todorov 1968) suggests that all narratives have – or at least unfold against the backdrop afforded by – a basic "shape" that involves progression from an initial condition of equilibrium, through a disruptive event, to a condition of equilibrium restored but on a different footing.

9 Monika Fludernik (2000) reviews some of the competing accounts, including Werlich's (1975, 1983) tripartite division between ideal types (= abstract models in readers' or speakers' minds), text forms (= specific text types), and text idioms (= actual instances of language in a given text); Adam's (1985) focus on deep-structural aspects of eight different text types; Virtanen and Wårvik's (1987) six-level model encompassing cognitive

processes, discourse functions, discourse types, text types, textual strategies, grammar, and actualized text; and Fludernik's own three-level model involving macrogenres (= text types in my account), genres/text types such as novels, conversational narratives, myths, etc., and discourse modes (such as report sequence, directives, dialogue, etc.). For her part, Dubrow (1982: 4–5) sets up the following taxonomy:

mode = narrative (or epic), drama, lyric
genre = *Bildungsroman*, comedy, epigram
subgenre = novel of manners, drawing-room comedy, country-house poem

10   For the same reason, as Hogan notes, "our prototypical dog in the context 'a farm in Maine' is different from our prototypical dog in the context 'Manhattan apartment'" (2003: 135).

11   In this connection, the circularity of generic definitions noted by Dubrow becomes a pertinent issue: "[the] definition of genres, like those of biological species, tend[s] to be circular: one establishes such a definition on the basis of a few examples, and yet the choice of those examples from the multitude of possible ones implies a prior decision about the characteristics of the genre" (1982: 46).

12   My thanks to the anonymous reviewer of an earlier draft of this book for helping me recast my discussion of this example.

13   For a fuller discussion of debates surrounding the CLM, see Herman (forthcoming b) and Klemke et al. (1998). Ankersmit (2005a) provides an overview of the use and critique of the CLM in historiography in particular; see also Ankersmit (2005b).

14   For more on this issue from a philosophy-of-mind rather than philosophy-of-science perspective, see the final section of chapter 6. That chapter also draws on research on the nexus of narrative and mind to revisit in more detail an issue broached in my next paragraph: namely, Levine's (1983) account of the explanatory gap between brain physiology and the felt, subjective character of conscious experience.

15   I am grateful to Arkady Plotnitsky and Meir Sternberg for their comments on earlier versions of parts of this chapter.

Chapter 5

1   Hence, as discussed in Herman (2002a: 9–22), the notion *storyworld* is consonant with a range of other concepts proposed by cognitive psychologists, discourse analysts, psycholinguists, philosophers of language, and others concerned with how people go about making sense of texts or discourses. Like *storyworld*, these other notions – including *deictic center*,

mental model, situation model, discourse model, contextual frame, and *possible world* – are designed to explain how interpreters rely on inferences triggered by textual cues to build up representations of the overall situation or world evoked but not fully explicitly described in the discourse. I discuss a number of these terms and concepts, and their relevance for the study of narrative ways of worldmaking in particular, later on in the present chapter.

2   In characterizing narrative texts as blueprints for building storyworlds, I am drawing implicitly on Reddy's (1979) critique of what he termed the conduit metaphor for communicative processes (see Green 1989: 10–13 for a useful discussion). According to this metaphor, linguistic expressions and other means for communication are viewed as mere vessels or vehicles for channeling back and forth thoughts, ideas, and meanings. Reddy suggested, instead, that sentences are like blueprints, planned artifacts whose design is tailored to the goal of enabling an interlocutor to reconstruct the situations or worlds after which the blueprints are patterned. Further, in contrast with the conduit metaphor, which blames miscommunication on a poorly chosen linguistic vessel, the blueprint analogy predicts that completely successful interpretation of communicative designs will be rare – given the complexity of the processes involved in planning, executing, and making sense of the blueprints.

3   On the notion of "what it is like" as a term of art used to describe the states of felt, subjective awareness associated with the having of conscious experiences, see Nagel (1974) and chapter 6. Further, on the relationships between narrativity (or the degree to which a representation is amenable to being interpreted as a story), occurrences that disrupt the canonical order of events in a storyworld, and reportability or tellability, see the final section of the present chapter.

4   As noted in chapter 3, deictic terms like *I, here,* and *now* are expressions whose meaning changes depending on who is uttering them in what discourse context.

5   Although literary narratives do not allow for "blended" spatial deixis of this sort, narrative fictions told in the second person can in some cases create analogous effects by way of *person deixis.* More specifically, some instances of narrative *you* can create blends by referring simultaneously (and ambiguously) to a narrator-protagonist and to a current recipient of the story, superimposing the space-time coordinates of a storyworld-internal entity upon those of a storyworld-external entity, and vice versa (see Herman 2002a: 331–71).

6   For example, in Labov's model clauses with past-tense verbs in the indicative mood correlate with the *complicating action* of a narrative, whereas *evaluation* or the signaling of the point of a story is marked by departures from this baseline narrative syntax.

7 See Bridgeman (2005) for a more extended discussion of how Emmott's model, in particular, can be adapted for the analysis of graphic narratives.

8 In "Hills," one of the few retrospections back to an earlier time-frame occurs when the narrator reports the male character's perception of the couple's suitcases as he and Jig prepare to board the train to Madrid: "He did not say anything but looked at the bags against the wall of the station. There were labels on them from all the hotels where they had spent nights" (Hemingway [1927] 1987: 214).

9 Zwigoff's film adaptation of the novel accentuates even more the increasingly divergent paths of the main characters. In the movie, Rebecca nags Enid to get a job so that they can get an apartment together and, in a moment suggesting incipient conformism on Rebecca's part, expresses particular admiration for a fold-out ironing board built into the wall of the apartment that she has leased.

10 In a compelling account of the relations between science and narrative, Plotnitsky argues that "the very idea of motion, which grounds all physics, cannot be conveyed without a narrative. 'Something moves' is a narrative. Accordingly, every time something begins to move a narrative begins, and, conversely, every time there is a narrative something begins to move or at least stands still (which still requires the idea of motion)" (2005: 514–15). From my perspective, however, this conception of narrative is overly inclusive. "Something moves" – or "something stands still" – is only potentially a narrative. For example, representations of a person's range of motion in a limb damaged by accident or illness are arguably best characterized as descriptions. By contrast, if a representation focuses on a person with a paralyzed limb who can suddenly move it, or conversely on a person who formerly had a normal range of motion in a limb but is suddenly stricken with paralysis, then the representation will display the critical property of disruptiveness or noncanonicalness required for narrative ways of worldmaking.

11 In several sections of the present chapter I have adapted material drafted for an essay in preparation for a volume titled *Teaching Narrative Theory*, coedited by David Herman, Brian McHale, and James Phelan and under consideration for publication by the Modern Language Association. I am grateful to Brian McHale and Jim Phelan for their comments on earlier versions of the material in question.

Chapter 6

1 Here my emphasis on consciousness, or the mental states bound up with conscious awareness, differs from Palmer's (2004) decision to background

this dimension of mind in his own study: "Generally, I use the term *mind* in preference to alternatives such as *consciousness* and *thought*. The use of the latter two terms is often accompanied by a tendency to see mental life mainly in terms of inner speech. In addition, consciousness can have the implication of self-consciousness, which I want to avoid because it deflects attention from non-consciousness and latent states of mind. The important point is that the mind refers to much more than what is normally thought of as consciousness or thought" (2004: 19; but see Palmer's discussion of qualia as aspects of nonverbal consciousness on pp. 97–8). Whereas Palmer's overall aim is to broaden the scope of investigations of fictional minds, and to enrich previous narratological approaches (e.g., Cohn 1978) with work in psychology, philosophy, anthropology, and other fields concerned with "the social mind in action," my own focus here is, by contrast, on the critical properties that make narrative modes of representation recognizable in the first place. I argue that one such critical property is the way stories evoke the impact of storyworld events on an experiencing consciousness, conveying what it's like for one or more human or human-like minds to undergo the events in question.

2   In this chapter, though I build on Fludernik's work to highlight the impact of storyworld events on experiencing minds as a basic element of narrative, I opt to use other terms besides *experientiality* to explore what I refer to in this and the previous section as the consciousness factor in stories. I adopt this strategy in part to avoid the implication that the other basic elements already discussed in previous chapters can be subordinated to experientiality as somehow less fundamental – as Fludernik's model prima facie implies (cf. Alber 2002 and my discussion below). In addition, my aim is to bring to bear on the study of representations of experiencing minds in storyworlds ideas developed in philosophy, among other fields (cf. Palmer 2004). Thus, to explore the role of the consciousness factor in narrative, I draw on Nagel's (1974) foundational study and refer to *the what-it's-like dimension of consciousness* or, more simply, *what it's like*, using that term more or less interchangeably with *qualia* and also with a third term that I further specify below, namely, *raw feels*.

3   For Wilson and Keil (1999) cognitive science includes six "confederated disciplines": philosophy; psychology; the neurosciences; computational intelligence; linguistics and language; and culture, cognition, and evolution.

4   For more on the larger debate concerning the question of conscious awareness and the status of qualia, see Blackmore (2004), Block, Flanagan, and Güzeldere (1997), Flanagan (1998), Freeman (2003), Hutto (1999, 2000), van Gulick (2004), and the other sources mentioned below. On the specific question of why we might have been equipped with consciousness – that is, what evolutionary advantage it may afford – Searle (1992: 108–9)

and van Gulick (2004: section 6) propose broadly similar answers. Searle suggests that conscious awareness affords flexibility, creativity, and powers of discrimination; van Gulick adds to these advantages an enhanced capacity for social coordination, a more unified representation of reality, and global informational access: "Making information conscious typically widens the sphere of influence and the range of ways it can be used to adaptively guide or shape both inner and outer behavior" (2004: section 6.5).

5   Critiquing Dennett's (1991) physicalist position, Searle (1997) writes: "the essential thing about the [sensation of] pain is that it is a specific internal qualitative feeling. The problem of consciousness in both philosophy and the natural sciences is to explain these subjective feelings. . . . The subjective feelings are the *data* that a theory of consciousness has to explain. . . . The peculiarity of Daniel Dennett's book can now be stated: he denies the existence of the data" (1997: 99). See Dennett (1997) for an elaboration of the argument that "when we look . . . at our original characterization of qualia, as ineffable, intrinsic, private, directly apprehensible properties of experience, we find that there is nothing to fill the bill" (1997: 639).

6   On problems with the very notion of zero-degree "behaviorist narrative" – that is, a mode of narration utterly devoid of clues about characters' dispositions, inferences, attitudes, etc. – see my discussion above and Palmer (2004: 205–39).

7   Compare here Hutto's (2006b) critique of what he terms the *Object Based Schema*. In Menary's (2006) account of Hutto's position, the Object Based Schema "is essentially committed to the view that contents and experiences are kinds of objects . . . typically, these are imagined to be mental objects with which we are directly phenomenally acquainted . . . or intentional contents to which we are psychologically related" (p. 8). In other words, a misplaced attachment to the Object Based Schema is the source of the philosophical tendency to reify experiences as inner objects with particular properties, e.g., phenomenal qualities like "redness" that come before the mind (Hutto 2006b). By contrast, Hutto himself characterizes "[e]xperiencing . . . as an extended temporal activity not as momentary inner occurrences. Likewise, experiencers must be understood as embodied and situated beings – whole organisms – not imaginary inner subjects or brains" (2006b: 52–3). Herman (2008a) explores implications of this line of argument for research on the problem of authorial intention in narrative contexts (cf. Herman 2008b). Further, the account proposed later in this section, in which narrative affords not just a means of expressing what it's like to experience events but moreover a basis or context for the having of (an) experience in the first place, can be viewed as an alternative to models of mind rooted in the Object Based Schema.

8   Note that both the narrower approach outlined by Hutto himself and the somewhat broader approach sketched in what follows can be viewed as generalizations of Hamburger's argument concerning the mind-evoking power of "epic fiction," that is, fictional narrative presented through third-person or heterodiegetic narration. According to Hamburger, "[e]pic fiction is the sole instance where third-person figures can be spoken of not, or not only[,] as objects, but also as subjects, where the subjectivity of a third-person figure *qua* that of a third-person can be portrayed" ([1957] 1993: 139). Or, to put the same point another way, "the content of narrative literature is fictive, i.e., not the experience-field of the narrator, but that of the fictive persons" ([1957] 1993: 122). Although it cuts against the grain of aspects of Hamburger's account, and in particular her claim that the worlds created through first-person versus third-person narration have a different ontological status, from another perspective the line of argument being developed here can be viewed as an extension of Hamburger's model. Not only fictional narrative but narrative more generally, the argument suggests, can be used to evoke or emulate the experiencing consciousness of another (cf. Fludernik 2007: 265–6). Meanwhile, for a wide-ranging discussion of types of empathy facilitated by such narrative emulations of consciousness (among other techniques used in novels), see Keen (2007).

Appendix

1   NSF Grant BCS-0236838 supported research on this narrative. See Christine Mallinson (2006: 61–115) for an extended discussion of the history and current sociocultural and ethnic profile of Texana; for a thumbnail sketch see <http://www.ncsu.edu/linguistics/ncllp/sites/texana.php>. As noted in chapter 1, I am greatly indebted both to Christine for her willingness to share insights about the Texana community and to Tyler Kendall, whose work on the North Carolina Sociolinguistic Archive and Analysis Project (NC SLAAP) made it possible for me to extract and download the digitized sound file containing Monica's story (see Kendall 2007).
2   It is worth commenting on Monica's use of the disjunction *or* in the phrase from the abstract ("UFO or the devil") that I have adopted as a title for her story. Insofar as she refuses to select definitively between a religious and a secular (if still supernatural) explanation for the experience on which her narrative centers, Monica can be interpreted as engaging in a complex form of self-positioning that is one of the hallmarks of her narrative as a whole (see my discussion of positioning theory in chapter 3). In parallel with Monica's use of the self-description that occurs later in this same line (*black asses*) – one that can be interpreted as aligning Monica with regional

as well as supraregional subgroups of the African American population, and thus against different elements of the dominant social order (see below) – her disjunctive explanation positions Monica amid competing sets of norms for telling stories about oneself, others, and the world.

3   As Mallinson (2008) notes, data from the 2000 U.S. Census indicate that about 230 people who self-identify as black live in Cherokee County, comprising just 1.6 percent of its total population.

4   As discussed in chapter 3, Enid Coleslaw is an anagram for Daniel Clowes (see Taylor 2001).

References

Aarts, B., D. Denison, E. Keizer, and G. Popova (eds.) (2004). *Fuzzy Grammar: A Reader.* Oxford: Oxford University Press.

Abbott, H. P. (2003). "Unnarratable Knowledge: The Difficulty of Understanding Evolution by Natural Selection." In D. Herman (ed.), *Narrative Theory and the Cognitive Sciences* (pp. 143–62). Stanford, CA: Center for the Study of Language and Information.

Abbott, H. P. (2005). "Narration." In D. Herman, M. Jahn, and M.-L. Ryan (eds.), *Routledge Encyclopedia of Narrative Theory* (pp. 339–44). London: Routledge.

Abbott, H. P. (2007). "Story, Plot, and Narration." In D. Herman (ed.), *The Cambridge Companion to Narrative* (pp. 39–51). Cambridge: Cambridge University Press.

Abbott, H. P. ([2002] 2008). *The Cambridge Introduction to Narrative.* 2nd edn. Cambridge: Cambridge University Press.

Adam, J.-M. (1985). "Quels types de textes?" *Le français dans le monde* 192, 39–43.

Adams, J.-K. (1996). *Narrative Explanation: A Pragmatic Theory of Discourse.* Frankfurt: Peter Lang.

Alber, J. (2002). "The 'Moreness' or 'Lessness' of 'Natural' Narratology: Samuel Beckett's 'Lessness' Reconsidered." *Style* 36(1), 54–75.

Ankersmit, F. (2005a). "Historiography." In D. Herman, M. Jahn, and M.-L. Ryan (eds.), *Routledge Encyclopedia of Narrative Theory* (pp. 217–21). London: Routledge.

Ankersmit, F. (2005b). "Narrative Explanation." In D. Herman, M. Jahn, and M.-L. Ryan (eds.), *Routledge Encyclopedia of Narrative Theory* (p. 354). London: Routledge.

Atran, S. (1990). *Cognitive Foundations of Natural History.* Cambridge: Cambridge University Press.

Baetens, J. (2002). "Revealing Traces: A New Theory of Graphic Enunciation." In R. Varnum and C. Gibbons (eds.), *The Language of Comics: Word and Image* (pp. 145–55). Jackson, MS: University Press of Mississippi.

Bakhtin, M. M. ([1937–8] 1981). "Forms of Time and of the Chronotope in the Novel." In M. Holquist (ed.), *The Dialogic Imagination*, trans. C. Emerson and M. Holquist (pp. 84–258). Austin: University of Texas Press.

Bakhtin, M. M. ([1953] 1986). "The Problem of Speech Genres," trans. V. W. McGee. In C. Emerson and M. Holquist (eds.), *Speech Genres and Other Late Essays* (pp. 60–102). Austin: University of Texas Press.

Bal, M. ([1980] 1997). *Narratology: Introduction to the Theory of Narrative*, trans. C. van Boheemen. 2nd edn. Toronto: University of Toronto Press.

Bamberg, M. (ed.) (1997a). Special issue on "Oral Versions of Personal Experience: Three Decades of Narrative Analysis." *Journal of Narrative and Life History* 7(1–4), 1–415.

Bamberg, M. (1997b). "Positioning between Structure and Performance." *Journal of Narrative and Life History* 7(1–4), 335–42.

Bamberg, M. (2004a). "Positioning with Davie Hogan: Stories, Tellings, and Identities." In C. Daiute and C. Lightfoot (eds.), *Narrative Analysis: Studying the Development of Individuals in Society* (pp. 133–57). London: Sage.

Bamberg, M. (2004b). "Talk, Small Stories, and Adolescent Identities." *Human Development* 47, 366–9.

Bamberg, M. (2005). "Positioning." In D. Herman, M. Jahn, and M.-L. Ryan (eds.), *Routledge Encyclopedia of Narrative Theory* (pp. 445–6). London: Routledge.

Bamberg, M. (2006). Special issue on "Narrative – State of the Art." *Narrative Inquiry* 16(1), 1–228.

Bamberg, M., and M. Andrews (eds.) (2004). *Considering Counternarratives: Narrating, Resisting, Making Sense*. Amsterdam: John Benjamins.

Banfield, A. (1982). *Unspeakable Sentences: Narration and Representation in the Language of Fiction*. Boston: Routledge & Kegan Paul.

Barnes, B. (1990). "Sociological Theories of Scientific Knowledge." In R. C. Olby, G. N. Cantor, J. R. R. Christie, and M. J. S. Hodge (eds.), *Companion to the History of Modern Science* (pp. 60–73). London: Routledge.

Barthes, R. ([1957] 1972). *Mythologies*, trans. A. Lavers. New York: Hill & Wang.

Barthes, R. ([1966] 1977). "Introduction to the Structural Analysis of Narratives," trans. S. Heath. In *Image Music Text* (pp. 79–124). New York: Hill & Wang.

Barthes, R. ([1968] 1977). "From Work to Text," trans. S. Heath. In *Image Music Text* (pp. 155–64). New York: Hill & Wang.

Benson, J. J. (ed.) (1990). *New Critical Approaches to the Short Stories of Ernest Hemingway*. Durham: Duke University Press.

Beowulf (1993). Trans. E. T. Donaldson, in M. H. Abrams (ed.), *The Norton Anthology of English Literature*, vol. 1, 6th edn. (pp. 27–68). New York: W. W. Norton.

Berkenkotter, C., and T. N. Huckin (1995). *Genre Knowledge in Disciplinary Communication: Cognition/Culture/Power*. Mahwah, NJ: Lawrence Erlbaum Associates.

Berlin, B. (1992). *Ethnobiological Classification: Principles of Categorization of Plants and Animals in Traditional Societies*. Princeton: Princeton University Press.

Berlin, B., D. E. Breedlove, and P. H. Raven (1973). "General Principles of Classi-fication and Nomenclature in Folk Biology." *American Anthropologist* 75, 214–42.

Blackmore, S. (2004). *Consciousness: An Introduction*. Oxford: Oxford University Press.

Blackmore, S. (2005). *Consciousness: A Very Short Introduction*. Oxford: Oxford University Press.

Block, N., O. Flanagan, and G. Güzeldere (eds.) (1997). *The Nature of Conscious-ness: Philosophical Debates*. Cambridge, MA: MIT Press.

Bolter, J. D., and R. Grusin (1999). *Remediation: Understanding the New Media*. Cambridge, MA: MIT Press.

Booth, W. C. ([1961] 1983). *The Rhetoric of Fiction*. 2nd edn. Chicago: University of Chicago Press.

Booth, W. C. (2005). "Resurrection of the Implied Author: Why Bother." In J. Phelan and P. J. Rabinowitz (eds.), *A Companion to Narrative Theory* (pp. 75–88). Oxford: Blackwell.

Borges, J. L. (1964). *Labyrinths: Selected Stories and Other Writings*, ed. D. A. Yates and J. E. Irby. New York: New Directions.

Bremond, C. (1964). "Le Message narratif." *Communications* 4, 4–32.

Bremond, C. (1980). "The Logic of Narrative Possibilities," trans. E. D. Cancalon. *New Literary History* 11, 387–411.

Bridgeman, T. (2005). "Figuration and Configuration: Mapping Imaginary Worlds in Bande Dessinee." In C. Forsdick, L. Grove and L. McQuillan (eds.), *The Francophone Bande Dessinee* (pp. 115–36). Amsterdam: Rodopi, 2005.

Bruner, J. (1986). *Actual Minds, Possible Worlds*. Cambridge, MA: Harvard University Press.

Bruner, J. (1987). "Life as Narrative." *Social Research* 54, 11–32.

Bruner, J. (1990). *Acts of Meaning*. Cambridge, MA: Harvard University Press.

Bruner, J. (1991). "The Narrative Construction of Reality." *Critical Inquiry* 18, 1–21.

Buchholz, S., and M. Jahn (2005). "Space in Narrative." In D. Herman, M. Jahn, and M.-L. Ryan (eds.), *Routledge Encyclopedia of Narrative Theory* (pp. 551–5). London: Routledge.

Carrier, D. (2000). *The Aesthetics of Comics*. University Park, PA: Pennsylvania State University Press.

Chafe, W. (1994). *Discourse, Consciousness, and Time: The Flow and Displacement of Conscious Experience in Speaking and Writing*. Chicago: University of Chicago Press.

Chalmers, D. J. (1996). *The Conscious Mind: In Search of a Fundamental Theory*. New York: Oxford University Press.

Chatman, S. (1978). *Story and Discourse: Narrative Structure in Fiction and Film*. Ithaca, NY: Cornell University Press.

Chatman, S. (1990). *Coming to Terms: The Rhetoric of Narrative in Fiction and Film.* Ithaca, NY: Cornell University Press.

Clark, A. (1998). "Embodied, Situated, and Distributed Cognition." In W. Bechtel and G. Graham (eds.), *A Companion to Cognitive Science* (pp. 506–17). Oxford: Blackwell.

Clark, G. (1990). *Beowulf.* Boston: Twayne.

Clover, C. J. (1980). "The German Context of the Unferþ Episode." *Speculum* 55, 444–68.

Clowes, D. (1997). *Ghost World.* Seattle, WA: Fantagraphics Books.

Cohn, D. (1978). *Transparent Minds: Narrative Modes for Presenting Consciousness in Fiction.* Princeton: Princeton University Press.

Cohn, D. (1999). *The Distinction of Fiction.* Baltimore: Johns Hopkins University Press.

Crystal, D. (1997). *A Dictionary of Linguistics and Phonetics.* 4th edn. Oxford: Blackwell.

Culler, J. (1975). *Structuralist Poetics: Structuralism, Linguistics, and the Study of Literature.* Ithaca, NY: Cornell University Press.

Culler, J. (1998). *A Very Short Introduction to Literary Theory.* Oxford: Oxford University Press.

Dannenberg, H. (2008). *Convergent and Divergent Lives: Plotting Coincidence and Counterfactuality in Narrative Fiction.* Lincoln: University of Nebraska Press.

Danto, A. C. (1985). *Narration and Knowledge* (including the integral text of *Analytical Philosophy of History*). New York: Columbia University Press.

Davies, M. (1999). "Consciousness." In R. A. Wilson and F. C. Keil (eds.), *The MIT Encyclopedia of the Cognitive Sciences* (pp. 190–3). Cambridge, MA: MIT Press.

Dennett, D. (1991). *Consciousness Explained.* Boston: Little, Brown.

Dennett, D. (1997). "Quining Qualia." In N. Block, O. Flanagan, and G. Güzeldere (eds.), *The Nature of Consciousness: Philosophical Debates* (pp. 619–42). Cambridge, MA: MIT Press.

Derrida, J. ([1980] 1991). "The Law of Genre." In D. Attridge (ed.), *Acts of Literature* (pp. 221–52). New York: Routledge.

Doležel, L. (1980). "Truth and Authenticity in Narrative." *Poetics Today* 1, 7–25.

Doležel, L. (1998). *Heterocosmica: Fiction and Possible Worlds.* Baltimore: Johns Hopkins University Press.

Drew, P., and J. Heritage (eds.) (1992). *Talk at Work.* Cambridge: Cambridge University Press.

Dubrow, H. (1982). *Genre.* London: Methuen.

Edwards, D. (1997). *Discourse and Cognition.* London: Sage.

Edwards, D. (2006). "Discourse, Cognition and Social Practices: The Rich Surface of Language and Social Interaction." *Discourse Studies* 8(1), 41–9.

Edwards, D., and J. Potter (1992). *Discursive Psychology.* London: Sage.

Eggins, S., and D. Slade (1997). *Analysing Casual Conversation.* London: Cassell.

Eisner, W. (1996). *Graphic Storytelling and Visual Narrative.* Tamarac: Poorhouse Press.

Ellen, R. (1993). *The Cultural Relations of Classification.* Cambridge: Cambridge University Press.

Emmott, C. (1997). *Narrative Comprehension: A Discourse Perspective.* Oxford: Oxford University Press.

Ewert, J. C. (2004). "Art Spiegelman's *Maus* and the Graphic Narrative." In M.-L. Ryan (ed.), *Narrative Across Media: The Languages of Storytelling* (pp. 178–93). Lincoln: University of Nebraska Press.

Ewert, J. C. (2005). "Comics and Graphic Novel." In D. Herman, M. Jahn, and M.-L. Ryan (eds.), *Routledge Encyclopedia of Narrative Theory* (pp. 71–3). London: Routledge.

Flanagan, O. (1998). "Consciousness." In W. Bechtel and G. Graham (eds.), *A Companion to Cognitive Science* (pp. 176–85). Oxford: Blackwell.

Fludernik, M. (1993). *The Fictions of Language and the Languages of Fiction: The Linguistic Representation of Speech and Consciousness.* London: Routledge.

Fludernik, M. (1996). *Towards a "Natural" Narratology.* London: Routledge.

Fludernik, M. (2000). "Genres, Text Types, or Discourse Modes?" *Style* 34(2), 274–92.

Fludernik, M. (2003). "Natural Narratology and Cognitive Parameters." In D. Herman (ed.), *Narrative Theory and the Cognitive Sciences* (pp. 243–67). Stanford, CA: Center for the Study of Language and Information.

Fludernik, M. (2005). "Histories of Narrative Theory (II): From Structuralism to the Present." In J. Phelan and P. J. Rabinowitz (eds.), *A Companion to Narrative Theory* (pp. 36–59). Oxford: Blackwell.

Fludernik, M. (2007). "Identity/Alterity." In D. Herman (ed.), *The Cambridge Companion to Narrative* (pp. 260–73). Cambridge: Cambridge University Press.

Frawley, W. (1992). *Linguistic Semantics.* Hillsdale, NJ: Lawrence Erlbaum

Freeman, A. (2003). *Consciousness: A Guide to the Debates.* Santa Barbara, CA: ABC-Clio.

Gallagher, S. (2006). "The Narrative Alternative to Theory of Mind." In R. Menary (ed.), *Radical Enactivism: Intentionality, Phenomenology, and Narrative: Focus on the Philosophy of Daniel D. Hutto* (pp. 223–9). Amsterdam: John Benjamins.

Garcia Landa, J. A. (2004). "Overhearing Narrative." In J. Pier (ed.), *The Dynamics of Narrative Form: Studies in Anglo-American Narratology* (pp. 191–214). Berlin: Walter de Gruyter.

Garfinkel, H. (1967). *Studies in Ethnomethdology.* Englewood Cliffs, NJ: Prentice Hall.

Genette, G. ([1972] 1980). *Narrative Discourse: An Essay in Method,* trans. J. E. Lewin. Ithaca, NY: Cornell University Press.

Genette, G. ([1966] 1982). "Frontiers of Narrative." In *Figures of Literary Discourse*, trans. A. Sheridan (pp. 127–42). New York: Columbia University Press.

Genette, G. ([1983] 1988). *Narrative Discourse Revisited*, trans. J. E. Lewin. Ithaca, NY: Cornell University Press.

Genette, G. ([1991] 1993). *Fiction and Diction*, trans. Catherine Porter. Ithaca, NY: Cornell University Press.

Genette, G. ([1982] 1997). *Palimpsests: Literature in the Second Degree*, trans. C. Newman and C. Doubinsky. Lincoln: University of Nebraska Press.

Georgakopoulou, A. (2005). "Text-Type Approach to Narrative." In D. Herman, M. Jahn, and M.-L. Ryan (eds.), *The Routledge Encyclopedia of Narrative Theory* (pp. 594–6). London: Routledge.

Georgakopoulou, A. (2007). *Small Stories, Interaction and Identities*. Amsterdam: John Benjamins.

Gerrig, R. J. (1993). *Experiencing Narrative Worlds: On the Psychological Activities of Reading*. New Haven: Yale University Press.

Goffman, E. (1974). *Frame Analysis: An Essay on the Organization of Experience*. New York: Harper & Row.

Goffman, E. (1981). *Forms of Talk*. Philadelphia: University of Pennsylvania Press.

Goodman, N. (1978). *Ways of Worldmaking*. Indianapolis: Hackett.

Goodwin, M. H. (1990). *He-Said-She-Said: Talk as Organization among Black Children*. Bloomington: Indiana University Press.

Görlach, M. (2004). *Text Types and the History of English*. Berlin: Mouton de Gruyter.

Green, G. M. (1989). *Pragmatics and Natural Language Understanding*. Hillsdale, NJ: Lawrence Erlbaum.

Greimas, A. J. ([1966] 1983). *Structural Semantics: An Attempt at a Method*, trans. D. McDowell, R. Schleifer, and A. Velie. Lincoln: University of Nebraska Press.

Groensteen, T. (2007). *The System of Comics*, trans. Bart Beaty and Nick Nguyen. Jackson: University of of Mississippi Press.

Gumperz, J. J. (1982). *Discourse Strategies*. Cambridge: Cambridge University Press.

Halliday, M. A. K. (1994). *An Introduction to Functional Grammar*. 2nd edn. London: Edward Arnold.

Hamburger, K. ([1957] 1993). *The Logic of Literature*. 2nd, revised, edn., trans. M. J. Rose. Bloomington: Indiana University Press.

Hamon, P. (1982). "What Is a Description?" In P. Hamon (ed.), *French Literary Theory Today* (pp. 147–78). Cambridge: Cambridge University Press.

Hansen, P. K. (2007). "Reconsidering the Unreliable Narrator." *Semiotica* 165(1/4), 227–46.

Harré, R. (2001). "The Discursive Turn in Social Psychology." In D. Schiffrin, D. Tannen, and H. E. Hamilton (eds.), *The Handbook of Discourse Analysis* (pp. 688–706). Oxford: Blackwell.

Harré, R., and G. Gillett (1994). *The Discursive Mind*. London: Sage.

Harré, R., and L. van Langenhove (eds.) (1999). *Positioning Theory: Moral Contexts of Intentional Action*. Oxford: Blackwell.

Harré, R., and P. Stearns (eds.) (1995). *Discursive Psychology in Practice*. Thousand Oaks, CA: Sage.

Hemingway, E. ([1927] 1987). "Hills Like White Elephants." In *The Complete Short Stories of Ernest Hemingway* (pp. 211–14). New York: Charles Scribner's Sons.

Hempel, C. ([1948] 1998). "Studies in the Logic of Explanation." In E. D. Klemke, R. Hollinger, and D. W. Rudge, with A. D. Kline (eds.), *Introductory Readings in the Philosophy of Science* (pp. 206–24). Amherst, NY: Prometheus Books.

Herman, D. (1998). "Narrative, Science, and Narrative Science." *Narrative Inquiry* 8(2), 379–90.

Herman, D. (1999a). "Introduction." In David Herman (ed.), *Narratologies: New Perspectives on Narrative Analysis* (pp. 1–30). Columbus: Ohio State University Press.

Herman, D. (1999b). "Towards a Socionarratology." In D. Herman (ed.), *Narratologies: New Perspectives on Narrative Analysis* (pp. 1–30). Columbus: Ohio State University Press.

Herman, D. (2000). "Pragmatic Constraints on Narrative Processing: Actants and Anaphora Resolution in a Corpus of North Carolina Ghost Stories." *Journal of Pragmatics* 32(7), 959–1001.

Herman, D. (2001a). "Spatial Reference in Narrative Domains." *TEXT: An Interdisciplinary Journal for the Study of Discourse* 21(4), 515–41.

Herman, D. (2001b). "Sciences of the Text." *Postmodern Culture* 11(3) <http://www.iath.virginia.edu/pmc/text-only/issue.501/11.3herman.txt>.

Herman, D. (2002a). *Story Logic: Problems and Possibilities of Narrative*. Lincoln: University of Nebraska Press.

Herman, D. (2002b). "Narrative: A User's Manual." *Style* 36(2), 560–8.

Herman, D. (2003a). "Stories as a Tool for Thinking." In D. Herman (ed.), *Narrative Theory and the Cognitive Sciences* (pp. 163–92). Stanford, CA: Publications of the Center for the Study of Language and Information.

Herman, D. (2003b). "Regrounding Narratology: The Study of Narratively Organized Systems for Thinking." In T. Kindt and H.-H. Müller (eds.), *What Is Narratology? Questions and Answers Regarding the Status of a Theory* (pp. 303–32). Berlin: Walter de Gruyter.

Herman, D. (2004). "Toward a Transmedial Narratology." In M.-L. Ryan (ed.), *Narrative across Media: The Languages of Storytelling* (pp. 47–75). Lincoln: University of Nebraska Press.

Herman, D. (2005a). "Histories of Narrative Theory (I): A Genealogy of Early Developments." In J. Phelan and P. J. Rabinowitz (eds.), *The Blackwell Companion to Narrative Theory* (pp. 19–35). Oxford: Blackwell.

Herman, D. (2005b). "Quantitative Methods in Narratology: A Corpus-Based Study of Motion Events in Stories." In J.-C. Meister (ed.), *Narratology Beyond Literary Criticism* (pp. 125–49). (Edited in cooperation with T. Kindt, W. Schernus, and M. Stein). Berlin: Walter de Gruyter.

Herman, D. (2006a). "Narrative: Cognitive Approaches." In K. Brown (ed.), *Encyclopedia of Language and Linguistics*, 2nd edn., vol. 8 (pp. 452–9). (Section editor C. Emmott.) Oxford: Elsevier.

Herman, D. (2006b). "Dialogue in a Discourse Context: Scenes of Talk in Fictional Narrative." *Narrative Inquiry* 16(1), 79–88.

Herman, D. (2006c). "Genette Meets Vygotsky: Narrative Embedding and Distributed Intelligence." *Language and Literature* 15(4), 375–98.

Herman, D. (2007a). "Nonfactivity, Tellability, and Narrativity." Presentation for a Workshop on "Events, Eventfulness, and Tellability" sponsored by the University of Hamburg's Interdisciplinary Centre for Narratology and the University of Ghent; Ghent, Belgium, February 2007.

Herman, D. (2007b). "Storytelling and the Sciences of Mind: Cognitive Narratology, Discursive Psychology, and Narratives in Face-to-Face Interaction." *Narrative* 15(3), 306–34.

Herman, D. (2007c). "Cognition, Emotion, and Consciousness." In D. Herman (ed.), *The Cambridge Companion to Narrative* (pp. 245–59). Cambridge: Cambridge University Press.

Herman, D. (2008a). "Narrative Theory and the Intentional Stance." *Partial Answers* 6(2), 233–60.

Herman, D. (2008b). "Narrative and Intentionality." Presentation for a panel on "Intentionalities" at the annual meeting of the International Society for the Study of Narrative; Austin, Texas, May 2008.

Herman, D. (forthcoming a). "Narrative Theory after the Second Cognitive Revolution." In L. Zunshine (ed.), *Introduction to Cognitive Cultural Studies*. Baltimore: Johns Hopkins University Press.

Herman, D. (forthcoming b). "Description, Narrative, and Explanation: Text-Type Categories and the Cognitive Foundations of Discourse Competence." *Poetics Today* 29(3).

Herman, D. (forthcoming c). "Word-Image/Utterance-Gesture: Case Studies in Multimodal Storytelling." New Perspectives on *Narrative and Multimodality*. Ed. R. Page. London: Routledge.

Herman, D., and B. Childs (2003). "Narrative and Cognition in *Beowulf*." *Style* 37(2), 177–202.

Herman, D., and S. Moss (2007). "Plant Names and Folk Taxonomies: Frameworks for Ethnosemiotic Inquiry." *Semiotica* 167(1/4), 1–11.

Herman, L., and B. Vervaeck (2005a). *Handbook of Narrative Analysis*. Lincoln: University of Nebraska Press.

Herman, L., and B. Vervaeck (2005b). "Postclassical Narratology." In D. Herman, M. Jahn, and M.-L. Ryan (eds.), *The Routledge Encyclopedia of Narrative Theory* (pp. 450–1). London: Routledge.

Hogan, P. C. (2003). *Cognitive Science, Literature, and the Arts: A Guide for Humanists*. London: Routledge.

Hutto, D. D. (1999). *The Presence of Mind*. Amsterdam: John Benjamins.

Hutto, D. D. (2000). *Beyond Physicalism*. Amsterdam: John Benjamins.

Hutto, D. D. (2006a). "Narrative Practice and Understanding Reasons: Reply to Gallagher." In R. Menary (ed.), *Radical Enactivism: Intentionality, Phenomenology, and Narrative: Focus on the Philosophy of Daniel D. Hutto* (pp. 231–47). Amsterdam: John Benjamins.

Hutto, D. D. (2006b). "Impossible Problems and Careful Expositions: Reply to Myin and De Nul." In R. Menary (ed.), *Radical Enactivism: Intentionality, Phenomenology, and Narrative: Focus on the Philosophy of Daniel D. Hutto* (45–64). Amsterdam: John Benjamins.

Hutto, D. D. (2007). "The Narrative Practice Hypothesis: Origins and Applications of Folk Psychology." In D. D. Hutto (ed.), *Narrative and Understanding Persons* (pp. 43–68). Cambridge: Cambridge University Press.

Hutto, D. D. (2008). *Folk Psychological Narratives: The Sociocultural Basis of Understanding Reasons*. Cambridge, MA: MIT Press.

Hutto, D. D., and M. Ratcliffe (eds.) (2007). *Folk Psychology Re-assessed*. Dordrecht: Springer.

Hymes, D. (1974). *Foundations in Sociolinguistics: An Ethnographic Approach*. Philadelphia: University of Pennsylvania Press.

Hyvärinen, M. (2006). "Towards a Conceptual History of Narrative." <http://www.helsinki.fi/collegium/e-series/volumes/volume_1/001_04_hyvarinen.pdf>. In M. Hyvärinen, A. Korhonen, and J. Mykkänen (eds.), *The Travelling Concept of Narrative* (pp. 20–41). Helsinki: Helsinki Collegium for Advanced Studies. <http://www.helsinki.fi/collegium/e-series/vol.s/vol._1/index.htm>.

Iser, W. (1974). *The Implied Reader: Patterns of Communication in Prose Fiction from Bunyan to Beckett*. Baltimore: Johns Hopkins University Press.

Jackson, F. (1982). "Epiphenomenal Qualia." *Philosophical Quarterly* 32, 127–36.

Jahn, M. (1996). "Windows of Focalization: Deconstructing and Reconstructing a Narratological Concept." *Style* 30(3), 241–67.

Jahn, M. (1997). "Frames, Preferences, and the Reading of Third-Person Narratives: Towards a Cognitive Narratology." *Poetics Today* 18, 441–68.

Jahn, M. (1999). "More Aspects of Focalization: Refinements and Applications." *GRAAT* 21 (Groupes de Recherches Anglo-Américaines de Tours) [Issue Topic: "Recent Trends in Narratological Research"], 85–110.

Jahn, M. (2005). "Focalization." In D. Herman, M. Jahn, and M.-L. Ryan (eds.), *Routledge Encyclopedia of Narrative Theory* (pp. 173–7). London: Routledge.

Jahn, M. (2007). "Focalization." In D. Herman (ed.), *The Cambridge Companion to Narrative* (pp. 94–108). Cambridge: Cambridge University Press.

Jakobson, R. (1960). "Closing Statement: Linguistics and Poetics." In T. A. Sebeok (ed.), *Style in Language* (pp. 350–77). Cambridge, MA: MIT Press.

Jannidis, F. (2003). "Narratology and the Narrative." In T. Kindt and H.-H. Müller (ed.), *What Is Narratology? Questions and Answers Regarding the Status of a Theory* (pp. 35–54). Berlin: Walter de Gruyter.

Jauss, H. R. (1982). *Toward an Aesthetic of Reception*, trans. Timothy Bahti. Minneapolis: University of Minnesota Press.

Jefferson, G. (1984). "Transcription Notation." In J. M. Atkinson and J. Heritage (eds.), *Structures of Social Action: Studies in Conversation Analysis* (pp. ix–xvi). Cambridge: Cambridge University Press.

Jewitt, C. (2006). *Technology, Literacy, and Learning: A Multimodal Approach*. London: Routledge.

Johnston, K. G. (1987). *The Tip of the Iceberg: Hemingway and the Short Story*. Greenwood, FL: Penkevill.

Johnstone, B. (2000). *Qualitative Methods in Sociolinguistics*. Oxford: Oxford University Press.

Kafalenos, E. (2006). *Narrative Causalities*. Columbus: Ohio State University Press.

Keen, S. (2007). *Empathy and the Novel*. Oxford: Oxford University Press.

Kendall, T. (2007). "Enhancing Sociolinguistic Data Collections: The North Carolina Sociolinguistic Archive and Analysis Project." *Penn Working Papers in Linguistics* 13(2), 15–26. <http://repository.upenn.edu/pwpl/vol13/iss2/>.

Kindt, T., and H.-H. Müller (2006). *The Implied Author: Concept and Controversy*. Berlin: Walter de Gruyter.

Kirk, R. (2003). "Zombies." In E. N. Zalta (ed.), *The Stanford Encyclopedia of Philosophy* (Fall 2003 edn.).<http://plato.stanford.edu/archives/fall2003/entries/zombies/>.

Kittay, J. (1981). "Descriptive Limits." *Yale French Studies* 61, 225–43.

Klemke, E. D., R. Hollinger, and D. W. Rudge, with A. D. Kline (eds.) (1998). *Introductory Readings in the Philosophy of Science*. Amherst, NY: Prometheus Books.

Kraus, W. (2005). "The Eye of the Beholder: Narratology as Seen by Social Psychology." In J.-C. Meister (ed.), *Narratology Beyond Literary Criticism* (pp. 265–87). (Edited in cooperation with T. Kindt, W. Schernus, and M. Stein). Berlin: Walter de Gruyter.

Kreiswirth, M. (2005). "Narrative Turn in the Humanities." In D. Herman, M. Jahn, and M.-L. Ryan (eds.), *Routledge Encyclopedia of Narrative Theory* (pp. 377–82). London: Routledge.

Kress, G., and T. van Leeuwen (2001). *Multimodal Discourse: The Modes and Media of Contemporary Communication*. London: Arnold.

Labov, W. (1972). "The Transformation of Experience in Narrative Syntax." In *Language in the Inner City* (pp. 354–96). Philadelphia: University of Pennsylvania Press.

Labov, W., and J. Waletzky (1967). "Narrative Analysis: Oral Versions of Personal Experience." In J. Helm (ed.), *Essays on the Verbal and Visual Arts* (pp. 12–44). Seattle: University of Washington Press.

Lacey, A. R. (1986). *A Dictionary of Philosophy*. 2nd edn. London: Routledge.

Lakoff, G. (1987). *Women, Fire and Dangerous Things: What Categories Reveal about the Mind*. Chicago: University of Chicago Press.

Lakoff, G. ([1987] 2004). "The Importance of Categorization." In B. Aarts, D. Denison, E. Keizer, and G. Popova (eds.), *Fuzzy Grammar: A Reader* (pp. 139–77). Oxford: Oxford University Press.

Lambert, K., and G. Britten ([1970] 1998). "Laws and Conditional Statements." In E. D. Klemke, R. Hollinger, and D. W. Rudge, with A. D. Kline (eds.), *Introductory Readings in the Philosophy of Science* (pp. 225–32). Amherst, NY: Prometheus Books.

Lambrou, M. (2008). "Oral Narratives of Personal Experiences: When Is a Narrative not a Narrative but a Recount?" In M. Lambrou and P. Stockwell (eds.), *Contemporary Stylistics* (pp. 196–208). London: Continuum.

Lanser, S. S. (1981). *The Narrative Act: Point of View in Prose Fiction*. Princeton: Princeton University Press.

Lanser, S. S. (1992). *Fictions of Authority: Women Writers and Narrative Voice*. Ithaca, NY: Cornell University Press.

Leech, G., and M. Short ([1981] 2007). *Style in Fiction: A Linguistic Introduction to English Fictional Prose*. 2nd edn. Harlow: Pearson/Longman.

Lejeune, P. (1989). "The Autobiographical Pact." In *On Autobiography*, ed. P. J. Eakin, trans. K. Leary (pp. 3–30). Minneapolis: University of Minnesota Press.

Levi, P. (1961). *Survival in Auschwitz*, trans. S. Woolf. New York: Collier.

Levin, J. (1999). "Qualia." In R. A. Wilson and F. C. Keil (eds.), *The MIT Encyclopedia of the Cognitive Sciences* (pp. 693–4). Cambridge, MA: MIT Press.

Levine, J. (1983). "Materialism and Qualia: The Explanatory Gap." *Pacific Philosophical Quarterly* 64(4), 354–61.

Levinson, S. ([1979] 1992). "Activity Types and Language." In P. Drew and J. Heritage (eds.), *Talk at Work* (pp. 66–100). Cambridge: Cambridge University Press.

Lewis, D. (1979). "Scorekeeping in a Language Game." *Journal of Philosophical Logic* 8, 339–59.

Linde, C. (1993). *Life Stories: The Creation of Coherence*. New York: Oxford University Press.

Lodge, D. (2002). "Consciousness and the Novel." In *Consciousness and the Novel: Connected Essays* (pp. 1–91). Cambridge, MA: Harvard University Press.

Longino, H. (1990). *Science as Social Knowledge: Values and Objectivity in Scientific Inquiry*. Princeton: Princeton University Press.

Longino, H. (2002). "The Social Dimensions of Scientific Knowledge." In E. N. Zalta (ed.), *The Stanford Encyclopedia of Philosophy*. <http://plato.stanford.edu/entries/scientific-knowledge-social/>.

Lönneker, B. (2005). "Narratological Knowledge for Natural Language Generation." In G. Wilcock, K. Jokinen, C. Mellish, and E. Reiter (eds.), *Proceedings of the 10th European Workshop on Natural Language Generation* (= ENLG 2005) (pp. 91–100). Aberdeen, Scotland, August 8–10, 2005. <http://www1.uni-hamburg.de/story-generators//Birte/Narratological_Knowledge.pdf>.

Lord, A. B. (1995). *The Singer Resumes the Tale*, ed. M. L. Lord. Ithaca, NY: Cornell University Press.

Lubbock, P. ([1921] 1957). *The Craft of Fiction*. London: Jonathan Cape.

Lukács, G. ([1936] 1970). "Narrate or Describe?" In *Writer and Critic and Other Essays*, trans. and ed. A. D. Kahn (pp. 110–48). New York: Grosset & Dunlap.

Lyotard, J.-F. ([1979] 1984). *The Postmodern Condition: A Report on Knowledge*, trans. G. Bennington and B. Massumi. Minneapolis: University of Minnesota Press.

MacIntyre, A. (1984). *After Virtue: A Study of Moral Theory*. 2nd edn. South Bend: University of Notre Dame Press.

Mallinson, C. (2006). "The Dynamic Construction of Race, Class, and Gender through Linguistic Practice among Women in a Black Appalachian Community." Unpublished doctoral dissertation. Department of Sociology, North Carolina State University.

Mallinson, C. (2008). "The Linguistic Negotiation of Complex Racialized Identities by Black Appalachian Speakers." In K. King, N. Schilling-Estes, L. Fogle, J. Lou, and B. Soukup (eds.), *Sustaining Linguistic Diversity: Endangered and Minority Languages and Language Varieties* (pp. 67–80). Washington, DC: Georgetown University Press.

Malt, B. C. (1995). "Category Coherence in Cross-Cultural Perspective." *Cognitive Psychology* 29, 85–148.

Margolin, U. (1990a). "The What, the When, and the How of Being a Character in a Literary Narrative." *Style* 24, 453–68.

Margolin, U. (1990b). "Individuals in Narrative Worlds: An Ontological Perspective." *Poetics Today* 11, 843–71.

Margolin, U. (1999). "Of What Is Past, Is Passing, or To Come: Temporality, Aspectuality, Modality, and the Nature of Narrative." In D. Herman (ed.), *Narratologies: New Perspectives on Narrative Analysis* (pp. 142–66). Columbus: Ohio State University Press.

Margolin, U. (2005a). "Character." In D. Herman, M. Jahn, and M.-L. Ryan (eds.), *Routledge Encyclopedia of Narrative Theory* (pp. 52–7). London: Routledge.

Margolin, U. (2005b). "Authentication." In D. Herman, M. Jahn, and M.-L. Ryan (eds.), *Routledge Encyclopedia of Narrative Theory* (pp. 32–3). London: Routledge.

Margolin, U. (2007). "Character." In D. Herman (ed.), *The Cambridge Companion to Narrative* (pp. 66–79). Cambridge: Cambridge University Press.

Martin, T. (2004). *Poiesis and Possible Worlds: A Study in Modality and Literary Theory*. Toronto: University of Toronto Press.

Martin, W. (1986). *Recent Theories of Narrative*. Ithaca, NY: Cornell University Press.

Mateas, M., and P. Senger (2003). *Narrative Intelligence*. Amsterdam: John Benjamins.

McCloud, S. (1993). *Understanding Comics*. New York: HarperCollins.

McEwan, I. (1978). *The Cement Garden*. London: Jonathan Cape.

McHale, B. (1987). *Postmodernist Fiction*. London: Methuen.

Meister, J. C. (2003). *Computing Action: A Narratological Approach*. Berlin: Walter de Gruyter.

Menary, R. (2006). "Introduction: What is Radical Enactivism?" In R. Menary (ed.), *Radical Enactivism: Intentionality, Phenomenology, and Narrative: Focus on the Philosophy of Daniel D. Hutto* (pp. 1–12). Amsterdam: John Benjamins.

Mildorf, J. (2007). *Storying Domestic Violence: Constructions and Stereotypes of Abuse in the Discourse of General Practitioners*. Lincoln: University of Nebraska Press.

Miller, C. R. (1984). "Genre as Social Action." *Quarterly Journal of Speech* 70, 151–67.

Miller, J. E. (ed.) (1972). *Theory of Fiction: Henry James*. Lincoln: University of Nebraska Press.

Mink, L. (1978). "Narrative Form as Cognitive Instrument." In R. H. Canary and H. Kozicki (eds.), *The Writing of History: Literary Form and Historical Understanding* (pp. 129–49). Madison: University of Wisconsin Press.

Moisinnac, L. (2008). "Positioning in Conversational Stories: Advances in Theory and Practice." Prospectus of panel discussion held at the Georgetown University Roundtable in Linguistics, March 2008. < http://www8.georgetown.edu/college/gurt/2008/>.

Moore, A., D. Gibbons, and J. Higgins (1987). *Watchmen*. New York: DC Comics.

Morgan, R. (2002). *Altered Carbon*. New York: Del Rey.

Morrison, J. (forthcoming). "Narrative Theory in the Film Studies Classroom; or, Old Movies and the New Disorder." In D. Herman, B. McHale, and J. Phelan (eds.), *Teaching Narrative Theory*. New York: Modern Language Association of America.

Mosher, H. F., Jr. (1991). "Towards a Poetics of Descriptized Narration." *Poetics Today* 3, 425–45.

Nagel, T. (1974). "What Is It Like To Be a Bat?" *The Philosophical Review* 83(4), 435–50.

Nelson, L. H. (1990). *Who Knows: From Quine to Feminist Empiricism*. Philadelphia, PA: Temple University Press.

Nieragden, G. (2002). "Focalization and Narration: Theoretical and Terminological Refinements." *Poetics Today* 23(4), 685–97.

Norrick, N. R. (1992). "Twice-Told Tales: Collaborative Narration of Familiar Stories." *Language in Society* 26, 199–220.

Norrick, N. R. (2000). *Conversational Narrative*. Amsterdam: John Benjamins.

Norrick, N. R. (2007). "Conversational Storytelling." In D. Herman (ed.), *The Cambridge Companion to Narrative* (127–41). Cambridge: Cambridge University Press.

Nünning, A. (1997). "Deconstructing and Reconceptualizing the Implied Author." *Anglistik* 8(2), 95–116.

Nünning, A. (2003). "Narratology or Narratologies? Taking Stock of Recent Developments: Critique and Modest Proposals for Future Usages of the Term." In T. Kindt and H.-H. Müller, *What Is Narratology? Questions and Answers Regarding the Status of a Theory* (pp. 239–75). Berlin: Walter de Gruyter.

Nünning, A. (2005). "Reconceptualizing Unreliable Narration." In J. Phelan and P. J. Rabinowitz (eds.), *A Companion to Narrative Theory* (pp. 89–107). Oxford: Blackwell.

Oatley, K. (1999). "Emotions." In R. A. Wilson and F. C. Keil (eds.), *The MIT Encyclopedia of the Cognitive Sciences* (pp. 273–5). Cambridge, MA: MIT Press.

Ochs, E., and L. Capps (2001). *Living Narrative: Creating Lives in Everyday Storytelling*. Cambridge, MA: Harvard University Press.

Ochs, E., C. Taylor, D. Rudolph, and R. Smith (1992). "Storytelling as Theory-Building Activity." *Discourse Processes* 15, 37–72.

Page, R. (2006). *Literary and Linguistic Approaches to Feminist Narratology*. Basingstoke: Palgrave Macmillan.

Palmer, A. (2003). "The Mind Beyond the Skin." In D. Herman (ed.), *Narrative Theory and the Cognitive Sciences* (pp. 322–48). Stanford, CA.: Center for the Study of Language and Information.

Palmer, A. (2004). *Fictional Minds*. Lincoln: University of Nebraska Press.

Pavel, T. (1976). *Syntaxe narrative des tragédies de Corneille*. Paris: Klincksieck.

Pavel, T. (1985). *The Poetics of Plot*. Minneapolis: University of Minnesota Press.

Pavel, T. (1986). *Fictional Worlds*. Cambridge, MA: Harvard University Press.

Pflugmacher, T. (2005). "Description." In D. Herman, M. Jahn, and M.-L. Ryan (eds.), *Routledge Encyclopedia of Narrative Theory* (pp. 101–2). London: Routledge.

Phelan, J. (1989). *Reading People, Reading Plots*. Chicago: University of Chicago Press.

Phelan, J. (2005a). *Living to Tell about It: A Rhetoric and Ethics of Character Narration.* Ithaca, NY: Cornell University Press.

Phelan, J. (2005b). "Who's Here? Thoughts on Narrative Identity and Narrative Imperialism." *Narrative* 13(3), 205–10.

Pike, K. L. (1982). *Linguistic Concepts: An Introduction to Tagmemics.* Lincoln: University of Nebraska Press.

Plotnitsky, A. (2005). "Science and Narrative." In D. Herman, M. Jahn, and M.-L. Ryan (eds.), *Routledge Encyclopedia of Narrative Theory* (pp. 514–18). London: Routledge.

Plum, G. A. (1988). "Text and Contextual Conditioning in Spoken English: A Genre-Based Approach." Unpublished doctoral dissertation. University of Sydney.

Potter, J., and M. Wetherell (1987). *Discourse and Social Psychology.* London: Sage.

Pratt, M. L. (1977). *Toward a Speech Act Theory of Literary Discourse.* Bloomington: Indiana University Press.

Prince, G. (1973). *A Grammar of Stories.* The Hague: Mouton.

Prince, G. (1980). "Aspects of a Grammar of Narrative." *Poetics Today* 1, 49–63.

Prince, G. (1982). *Narratology: The Form and Functioning of Narrative.* The Hague: Mouton.

Prince, G. (1983). "Narrative Pragmatics, Message, and Point." *Poetics* 12, 527–36.

Prince, G. (1999). "Revisiting Narrativity." In W. Grünzweig and A. Solbach (eds.), *Transcending Boundaries: Narratology in Context* (pp. 43–51). Tübingen: Narr.

Prince, G. ([1987] 2003). *A Dictionary of Narratology.* 2nd edn. Lincoln: University of Nebraska Press.

Prince, G. (2005). "Narrativity." In D. Herman, M. Jahn, and M.-L. Ryan (eds.), *Routledge Encyclopedia of Narrative Theory* (pp. 387–8). London: Routledge.

Propp, V. ([1928] 1968). *Morphology of the Folktale,* 2nd edn. trans. L. Scott; revised L. A. Wagner. Austin: University of Texas Press.

Quine, W. V. O. (1951). "Two Dogmas of Empiricism." *The Philosophical Review* 60, 20–43.

Rabinowitz, P. J. ([1977] 1996). "Truth in Fiction: A Reexamination of Audiences." In D. H. Richter (ed.), *Narrative/Theory* (pp. 209–26). White Plains, NY: Longman.

Rabinowitz, P. J. (1998). *Before Reading: Narrative Conventions and the Politics of Interpretation.* Columbus: Ohio State University Press.

Reddy, M. J. (1979). "The Conduit Metaphor – a Case of Frame Conflict in Our Language about Language." In A. Ortony (ed.), *Metaphor and Thought* (pp. 284–324). Cambridge: Cambridge University Press.

Richardson, B. (2006). *Unnatural Voices: Extreme Narration in Modern and Contemporary Fiction.* Columbus: Ohio State University Press.

Ricoeur, P. (1990). *Time and Narrative*. Vol. 1. Trans. K. McLaughlin and D. Pellauer. Chicago: University of Chicago Press.

Rimmon-Kenan, S. ([1983] 2002). *Narrative Fiction: Contemporary Poetics*. 2nd edn. London: Routledge.

Robbe-Grillet, A. ([1957, 1959] 1965). *Two Novels, by Robbe-Grillet* [*La Jalousie* and *Dans le labyrinthe*], trans. R. Howard. New York: Grove Press.

Roberts, C. (1999). "Discourse." In R. A. Wilson and F. C. Keil (eds.), *The MIT Encyclopedia of the Cognitive Sciences* (pp. 231–2). Cambridge, MA: MIT Press.

Ronen, R. (1994). *Possible Worlds in Literary Theory*. Cambridge: Cambridge University Press.

Ronen, R. (1997). "Description, Narrative, and Representation." *Narrative* 3, 274–86.

Rosch, E. (1973). "Natural Categories." *Cognitive Psychology* 4, 328–50.

Rosch, E. ([1978] 2004). "Principles of Categorization." In B. Aarts, D. Denison, E. Keizer, and G. Popova (eds.), *Fuzzy Grammar: A Reader* (pp. 91–108). Oxford: Oxford University Press.

Rosch, E., C. Mervis, W. Gray, D. Johnson, and P. Boyes-Braem (1976). "Basic Objects in Natural Categories." *Cognitive Psychology* 8, 382–439.

Ryan, M.-L. (1991). *Possible Worlds, Artificial Intelligence, and Narrative Theory*. Bloomington: Indiana University Press.

Ryan, M.-L. (2001a). *Narrative as Virtual Reality: Immersion and Interactivity in Literature and Electronic Media*. Baltimore: Johns Hopkins University Press.

Ryan, M.-L. (2001b). "The Narratorial Functions: Breaking Down a Theoretical Primitive." *Narrative* 9(2), 146–52.

Ryan, M.-L. (ed.) (2004). *Narrative across Media: The Languages of Storytelling*. Lincoln: University of Nebraska Press.

Ryan, M.-L. (2005a). "Narrative." In D. Herman, M. Jahn, and M.-L. Ryan (eds.), *Routledge Encyclopedia of Narrative Theory* (pp. 344–8). London: Routledge.

Ryan, M.-L. (2005b). "Possible-Worlds Theory." In D. Herman, M. Jahn, and M.-L. Ryan (eds.), *Routledge Encyclopedia of Narrative Theory* (pp. 446–50). London: Routledge.

Ryan, M.-L. (2005c). "Tellability." In D. Herman, M. Jahn, and M.-L. Ryan (eds.), *Routledge Encyclopedia of Narrative Theory* (pp. 589–91). London: Routledge.

Ryan, M.-L. (2006). *Avatars of Story*. Minneapolis: University of Minnesota Press.

Ryan, M.-L. (2007). "Toward a Definition of Narrative." In D. Herman (ed.), *The Cambridge Companion to Narrative* (pp. 22–35). Cambridge: Cambridge University Press.

Sacco, J. (1994). *Palestine*. Seattle, WA: Fantagraphics Books.

Sacco, J. (2000). *Safe Area Gorazde*. Seattle, WA: Fantagraphics Books.

Sacks, H. (1992). *Lectures on Conversation*. Vols. 1 and 2, ed. G. Jefferson. Oxford: Blackwell.

Sacks, H., E. Schegloff, and G. Jefferson (1974). "A Simplest Systematics for the Organization of Turn-Taking for Conversation." *Language* 50, 696–735.

Salway, A., M. Graham, E. Tomadaki, and Y. Xu (2003). "Linking Video and Text via Representations of Narrative." *Intelligent Media Management: Papers from the AAAI 2003 Spring Symposium: Technical Report SS-03-08* (pp. 104–12). Menlo Park, CA: American Association for Artificial Intelligence.

Saussure, F. de ([1916] 1959). *Course in General Linguistics*, ed. C. Bally and A. Sechehaye, in collaboration with A. Riedlinger, trans. W. Baskin. New York: The Philosophical Library.

Saville-Troike, M. (2002). *The Ethnography of Communication: An Introduction*. 3rd edn. Oxford: Blackwell.

Schechtman, M. (1997). *The Constitution of Selves*. Ithaca: Cornell University Press.

Schegloff, E. A. (1981). "Discourse as an Interactional Achievement." In D. Tannen (ed.), *Analyzing Discourse: Text and Talk* (pp. 71–93). Washington, DC: Georgetown University Press.

Schegloff, E. A. (1997). "Narrative Analysis Thirty Years Later." *Journal of Narrative and Life History* 7(1–4), 97–106.

Schegloff, E. A. (n.d.). "Transcription Module." <http://www.sscnet.ucla.edu/soc/faculty/schegloff/TranscriptionProject/index.html>.

Schiffrin, D. (1987). *Discourse Markers*. Cambridge: Cambridge University Press.

Scholes, R., and R. Kellogg (1966). *The Nature of Narrative*. Oxford: Oxford University Press.

Schutz, A. (1962). "Common-Sense and the Scientific Interpretation of Human Action." In *Collected Papers*, vol. 1, ed. M. Natanson (pp. 3–47). The Hague: Martinus Nijhoff.

Searle, J. R. (1992). *The Rediscovery of the Mind*. Cambridge, MA: MIT Press.

Searle, J. R. (1997). *The Mystery of Consciousness*. New York: The New York Review of Books.

Sebald, W. G. ([1992] 1996). *The Emigrants*, trans. M. Hulse. New York: New Directions.

Sebald, W. G. (2001). *Austerlitz*, trans. A. Bell. New York: Random House.

Segal, E. M. (1995). "Narrative Comprehension and the Role of Deictic Shift Theory." In J. F. Duchan, G. A. Bruder, and L. E. Hewitt (eds.), *Deixis in Narrative: A Cognitive Science Perspective* (pp. 3–17). Hillsdale, NJ: Lawrence Erlbaum.

Shaw, H. (2005). "Why Won't Our Terms Stay Put? The Narrative Communication Diagram Scrutinized and Historicized." In J. Phelan and P. J. Rabinowitz (eds.), *A Companion to Narrative Theory* (pp. 299–311). Oxford: Blackwell.

Shklovskii, V. ([1929 [1990]). *Theory of Prose*, trans. B. Sher. Elmwood Park, IL: Dalkey Archive Press.

Stanzel, F. K. ([1979] 1984). *A Theory of Narrative*, trans. C. Goedsche. Cambridge: Cambridge University Press.

Sternberg, M. (1978). *Expositional Modes and Temporal Ordering in Fiction.* Baltimore: Johns Hopkins University Press.

Sternberg, M. (1981). "Ordering the Unordered: Time, Space and Descriptive Coherence." *Yale French Studies* 61, 61–88.

Sternberg, M. (1982). "Proteus in Quotation-Land: Mimesis and the Forms of Reported Discourse." *Poetics Today* 3(2), 107–56.

Sternberg, M. (1990). "Telling in Time (I): Chronology and Narrative Theory." *Poetics Today* 11, 901–48.

Sternberg, M. (1992). "Telling in Time (II): Chronology, Teleology, Narrativity." *Poetics Today* 13, 463–541.

Sternberg, M. (2001). "How Narrativity Makes a Difference." *Narrative* 9(2), 115–22.

Strawson, G. (2004). "Against Narrativity." *Ratio* 17, 428–52.

Tammi, P. (2006). "Against Narrative: A Boring Story." *Partial Answers* 4(2), 19–40.

Tannen, D. (ed.) (1993). *Framing in Discourse*. Oxford: Oxford University Press.

Taylor, Charles (1989). *Sources of the Self*. Cambridge: Cambridge University Press.

Taylor, Craig (2001). "Girls World." *The Guardian*, Saturday, November 3, 2001. <http://www.guardian.co.uk/Archive/Article/0,4273,4290067,00.html>

Teahan, S. (1995). *The Rhetorical Logic of Henry James*. Baton Rouge: Louisiana State University Press.

Todorov, T. (1968). "La Grammaire du récit." *Langages* 12, 94–102.

Todorov, T. (1969). *Grammaire du "Décaméron."* The Hague: Mouton.

Todorov, T. ([1978] 1990). *Genres in Discourse*, trans. Catherine Porter. Cambridge: Cambridge University Press.

Tomasello, M. (1999). *The Cultural Origins of Human Cognition*. Cambridge, MA: Harvard University Press.

Tomasello, M. (2003). *Constructing a Language: A Usage-Based Theory of Language Acquisition*. Cambridge, MA: Harvard University Press.

Tomashevskii, B. ([1925] 1965). "Thematics." In L. T. Lemon and M. J. Reis (eds.), *Russian Formalist Criticism* (pp. 61–95). Lincoln: University of Nebraska Press.

Toolan, M. ([1988] 2001). *Narrative: A Critical Linguistic Introduction*. 2nd edn. London: Routledge.

Turner, M. (ed.) (2006). *The Artful Mind: Cognitive Science and the Riddle of Human Creativity*. Oxford: Oxford University Press.

Tye, M. (2003). "Qualia." In E. N. Zalta (ed.), *The Stanford Encyclopedia of Philosophy* (Summer 2003 edn.). <http://plato.stanford.edu/archives/sum2003/entries/qualia/>.

Van Gulick, R. (2004). "Consciousness." In E. N. Zalta (ed.), *The Stanford Encyclopedia of Philosophy* (Fall 2004 edn.). <http://plato.stanford.edu/archives/fall2004/entries/consciousness/>.

Virtanen, T. (1992). "Issues of Text Typology: Narrative–a 'Basic' Type of Text?" *TEXT* 12, 293–310.

Virtanen, T., and B. Wårvik (1987). "Observations sur les types de texte." *Communications: Recontre des professeurs de français de l'enseignement supérieur* 8, 161–9.

Wagner-Martin, L. (ed.) (1998). *Ernest Hemingway: Seven Decades of Criticism.* East Lansing: Michigan State University Press.

Walsh, R. (2007). *The Rhetoric of Fictionality: Narrative Theory and the Idea of Fiction.* Columbus: Ohio State University Press.

Walton, K. (1990). *Mimesis as Make-Believe: On the Foundations of the Representational Arts.* Cambridge, MA: Harvard University Press.

Ward, G., and J. Hirschberg (1985). "Implicating Uncertainty: The Pragmatics of Fall-Rise Intonation." *Language* 61(4), 747–76.

Warhol, R. (1989). *Gendered Interventions: Narrative Discourse in the Victorian Novel.* New Brunswick: Rutgers University Press.

Warhol, R. (2003). *Having a Good Cry: Effeminate Feelings and Popular Forms.* Columbus: Ohio State University Press.

Warhol, R. (2005). "Neonarrative; or, How to Render the Unnarratable in Realist Fiction and Contemporary Film." In J. Phelan and P. J. Rabinowitz (eds.), *A Companion to Narrative Theory* (pp. 220–31). Oxford: Blackwell.

Welty, E. ([1941] 2006). "A Worn Path." In E. V. Roberts and H. E. Jacobs (eds.), *Literature: An Introduction to Reading and Writing,* 8th edn. (pp. 138–43). Upper Saddle River, NJ: Prentice Hall.

Werlich, E. (1975). *Typologie der Texte: Entwurf eines textlinguistischen Modells zur Grundlegung einer Textgrammatik.* Heidelberg: Quelle & Meyer.

Werlich, E. (1983). *A Text Grammar of English,* 2nd edn. Heidelberg: Quelle & Meyer.

Werth, P. (1999). *Text Worlds: Representing Conceptual Space in Discourse.* London: Longman.

Wilson, R., and F. Keil (eds.) (1999). *The MIT Encyclopedia of the Cognitive Sciences.* Cambridge, MA: MIT Press.

Wimsatt, W., and M. Beardsley ([1947] 2001). "The Intentional Fallacy." In V. B. Leitch et al. (eds.), *The Norton Anthology of Theory and Criticism* (pp. 1374–89). New York: W. W. Norton.

Wittgenstein, L. ([1953] 1958). *Philosophical Investigations,* ed. G. E. M. Anscombe and R. Rhees, trans. G. E. M. Anscombe, 3rd edn. Oxford: Blackwell.

Woodward, J. (2003). "Scientific Explanation." In E. N. Zalta (ed.), *The Stanford Encyclopedia of Philosophy.* <http://plato.stanford.edu/entries/scientific-explanation/>.

Young, K. G. (1987). *Taleworlds and Storyrealms: The Phenomenology of Narrative.* Dordrecht: Martinus Nijhoff.

Zoran, G. (1984). "Towards a Theory of Space in Narrative." *Poetics Today* 5(2), 309–35.

Zubin, D., and L. E. Hewitt (1995). "The Deictic Center: A Theory of Deixis in Narrative." In J. F. Duchan, G. A. Bruder, and L. E. Hewitt (eds.), *Deixis in Narrative: A Cognitive Science Perspective* (pp. 129–55). Hillsdale, NJ: Lawrence Erlbaum.

Zunshine, L. (2006). *Why We Read Fiction: Theory of Mind and the Novel.* Columbus: Ohio State University Press.

Zwigoff, T. (2001). *Ghost World.* MGM.

Index